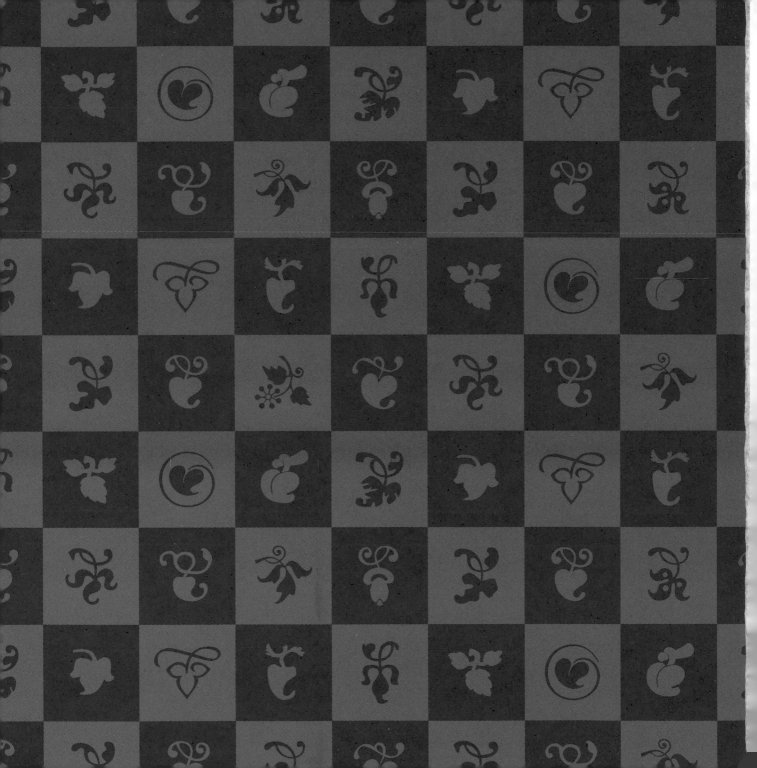

INDIE **FONTS 2**

A Compendium of Digital Type from Independent Foundries

Richard Kegler
James Grieshaber
Tamye Riggs
Editors

GLOUCESTER MASSACHUSETTS

ROCKPORT PUBLISHERS

ROCKPORT

Library of Congress Control Number: 2002117837

ISBN: 1-59253-124-5

Published by
Rockport Publishers, Inc.
33 Commercial Street
Gloucester, MA 01930-5089
Phone: 978.282.9590
Fax: 978.283.2742
www.rockpub.com

Designed in the USA
Printed in China

Contents

Introduction

Considering the firmly physical origins of type (thank you, Mr. Gutenberg), it's a bit ironic that the internet is now the primary vehicle for buying and selling typefaces. And why not? It's much cheaper to design and build a website, even one with a robust ecommerce system, than it is to continually design, produce, and deliver printed catalogs to potential customers.

What's more, personal computing and the net have contributed to a literal explosion in the number of available typefaces. These days, anyone with a computer and the right software can create fonts. It still takes years of study and practice (and talent, creativity, and dedication) to design quality typefaces—that will never change. But more people are making faces than ever before, and the number of fonts available to computer users continues to grow exponentially.

The inevitable questions come to mind: "Does the world really need more fonts? Hasn't everything already been done? Can't we just use what we already have?" It's only the alphabet, after all...

Let's put to rest right now the notion that we don't need new fonts. If designers had stopped making new fonts, we wouldn't have the exquisite *Dotic*, Miguel Hernández' bitmap fraktur designed for the screen. What would the world be like if František Štorm hadn't drawn his own version of the glorious *Baskerville*, and created its companion grotesk, *John Sans*? These are but a few examples of innovation in contemporary type design—the possibilities are virtually limitless.

In the fall of 2002, the first volume of *Indie Fonts* was published, showcasing nearly 2,000 fonts from 18 independent digital type foundries. Less than a year later, we're pleased to bring you *Indie Fonts 2*, featuring the creations of 19 additional foundries. These type makers range from those who've been around since the days of hot metal to others who opened up shop just this year.

Regardless of the length of time they've been producing type, these foundries share a common goal—they are dedicated to making original digital fonts imbued with a love of the craft, and are committed to bringing their creations to the people that need them.

Although most of the typefaces presented in the *Indie Fonts* series are available for review and purchase on the web, the participating foundries elected to show their designs in the media that type was invented for: print. Ink on paper is still the best way to display a typeface, and there are few things as delicious as the anticipation of turning the pages of a brand new book.

Enjoy the view.

The Editors

Font Style Index

282	*Jannon T Moderne Swash Ital.*
282	JANNON T MOD. SC PLAIN
282	*JANNON T MOD. SC ITALIC*
282	**Jannon T Moderne Bold**
282	***Jannon T Mod. Bold Italic***
282	**JANNON T MOD. SC BOLD**
282	***JANNON T MOD. SC B.ITAL.***
282	Jannon Text Plain
282	*Jannon Text Italic*
282	Jannon Text Medium
282	*Jannon Text Med. Italic*
282	JANNON TEXT MED SC
282	*JANNON TEXT MED SC ITAL.*
282	**Jannon Text Bold**
282	***Jannon Text Bold Italic***
285	John Baskerville Plain
285	*John Baskerville Italic*
285	JOHN BASKERVILLE CAPS
285	*JOHN BASKERVILLE CAPS ITALIC*
285	John Baskerville Medium
285	*John Baskerville Medium Italic*
285	**John Baskerville Bold**
285	***John Baskerville Bold Italic***
285	JOHN BASKERVILLE CAPS BOLD
285	*JOHN BASKERVILLE CAPS B.ITALIC*
130	Josefov Leicht
130	**Josefov Normal**
295	Juvenis Light
295	*Juvenis Light Italic*
295	Juvenis Book
295	*Juvenis Book Italic*
295	**Juvenis Book Bold**
295	***Juvenis Book Bold Ital.***
295	**Juvenis Medium Bold**
295	***Juvenis Med. Bold Ital.***
295	Juvenis Text
295	*Juvenis Text Italic*
295	**Juvenis Text Bold**
295	***Juvenis T. Bold Ital.***
272	Kandal Book
272	*Kandal Book Italic*
272	Kandal Medium
272	*Kandal Medium Italic*
272	**Kandal Bold**
272	***Kandal Bold Italic***
272	**Kandal Black**
272	***Kandal Black Italic***
204	Laguna Madre WBW
249	Latimer
249	LINDUM
195	Londonderry Air NF
246	Mayflower
246	*Mayflower Italic*
203	McKenna Handletter NF
203	*McKenna Handletter Italic NF*
203	**McKenna Handletter Bold NF**
68	McLemore Light
68	*McLemore Light Italic*
68	McLemore Regular
68	*McLemore Italic*
68	**McLemore Bold**
68	***McLemore Bold Italic***
68	**McLemore Black**
68	***McLemore Black Italic***
248	Mercian
50	FTF Merlo Roman
50	*FTF Merlo Italic*
50	FTF MERLO CAPS
50	*FTF MERLO CAPS ITALIC*
199	Mrs Bathhurst FGC
220	MS KITTY
220	MS KITTY BOLD
210	ITC Oldrichium Light
210	*ITC Oldrichium Light Italic*
210	ITC Oldrichium Regular
210	*ITC Oldrichium Italic*
210	ITC Oldrichium Demi
210	*ITC Oldrichium Demi Italic*
210	**ITC Oldrichium Bold**
210	ITC Oldrichium Engraved
221	ParmaType
221	*ParmaType Italic*
221	**ParmaType Bold**
221	***ParmaType ItalicBold***
195	QUADRIVIUM NF
302	Rawlinson Regular
302	*Rawlinson Italic*
302	Rawlinson Medium
302	*Rawlinson Medium Italic*
303	**Rawlinson Bold**
303	***Rawlinson Bold Italic***
303	**Rawlinson Heavy**
303	***Rawlinson Heavy Italic***
304	Rawlinson Cond Regular
304	*Rawlinson Cond Italic*
304	Rawlinson Cond Medium

178	*Futura ND Cn Bold Oblique*	290	JohnSans White Italic	129	Josef Normal
179	**Futura ND Cn Extrabold**	290	JohnSans Lite	129	*Josef Kursiv*
179	***Futura ND Cn Extrabold Obliq***	290	*JohnSans Lite Italic*	129	**Josef Halbfett**
179	Futura ND Cn SCOsF Light	290	JohnSans Text	129	**Josef Fett**
179	*Futura ND Cn SCOsF Light Oblique*	290	*JohnSans Text Italic*	105	KANAL Ultra Light
179	Futura ND Cn SCOsF Medium	290	JohnSans Medium	105	*KANAL Ultra Light Italic*
179	*Futura ND Cn SCOsF Medium Oblique*	290	*JohnSans Medium Italic*	105	KANAL Light
179	**Futura ND Cn SCOsF Bold**	290	**JohnSans Bold**	105	*KANAL Light Italic*
179	***Futura ND Cn SCOsF Bold Oblique***	290	***JohnSans Bold Italic***	105	KANAL Normal
299	Giacomo Light	290	JohnSans Heavy	105	*KANAL Normal Italic*
299	*Giacomo Light Italic*	290	*JohnSans Heavy Italic*	105	**KANAL Regular**
299	Giacomo Regular	290	**JohnSans Black**	105	***KANAL Regular Italic***
299	*Giacomo Regular Italic*	290	***JohnSans Black Italic***	51	Bs-Mandrax Regular
300	Giacomo Medium	290	**JohnSans XBlack**	51	*Bs-Mandrax Italic*
300	*Giacomo Medium Italic*	290	***JohnSans XBlack Italic***	51	**Bs-Mandrax Bold**
300	**Giacomo Bold**	290	JohnSans White SC	51	**Bs-Mandrax Heavy**
300	***Giacomo Bold Italic***	290	*JohnSans White SC Italic*	267	Metallophile Sp 8 Light
301	**Giacomo Heavy**	290	JohnSans Lite SC	267	*Metallophile Sp 8 Light Italic*
301	***Giacomo Heavy Italic***	290	*JohnSans Lite SC Italic*	106	MONARK Light
301	**Giacomo Black**	290	JohnSans Text SC	106	*MONARK Light Italic*
301	***Giacomo Black Italic***	290	*JohnSans Text SC Italic*	106	MONARK Regular
218	Isbellium	290	JohnSans Medium SC	106	*MONARK Regular Italic*
218	*Isbellium Italique*	290	*JohnSans Medium SC Italic*	106	**MONARK Bold**
218	Isbellium Medium	290	**JohnSans Bold**	106	*MONARK Bold Italic*
218	*Isbellium Italique Medium*	129	***JohnSans Bold Italic***	106	**MONARK Black**
218	Isbellium DemiBold	129	**JohnSans Heavy SC**	106	***MONARK Black Italic***
218	*Isbellium Italique Demi*	129	***JohnSans Heavy SC Italic***	54	FTF Morgan Sn Regular
218	**Isbellium Bold**	129	**JohnSans Black SC**	54	*FTF Morgan Sn Oblique*
218	***Isbellium Italique Bold***	105	***JohnSans Black SC Italic***	54	**FTF Morgan Sn Bold**
218	**Isbellium ExtraBold**	105	**JohnSans XBlack SC**	54	***FTF Morgan Sn Bd Oblique***
218	***Isbellium Italique Extra***	105	***JohnSans XBlack SC Italic***	54	FTF MORGAN SN CP
290	JohnSans White	129	Josef Leicht	54	*FTF MORGAN SN CP OBLIQUE*

269	SANCTUARY REGULAR	213	*Tinman Bold Italic*	133	*Wendelin Normal Kursiv*
269	**SANCTUARY BOLD**	113	TRAK Fine	133	Wendelin Normal Kapitälchen
111	SEIZE Light	113	*TRAK Fine Italic*	133	Wendelin Kräftig
111	*SEIZE Light Italic*	113	TRAK Regular	133	*Wendelin Halbfett Kursiv*
111	SEIZE Regular	113	*TRAK Regular Italic*	133	**Wendelin Breitfett**
111	*SEIZE Regular Italic*	113	TRAK Semi-bold	133	**Wendelin Fett**
111	**SEIZE Bold**	113	*TRAK Semi-bold Italic*	133	***Wendelin Fett Kursiv***
111	***SEIZE Bold Italic***	113	**TRAK Bold**	115	WIRED Light
111	SEIZE Open	113	***TRAK Bold Italic***	115	*WIRED Light Italic*
111	*SEIZE Open Italic*	113	**TRAK Black**	115	WIRED Regular
270	Sharktooth Regular	113	***TRAK Black Italic***	115	*WIRED Regular Italic*
270	**Sharktooth Bold**	365	Ultramagnetic_Light	115	WIRED Black
270	**Sharktooth Heavy**	366	*Ultramagnetic_LightOblique*	115	*WIRED Black Italic*
214	SleepTickets	365	Ultramagnetic_Regular	348	Yumi UltraLight
214	**SleepTickets Bold**	366	*Ultramagnetic_Oblique*	348	Yumi Light
149	Spaulding Sans JF-Regular	365	**Ultramagnetic_Bold**	348	Yumi Normal
149	*Spaulding Sans JF-Italic*	366	***Ultramagnetic_BoldOblique***	348	Yumi Medium
345	squirrel regular	365	**Ultramagnetic_ExtraBold**	348	Yumi Bold
345	*squirrel italic*	366	***Ultramagnetic_ExtraBoldObliqu***		
345	**squirrel bold**	366	**Ultramagnetic_Black**		
345	***squirrel bolditalic***	366	***Ultramagnetic_BlackOblique***		
113	STAK Light	367	unisect_light		
113	*STAK Light Italic*	367	*unisect_lightoblique*		
113	STAK Regular	367	unisect_Regular		
113	*STAK Regular Italic*	367	*unisect_oblique*		
113	**STAK Bold**	367	**unisect_Bold**		
113	***STAK Bold Italic***	367	***unisect_Boldoblique***		
212	Tinman	367	**unisect_ExtraBold**		
213	*Tinman Italic*	367	***unisect_ExtraBoldoblique***		
212	Tinman DemiBold	367	**unisect_Black**		
213	*Tinman DemiBold Italic*	367	***unisect_Blackoblique***		
212	**Tinman Bold**	133	Wendelin Normal		

Display

353	6x7oct_ExtraLight	102	ANGOL SHARP Regular	85	BERIKA
353	6x7oct_ExtraLightAlt	102	ANGOL SHARP Bold	77	Bing Script
353	6x7oct_Light	102	ANGOL SHARP Black	77	**Bing Black**
353	6x7oct_LightAlt	196	*Annabelle Matinee NF*	77	Bing Inline
353	6x7oct_Regular	250	Aragon	354	blackgold_light
353	6x7oct_Alternate	47	**BS-ARCHAE REGULAR**	354	blackgold_Regular
353	6x7oct_Bold	47	**BS-ARCHAE BOLD**	354	**blackgold_bold**
353	6x7oct_ExtraBold	47	**BS-ARCHAE HEAVY**	354	**blackgold_extbold**
353	6x7oct_ExtraBold	341	ARE YOU IN? ~ regular	138	Blairesque JF-Curly
353	6x7oct_ExtraBoldAlt	227	Azuza Medium	138	Blairesque JF-Festive
353	6x7oct_Black	227	*Azuza Medium Italic*	139	Blairesque JF-Gothic
353	6x7oct_BlackAlt	227	**Azuza Bold**	354	blessed_extralight
102	45 DEGREES Ultra Light	227	***Azuza Bold Italic***	354	blessed_light
102	45 DEGREES Light	228	Balboa Wide Light	354	blessed_regular
102	*45 DEGREES Light Italic*	228	**Balboa Wide Medium**	354	blessed_semibold
102	45 DEGREES Regular	228	**Balboa Wide Bold**	354	blessed_bold
102	*45 DEGREES Regular Italic*	228	**Balboa Wide Extra Bold**	354	blessed_extrabold
345	Airbrake Regular	228	**Balboa Wide Black**	191	**BOOGALOO BLVDNF**
345	*Airbrake RegOblique*	229	Balboa Light	164	**MVB BOVINE REGULAR**
345	Airbrake Rounded	229	**Balboa Medium**	164	**MVB BOVINE ROUND**
345	*Airbrake RouOblique*	228	**Balboa Bold**	204	**BRAZOS WBW**
241	AMBOY	228	**Balboa Extra Bold**	140	*Bronson Gothic JF*
258	AMELIA	228	**Balboa Black**	140	Buena Park JF
339	Amp Light	229	Balboa Condensed	198	**Bundle of Joy NF**
339	Amp Regular	229	Balboa Extra Condensed	355	caliper_extrawide
339	**Amp Bold**	343	**Barbapapa**	355	caliper_wide
339	Amp Outline	84	Bebedot Blonde	355	caliper_Regular
119	**Anatole France**	84	**Bebedot Black**	355	caliper_Alternate
102	ANGOL ROUND Regular	236	Benicia Medium	355	caliper_unicase
102	ANGOL ROUND Bold	236	*Benicia Medium Italic*	355	caliper_stairstep
102	ANGOL ROUND Black	236	Benicia Bold	355	caliper_lightcubed
		236	*Benicia Bold Italic*	196	cambridge pinstripe nf

19

363 REVERSION_EXB	324 *Sauna Italic Swash*	205 SPINDLETOP WBW
363 REVERSION_TE	324 *Qu Ch Ct ffi St It Sw Lig*	89 Submarine Extra Light
363 REVERSION_ELB	324 SAUNA SMALLCAPS	89 Submarine Light
363 REVERSION_LBA	323 **Sauna Bold**	89 Submarine Regular
363 REVERSION_RB	325 **Sauna Bold Italic**	89 **Submarine Bold**
363 REVERSION_SBB	325 **Sauna Bold Italic Swash**	89 **Submarine Extra Bold**
237 Richmond Light	323 **Sh kk ffl zz Bld It Sw Lig**	197 SUPER BOB TRILINE NF
237 *Richmond Light Italic*	323 **Sauna Black**	232 Sutro Light
237 Richmond Medium	322 **Sauna Black Italic**	232 Sutro Medium
237 *Richmond Medium Italic*	322 **Sauna Black Italic Sw**	232 Sutro Bold
237 **Richmond Bold**	322 **Ck ff ll St Blk It Sw Lig**	232 Sutro Extra Bold
237 **Richmond Bold Italic**	132 Schwabacher Deutsche Reichsbahn	233 SUTRO BLACK
237 Richmond Light Condensed	364 Selector_Light	233 SUTRO SHADED
237 Richmond Medium Condensed	364 Selector_Regular	337 Swingo Regular
237 Richmond Bold Condensed	364 **Selector_Bold**	337 **Swingo Bold**
237 **Richmond Extra Bold Condensed**	364 **Selector_ExtraBold**	343 Systemaz Extra Light
237 RICHMOND INITIALS	112 SHARP Light	343 Systemaz Light
205 **Rio Grande WBW**	112 SHARP Light Italic	343 Systemaz Regular
197 ROBOT MONSTER NF	112 SHARP Regular	343 **Systemaz Bold**
111 ROBUSTIK Light	112 SHARP Regular Italic	343 Systemaz Extra Light Force
111 ROBUSTIK Light Obliq	112 SHARP Bold	343 Systemaz Light Force
111 ROBUSTIK Regular	112 SHARP Bold Italic	343 Systemaz Force
111 ROBUSTIK Reg Obliq	112 SHARP Ultra	343 Systemaz Bold Force
111 ROBUSTIK Bold	112 SHARP Ultra Italic	343 Systemaz Extra Bold Force
111 ROBUSTIK Bld Oblique	160 MVB Sirenne Eighteen Roman	294 Teuton Weiss
65 **Robusto Black**	160 MVB *Sirenne Eighteen Italic*	294 Teuton Hell
194 Rocketman XV-7 NF	160 MVB SIRENNE EIGHTEEN SC	294 Teuton Mager
199 **Roman Holiday NF**	160 MVB Sirenne Seventy-Two Roman	294 **Teuton Mager Bold**
194 **SABRINA ZAFTIG NF**	160 MVB *Sirenne Seventy-Two Italic*	294 Teuton Normal
148 SAHARAN JF	161 MVB SIRENNE SEVENTY-TWO SC	294 **Teuton Normal Bold**
322 Sauna Roman	149 *Southland JF*	294 **Teuton Fett Bold**
322 *Sauna Italic*	205 **Spaghetti Western WBW**	201 Thai Foon HB

Script

137	Acroterion JF
137	Adage Script JF
254	Afton
137	**Alpengeist JF**
137	Annabelle JF
201	Artemisia NF
255	Avocet Light
140	**Boxer Script JF**
167	MVB Café Mimi Regular
167	**MVB Café Mimi Bold**
181	CarloMagno ND
165	MVB Chanson d'Amour
141	Charade JF
337	Chuba Thin
337	Chuba Thin Italic
337	Chuba Tubby
337	Chuba Tubby Italic
337	**Chuba Fat**
337	**Chuba Fat Italic**
356	Cinahand_Light
356	Cinahand LightAlternate
356	**Cinahand_Regular**
356	**Cinahand Alternate**
264	Coquette Light
264	Coquette Regular
264	**Coquette Bold**
141	Debonair JF
123	Deutsche Schrift Lettung
216	DogButter Extra Light
216	DogButter Regular
217	DogButter Medium
217	DogButter DemiBold
217	**DogButter Bold**
250	Elven
167	MVB Emmascript Regular
167	**MVB Emmascript Bold**
241	Felt Tip Roman
241	**Felt Tip Roman Bold**
241	**Felt Tip Roman Heavy**
241	Felt Tip Senior
241	Felt Tip Woman
241	**Felt Tip Woman Bold**
142	Fenway Park JF
128	FKGrun
167	MVB Greymantle Regular
143	Jeffriana JF
130	**KLEX**
144	Kon Tiki JF-Enchanted
145	Kon Tiki JF-Lounge
145	**Manual Script JF**
201	Margarita Ville NF
145	Mary Helen JF
201	Monte Carlo Script NF
146	Opulence JF
146	Peregroy JF
252	Plymouth
146	Primrose JF
146	Rambler Script JF
147	Retro Repro JF
253	Roanoke Script
148	Scriptorama JF-Hostess
148	**SCRIPTORAMA JF-MARKDOWN**
148	**Scriptorama JF-Tradeshow**
149	Shirley Script JF
150	Stanzie JF
254	Symphony
181	UNCIAL ROMANA ND
150	Valentina JF
150	Varsity Script JF
150	Viceroy JF
151	**Wonderboy JF**

23

Non-latin		Ornaments	
40	モイキチリラミ	180	
42		30	
		139	
		165	
		356	
		344	
		167	
		36	
		41	
		169	
		338	
		331	
		331	
		331	
		257	
		95	

25

ATOMIC MEDIA

Jaggies are good.

Retro-future fonts from Atomic Media are the comfort food for twenty-first century design. Great for on-screen and print use, these fonts and icons by Matthew Bardram, Susan Kare, and Miguel Hernández run the gamut of hardcore bitmap design from the past 20 years to the next 20 years to come. Cut the future, paste the past.

Arachnid

Matthew Bardram
1998

Regular

A quick black spider spins the lazy dog in silk

AaBbDdEeFf abcdefghijklmnopqrstuvwxyz ABCDEFGHIJKLMNOPQRSTUVWXYZ Don't be fooled by the tiny size { [(1 2 3 4 5 6 7 8 9 0)] }

Small Caps

CRAZY CAPPED SPIDER DANCES WITH PUZZLED FOX

AaBbCcDdEe ABCDEFGHIJKLMNOPQRSTUVWXYZ ABCDEFGHIJKLMNOPQRSTUVWXYZ Full character set included. { [(1 2 3 4 5 6 7 8 9 0)] }

Atomic

Matthew Bardram
1996

Inline

How I Learned To Stop

ABcd abcdefghijklmnopqrstuvwxyz12345 ABCDEFGHIJKLMNOPQRSTUVWX

Outline

Worrying And Love The

ABcd abcdefghijklmnopqrstuvwxyz12345 ABCDEFGHIJKLMNOPQRSTUVWX

Combine Inline and Outline styles for overlay effect.

BOMB

BOMB

BOMB

Susan Kare
2001

Pixel illustrations for bullets, watermarks, or borders.

fonts@atomicmedia.net

Matthew Bardram
2001

Regular

When we go back to Juarez, Mexico, do we fly

AaBbDdEeF

abcdefghijklmnopqrstuvwxyz
ABCDEFGHIJKLMNOPQRSTUVWXYZ

Don't be fooled by the tiny size

{ [(1 2 3 4 5 6 7 8 9 0)] }

Black

Over picturesque little Tucson, Arizona?

AaBbDdE

abcdefghijklmnopqrstuv
ABCDEFGHIJKLMNOPQRSTUV

Full character set included

{ [(1 2 3 4 5 6 7 8 9 0)] }

Regular

An inspired calligrapher can create pages

abcdefghijklmnopqrstuvwxyzABCDEFGHIJKLMNOPQRS
TUVWXYZ!@#$%^+*œéáóüãñîÉÁÓÜÃÎço≈---:+\\/·-.,~'º±«»

Don't be fooled by tiny size

{ [(1 2 3 4 5 6 7 8 9 0)] }

Bold

Of beauty using stick, ink, quill, brush

abcdefghijklmnopqrstuvwxyzABCDEFGHIJKLMNOPQRS
TUVWXYZ!@#$%^+*œéáóüãñîÉÁÓÜÃÎço ---:+\\/·-.,~'º±«»

All characters included

{ [(1 2 3 4 5 6 7 8 9 0)] }

Just yesterday Matthew Carter and I were out back referencing your Egyptian bowls. Ever since Seybold '84, there's been a trend towards pirating display ascenders. ··· Who knew that I would be considered a typographic genius simply by cutting recycled specimen books? ··· I'm teaching a course about reinventing disproportional ears.

Small Caps

Pick-axe, buzz saw, baked ham, or strawberry jam

abcdefghijklmnopqrstuvwxyzABCDEFGHIJKLMNOPQRS
TUVWXYZ!@#$%^+*œéáóüãñîÉÁÓÜÃÎço ---:+\\/·-.,~'º±«»

Don't be fooled by the tiny size

{ [(1 2 3 4 5 6 7 8 9 0)] }

Small Caps Bold

All a digital designer needs is this font

abcdefghijklmnopqrstuvwxyzABCDEFGHIJKLMNOPQRS
TUVWXYZ!@#$%^+*œéáóüãñîÉÁÓÜÃÎço ---:+\\/·-.,~'º±«»

All characters are included

{ [(1 2 3 4 5 6 7 8 9 0)] }

Matthew Bardram
2000

Regular

Forsaking monastic tradition, twelve jovial friars gave up their

abcdefghijklmnopqrstuvwxyzABCDEFGHIJKLMNOPQRS   Don't be fooled by this font's tiny size

TUVWXYZ!@#$%^ε*œéáóüãñîÉÁÓÜÃÎçø ---=:+\!/··.,~´≗≗«» 〈 [(1 2 3 4 5 6 7 8 9 0)] 〉

Bold

Vocation for a questionable move to flying trapeze

abcdefghijklmnopqrstuvwxyzABCDEFGHIJKLMNOPQRS   A full character set is included

TUVWXYZ!@#$%^ε*œéáóüãñîÉÁÓÜÃÎçø ---=:+\!/··.,~´≗≗«» 〈 [(1 2 3 4 5 6 7 8 9 0)] 〉

Sans Bold

Lazy movers quit hard-packing of papier-mâché

abcdefghijklmnopqrstuvwxyzABCDEFGHIJKLMNOPQRS   Yes, this font can speak French

TUVWXYZ!@#$%^ε*œéáóüãñîÉÁÓÜÃÎçø ---=:+\!/··.,~´≗≗«» 〈 [(1 2 3 4 5 6 7 8 9 0)] 〉

DON'T FORGET TO READ THE

Small Print

Tall

Forsaking monastic tradition, twelve jovial friars gave up their

abcdefghijklmnopqrstuvwxyzABCDEFGHIJKLMNOPQRS   Don't be fooled by this font's tiny size

TUVWXYZ!@#$%^ε*œéáóüãñîÉÁÓÜÃÎçø ---=:+\!/··.,~´≗≗«» 〈 [(1 2 3 4 5 6 7 8 9 0)] 〉

Bold

Vocation for a questionable move to flying trapeze

abcdefghijklmnopqrstuvwxyzABCDEFGHIJKLMNOPQRS   A full character set is included

TUVWXYZ!@#$%^ε*œéáóüãñîÉÁÓÜÃÎçø ---=:+\!/··.,~´≗≗«» 〈 [(1 2 3 4 5 6 7 8 9 0)] 〉

Sans Bold

Lazy movers quit hard-packing of papier-mâché

abcdefghijklmnopqrstuvwxyzABCDEFGHIJKLMNOPQRS   Yes, this font can speak French

TUVWXYZ!@#$%^ε*œéáóüãñîÉÁÓÜÃÎçø ---=:+\!/··.,~´≗≗«» 〈 [(1 2 3 4 5 6 7 8 9 0)] 〉

fonts@atomicmedia.net

¡A NEW DISPLAY PIXEL FONT!
AS PRESENTED BY THE INTERNACIONALLY ACCLAIMED AND
MOST RENOWNED AUTHORITHY
TYPOGRAPHER
ON EARTH
KNOWN FAR & WIDE AS THE GREAT
CIRCA
A CURIOUS BITMAP WONDER
BE AMUSED!

ABCDEFGHIJKLMNOPQRSTUVWXYZ

[1234567890]

¿¡?!@ª&ÆŒ/%.,:;[¢£¥$]

ÁÀÂÄÃÅÇÐÉÈÊËÍÌÎÏÑÓÒÔÖÕØÚÙÛÜÝŽ

1977-2003

Dotic

The New Dot Time.

AaBbCcDdEe

a b c d e f g h i j k l m n o p q r s t u v w x y z
ABCDEFGHIJKLMNOPQRSTUVWXYZ

A collector of books ran into an acquaintance who told him he had just thrown away an old Bible that he found in a dusty, old box. He happened to mention that "Guten–somebody–or–other" had printed it. "Not 'Gutenberg'?" gasped the collector. "Yes, that was it!" said the acquaintance. "You idiot!" yelled the collector. "You've thrown away one of the first books ever printed. A copy recently sold at auction for half a million dollars!" "Oh, I don't think this book would have been worth anything close to that much," replied the man. "It was scribbled all over in the margins by some dude named Martin Luther."

{ Ä Ç D É Ü Ô Ñ ä ç ó é ü ô ñ Æ œ Œ ∞ fi fl @ & ‡ ¢ £ ¥ € }

EVERETT QUICKLY VEXED BOLD ZEPHYRS

AaBbCcDdEeFfGgHhIiJjKkLlMmNnOoPpQqRrSsTtUuVvWwXxYyZz$1234567890!

WITH MOXIE AND IMPUNITY

THE FIVE FOXY GENE WIZARDS SPLICE QUICHLY

Regular
ABCDEFGHIJKLMNOPQRSTUVWXYZ$1234567890!+œÑÉÁÇÜÄ
GENETICA SPEAKS FRENCH, SPANISH, GERMAN & PORTUGUESE

Bold
ABCDEFGHIJKLMNOPQRS
TUVWXYZ$1234567890!

Matthew Bardram
2001

Square

A B C D E F G H I J K L M N O P Q R S T U V W X Y Z
A B C D E F G H I J K L M N O P Q R S T U V W X Y Z ([{1 2 3 4 5 6 7 8 9 0}])
@ # $ % ^ * € ¢ Ÿ Œ É Á Ó Ü Å Ñ Ì ç ø – — = + \ | / • - , " " ' ' º ª « » ‹ › ß ™ ¡ ¿ ! ?

Square Core

A B C D E F G H I J K L M N O P Q R S T U V W X Y Z
A B C D E F G H I J K L M N O P Q R S T U V W X Y Z ([{1 2 3 4 5 6 7 8 9 0}])
@ # $ % ^ * € ¢ Ÿ Œ É Á Ó Ü Å Ñ Ì ç ø – — = + \ | / • - , " " ' ' º ª « » ‹ › ß ™ ¡ ¿

Square Hollow

A B C D E F G H I J K L M N O P Q R S T U V W X Y Z
A B C D E F G H I J K L M N O P Q R S T U V W X Y Z ([{1 2 3 4 5 6 7 8 9 0}])
@ # $ % ^ * € ¢ Ÿ Œ É Á Ó Ü Å Ñ Ì ç ø – — = + \ | / • - , " " ' ' º ª « » ‹ › ß ™ ¡ ¿ ! ?

Crossed

A B C D E F G H I J K L M N O P Q R S T U V W X Y Z
A B C D E F G H I J K L M N O P Q R S T U V W X Y Z ([{1 2 3 4 5 6 7 8 9 0}])
@ # $ % ^ * € ¢ Ÿ Œ É Á Ó Ü Å Ñ Ì ç ø – — = + \ | / • - , " " ' ' º ª « » ‹ › ß ™ ¡ ¿ ! ?

Combine styles to create overlay effects.

SOLID PIXEL GENES
SOLID PIXEL GENES
SOLID PIXEL GENES

HARRY SPECIALIZED IN MAKING VERY QUAINT WAX TOYS

AaBbCcDdEeFfGgHhIiJjKkLlMmNnOoPpQqRrSsTtUuVvWwXxYyZz$1234567890!

A TRAIN, CAR, BOAT, DOLL, AND DOG

Pack my liquor box with five dozen vintage Atari ST joysticks, please.

abcdefghijklmnopqrstuvwxyzABCDEFGHIJKL   A Full Character Set
MNOPQRSTUVWXYZ@#$%^&*œéáóÚÑåÉÁÓÜÂÎç ø 1234567890!?}]}

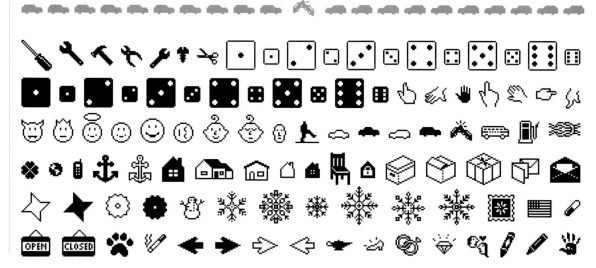

Regular

Watch all five questions asked by experts amaze the judge

AaBbCcDdEeFfGgHhIiJjKkLlMmNnOoPpQqRrSsTtUuVvWwXxYyZz{([\$1234567890!?])}

Yes, this font has diacritics and punct, and even your precious British currency: @#%^&*œñéáóüåçÉÁÓÜÅÎ£

Italic

How quickly five daft jumping zebras vex the lions

AaBbCcDdEeFfGgHhIiJjKkLlMmNnOoPpQqRrSsTtUuVvWwXxYyZz{([\$1234567890!?])}

*Italic also has diacritics and punct, and your precious British currency: @#%^&*œñéáóüåçÉ ÁÓÜÅÎ£*

Bold

Sphinx of black quartz, judge my five vows

AaBbCcDdEeFfGgHhIiJjKkLlMmNnOoPpQqRrSsTtUuVvWwXxYyZz{([\$1234567890!?])}

Bold also has all the good stuff, plus your fine British currency: @#%^&*ñéáóüåçÉÁÓÜÅÎ£

--- Set big fields of type with Kare Five Dots ---

Sure, Kare Five Dots can handle your copious body copy. Everything you need to churn out paragraphs of prose is included. "Quote" from a *Magazine*. **Bold random phrases** to your heart's content. Publish it all on any screen without fuzzy antialiasing. Unlike pixel fonts from other vendors, Kare Five Dots is Flash-compatible. Like all Atomic Media fonts, it is specially designed not to blur or fill. Jaggy is good.

Regular

A mix of big juicy steaks sizzled in a pan as

AaBbCcDdEeFfGgHhIiJjKkLlMmNnOoPpQqRrSsTtUuVvWwXxYyZz{([\$1234567890!?])}

Diacritics and punct, and even your lovely British currency: @#%^&*œñéáóüåçÉÁÓÜÅÎ£

Bold

Five workmen left the quarry to grub

AaBbCcDdEeFfGgHhIiJjKkLlMmNnOoPpQqRrSsTtUuVvWwXxYyZz1234567890!?

Diacritics and punct, and your British currency: {([\$@#%^&*ñéáóüåçÉÁÓÜÅÎ£

TINY TYPE YOU CAN READ.

How did Susan Kare fit legible letters into a space just 5 pixels high?

ANSWER: More than 20 YEARS of practicing BITMAPPY MAGIC.

Susan Kare
2001

Regular

Watch all six questions asked by experts amaze judge

AaBbCcDdEeFfGgHhIiJjKkLlMmNnOoPpQqRrSsTtUuVvWwXxYyZz{([$1234567890!?])}

Yes, this font has diacritics and punct, and even your precious British currency: @#%^&*œñéáóüåçÉÁÓÜÅÎî

Italic

How quickly six jumping zebras vex the lions

AaBbCcDdEeFfGgHhIiJjKkLlMmNnOoPpQqRrSsTtUuVvWwXxYyZz{([$1234567890!?])}

*Italic also has diacritics and punct, and your fine British currency: @#%^&*œñéáóüåçÉÁÓÜÅÎî*

Bold

Sphinx of black quartz, judge my six vows

AaBbCcDdEeFfGgHhIiJjKkLlMmNnOoPpQqRrSsTtUuVvWwXxYyZz{([$1234567890!?])}

Bold also has all the good stuff, plus your fine British currency: @#%^&*ñéáóüåçÉÁÓÜÅÎî

—— Set gobs of type with **Kare Six Dots** ——

Sure, Kare Six Dots can handle your copious body copy. Everything you need to churn out paragraphs of prose is included. "Quote" from a *Magazine*. **Bold random phrases** to your heart's content. Publish it all on any screen without fuzzy antialiasing. Unlike pixel fonts from other vendors, Kare Six Dots is Flash—compatible. Like all Atomic Media fonts, it is specially designed not to blur or fill. Jaggy is good.

Susan Kare
2001

Regular

A mix of juicy steaks sizzled in the pan as

AaBbCcDdEeFfGgHhIiJjKkLlMmNnOoPpQqRrSsTtUuVvWwXxYyZz{([$1234567890!?])}

Diacritics and punct, and even your lovely British currency: @#%^&*œñéáóüåçÉÁÓÜÅÎî

Bold

Five workmen left the quarry to grub

AaBbCcDdEeFfGgHhIiJjKkLlMmNnOoPpQqRrSsTtUuVvWwXxYyZz1234567890

Diacritics, punct, and your British currency: {([!?$@#%^&*ñéáóüåçÉÁÓÜÅÎî

SIX DOTS: **TINY TYPE YOU CAN READ.**

How did Susan Kare fit a legible letter into a space just 6 pixels high?

ANSWER: More than 20 YEARS of practicing BITMAPPY MAGIC.

Macroscopic A   M

WILT THE STILT HAS A POSSE
ABCDEFGHIJKLMNOPQRSTUVWXYZ
{[(1234567890)]}@#$%¢£¥Æœ
ÈÀÜÑÎÇªºßJ!? <>«»™©®

acroscopic B   M

WILT THE STILT HAS A POSSE
ABCDEFGHIJKLMNOPQRSTUVWXYZ
{[(1234567890)]}@#$%¢£¥Æœ

acroscopic C

WILT THE STILT HAS A POSSE
ABCDEFGHIJKLMNOPQRSTUVWXYZ
{[(1234567890)]}@#$%¢£¥Æœ
ÈÀÜÑÎÇªºßJ!? <>«»™©®

Macroscopic D

WILT THE STILT HAS A POSSE
ABCDEFGHIJKLMNOPQRSTUVWXYZ
{[(1234567890)]}@#$%¢£¥Æœ

Macroscopic E

WILT THE STILT HAS A POSSE
ABCDEFGHIJKLMNOPQRSTUVWXYZ
{[(1234567890)]}@#$%¢£¥Æœ

Macroscopic

Matthew Bardram
2001

All the Macroscopic styles are built with the same stem width, allowing them to be used together at the same point size to apply emphasis or create other effects.

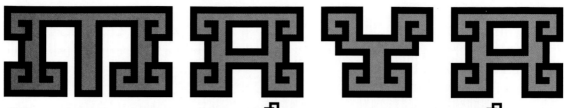

{ CHICHÉN ITZÁ }

ABCDEFGHIJKLMNOPQRSTUVWXYZ

‹ KUKULKÁN ›

[EYE$] (0123456789)

Megalon

Matthew Bardram
2000

A katakana font for Japanese text.

チコソシイチキクニマノ禾モミ

チコソシイハキクニマノリモミラセタスト力ナヒテサンツ

タテイスカンナ二ラセチトシハキクマノリレツサンヒコミモネル×ヌフアウエオヤ1ヨワホダディズガヱゼドジバギグツザゾビゴ

Methodic

Matthew Bardram
2001

Regular

FREIGHT ME PIXELS IN SIXTY DOZEN

ABCDEFGHIJKLMNOPQRSTUVWXYZABCDEFGHIJKLMNOPQRSTU
VWXYZ!1234567890@#$%^&*ŒÉÁÓÙÂÑÎÉÁÓÙÂÎçø ---=+\|/•-.,"?œ«»

Bold

QUART JARS & TWELVE SACKS

ABCDEFGHIJKLMNOPQRSTUVWXYZABCDEFGHIJKLMNOPQRSTUV
WXYZ!1234567890@#$%^&*ŒÉÁÓÙÂÑÎÉÁÓÙÂÎçø ---=+\|/•-.,"?œ«»

Microscopic

Matthew Bardram
2001

HIS CATS' NAMES ARE "ROCK, SCISSORS, AND PAPER"

MICROFONT

DON'T BE FOOLED BY THE TINY SIZE
{ [(1 2 3 4 5 6 7 8 9 0)] }
IT'S GOT DIACRITICS & PUNCT

ABCDEFGHIJKLMNOPQRSTUVWXYZ0#$%^&* [ONLY 4 PIXELS HIGH] ŒÉÁÓÙÂÑÎÉÁÓÙÂÎçø ---=+\|/•-.,"?œ«»

MiniFood

Susan Kare
2001

Pixel illustrations for bullets,
dividers, watermarks, or borders.

Atomic Media

BLACK SPHINX QUARTZ & JUDGE MONO

MONOCULE-IS-MONOSPACED ABCDEFGHIJKLMNOPQRSTUVWXYZ! 1234567890

@#$%^&*ŒÉÁÓÜÃÑÎÇØ ---=+\|/•.,"' ªº«»<>() <>ᴿᶜ™÷ FULL-CHAR-SET

⠈⠂⠇⠠⠐⠑⠒⠓⠔⠕⠖⠗⠘⠙⠚⠛⠜⠝⠞⠟⠠⠡⠢⠣⠤⠥⠦⠧⠨⠩⠪⠫⠬⠭⠮⠯⠰⠱⠲⠳

⠈⠂⠇⠠⠐⠑⠒⠓⠔⠕⠖⠗⠘⠙⠚⠛⠜⠝⠞⠟⠠⠡⠢⠣⠤⠥⠦⠧⠨⠩⠪⠫⠬⠭⠮⠯⠰⠱⠲⠳

JACKDAWS LOVE MY PURPLE LYNX MADE OF

DON'T BE FOOLED BY THE TINY SIZE

{ [(1 2 3 4 5 6 7 8 9 0)] }

IT'S GOT DIACRITICS & PUNCT

ABCDEFGHIJKLMNOPQRSTUVWXYZ@#$%^&*ŒÉÁÓÜÃÑÎÉÁÓÜÃÎÇØ ---=+\|/•.,"'ªº«»

A pixelated script for the nerd of distinction

AaBbCcDdEeFfGgHhIiJjKkLlMmNnOoPpQqRrSsTtUuVvWwXxYyZz1234567890!

He found love on the net

Regular

Hey guys! I've spent the past several days (that's right,

abcdefghijklmnopqrstuvwxyzABCDEFGHIJKLMNOPQRSTUVWXYZ Don't be fooled by the tiny size

!@#$%^&*œéáóüãñîÉÁÓÜÃÎçø ---=+\|/•.,"' ªº«» { [(1 2 3 4 5 6 7 8 9 0)] }

Bold

haven't eaten, slept, done any work...) playing a

abcdefghijklmnopqrstuvwxyzABCDEFGHIJKLMNOPQRSTUVWXYZ A full character set included

!@#$%^&*œéáóüãñîÉÁÓÜÃÎçø ---=+\|/•.,"' ªº«» { [(1 2 3 4 5 6 7 8 9 0)] }

Small

pre-release version of Silicon Beach's new game, Dark Castle.

abcdefghijklmnopqrstuvwxyzABCDEFGHIJKLMNOPQRSTUVWXYZ Don't be fooled by the tiny size

!@#$%^&*œéáóüãñîÉÁÓÜÃÎçø ---=+\|/•.,"' ªº«» { [(1 2 3 4 5 6 7 8 9 0)] }

Small Bold

This game is AMAZING! [comp.sys.mac 12.08.1986]

abcdefghijklmnopqrstuvwxyzABCDEFGHIJKLMNOPQRSTUVWXYZ A full character set is included

Announcing the long-awaited update of
Oregon Trail Deluxe!

Transformed from the MS-DOS version, far beyond the outdated graphics in the Apple][version. The hot new look supports the current industry standard of

256-Color Graphics!

abcdefghijklmnopqrstuvwxyzABCDEFGHIJKLMNOPQRSTUVWXYZ!
1234567890@#$%^&*œéáóüãñîíéñóüãîíçø ---=+\|/..,"'ao«»

The game is mouse-driven, making it even more accessible to all youngsters.
Retailing for $59.95

Oregon Trail requires 2 megabytes of RAM, a VGA graphics card, and a hard drive.
abcdefghijklmnopqrstuvwxyzABCDEFGHIJKLMNOPQRSTUVWXYZ!
1234567890@#$%^&*œéáóüãñîíéñóüãîíçø ---=+\|/..,"'ao«»

Scriptometer

Matthew Bardram
2001

Atomic Media

TWO HARDY BOXING KANGAROOS JET FROM

ABCDEFGHIJKLMNOPQRSTUVWXYZABCDEFGHIJKLMNOPQRSTUVWXYZ

!1234567890@#$x^+*œÉÁÓÜÃÑÎÇ8 ---:+\|/.., "'88«»

SALT LAKE TO ZAMBIA BY PIXEL PLANE

ABCDEFGHIJKLMNOPQRSTUVWXYZABCDEFGHIJKLMNOPQRSTUVWXYZ

!1234567890@#$x^+*œÉÁÓÜÃÑÎÇ8 ---:+\|/.., "'88«»

Wired

Matthew Bardram
1999

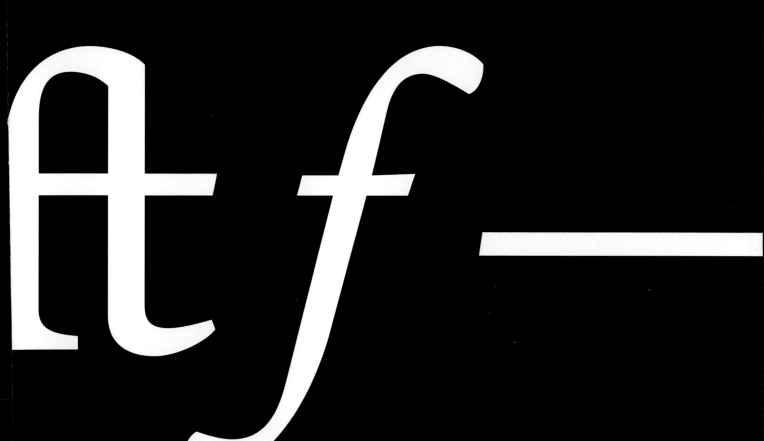

FELICIANO
TYPE
FOUNDRY

Feliciano Type Foundry is an independent
type foundry based in Lisbon, providing quality
font software for both platforms, Pc Windows
and Macintosh. The worldwide right to license
the typefaces BsArchae, BsKombat, BsLooper,
BsMandrax, BsMonofaked, BsRetchnov, FTF Merlo,
FTF Morgan Sans, FTF Morgan Sans Condensed,
FTF Morgan Bog, FTF Morgan Poster, FTF Morgan
Tower, FTF Rongel, and FTF Stella, belongs
exclusively to the Feliciano Type Foundry.

T: +351 21 390 61 40
F: +351 21 394 07 04
E: ftfinfo@secretonix.pt

To buy online go to myfonts.com

Bs-Archae Regular

AaBCDEEFGHIiJKLMMNNOPQRrSTbUVWXYYZ,&1234567890!?

Bs-Archae Bold

AaBCDEEFGHIiJKLMMNNOPQRrSTbUVWXYYZ,&12345678

Bs-Archae Heavy

AaBCDEEFGHIiJKLMMNNOPQRrSTbUVWXYYZ,&12345

Bs-Archae

Mário Feliciano
1999

Regular, Bold, Heavy

STAR

SUPERJET AIRCRAFTS

WIN

ENDLESS

DIFFERENT TIME ZONES

MICKEY SPILLANE

JACK

GRAVITY IS LESS ON THE

BRAIN

MR

SIR

GARFIELD

ARTHUR STERLING

THE

INVENTOR

Bs-Kombat

Mário Feliciano
1998

Normal, Alternate

Bs-Kombat & Kombat Alternate

ABCDEFGHIJKLMNOPQRSTUVWXYZ abcdefghijklmnopqrstuvwxyz áâàãäå ç

1234567890&!?.,,: — aemnrsty ÁÂÀÃÄ ç % $£ Ꝏꜵꜵꜹꜻꜽ ꜱꜱꜱ ꜰꜰꜰ ª⁰ ¶

FRESH

AIR

SEQUENCE

GR165

spacecraft

SUDDENLY

BASS

Electronique

DRIVERS

Science instruments

Mário Feliciano
2000

Regular Stencil, Black Stencil

Bs-Looper Black Stencil

ABCDEFGHIJKLMNOPQRSTU
VWXYZÆŒ&1234567890!?.;

B-53

SPECTROMETER

HANDUBES

SOUTH OF THE BORDER

ROCKIE

Bs-Looper Regular Stencil

ABCDEFGHIJKLMNOPQRSTU
VWXYZÆŒ&1234567890!?.;

ftfinfo@secretonix.pt

Bs-Mandrax Bold, Regular e Italic 7.5pt

There are approximately two billion children (persons under 18) in
the world. However, since Santa does not visit children of Muslim, Hindu,
Jewish or Buddhist religions, this reduces the workload for Christmas
night to 15% of the total, or 378 million (according to the population
reference bureau). At an average rate of 3.5 children per household, that
comes to 108 million homes, presuming that there is at least one good
child in each. Santa has about 31 hours of Christmas to work with, thanks
to the different time zones and the rotation of the earth, assuming he
travels east to west. This works out to 967.7 visits per second. This is to
say that, for each Christian household with a good child, Santa has around
1/1000th of a second to park the sleigh, hop out, jump down the chimney,
fill the stockings, distribute the remaining presents under the tree, eat
whatever snacks have been left for him, get back up the chimney, jump into
the sleigh, and get on to the next house. Assuming that each one of these
108 million stops is evenly distributed around the earth (which, of course,
we know to be false, but will accept for the purposes of our calculations), we
are now talking about 0.78 miles per household; a total trip of 75.5 million
miles, not counting bathroom stops or breaks. This means Santa's sleigh is
moving at 650 miles per second (3000 times the speed of sound). For
purposes of comparison, the fastest man-made vehicle, the Ulysses space
probe, moves at a poky 27.4 miles per second, and a conventional

Bs-Mandrax Regular 6pt

The payload of the sleigh adds another
interesting element. Assuming that each
child gets nothing more than a medium-sized
Lego set (two pounds), the sleigh is carrying
over 500 thousand tons, not counting Santa
himself. On land, a conventional reindeer
can pull no more than 300 pounds. Even
granting that the flying reindeer could pull
10 times that amount, the job can't be done
with eight or even nine of them; Santa would
need 360,000 of them. This increases the

Bs-Mandrax Italic 6pt

The payload of the sleigh adds another
interesting element. Assuming that each
child gets nothing more than a medium-sized
Lego set (two pounds), the sleigh is carrying
over 500 thousand tons, not counting Santa
himself. On land, a conventional reindeer can
pull no more than 300 pounds. Even granting
that the flying reindeer could pull 10 times
that amount, the job can't be done with eight
or even nine of them; Santa would need
360,000 of them. This increases the

Bs-Mandrax

Mário Feliciano
2000

Regular, Italic, Bold, Heavy

Feliciano

There are approximately two billion children in the world

Thermoelectric converter

Ultraviolet

The instrument looks for specific colors

Bs-Mandrax Regular complete character set

abcdefghijklmnopqrstuvwxyzABCDEFGHIJKLMNOPQRSTUVWXYZ_12345678
90,%‰!?&æœøßÆŒØ.:,; fifl° # ªº «»"‹›"''(—) †‡*¡¿-¥€f¢$©\|// [@] ™ [•] áâàäåå
çéêèëíîìïñóôòöõúûùüÿÁÂÀÄÃÅÇÉÊÈËÍÎÌÏÑÓÔÒÖÕÚÛÙÜŸ+−×÷<=>´ˆ`¨˜

FTF Merlo

Mário Feliciano
1997–2003

Roman (osf, lining, caps, figures, pi font), Italic (osf, lining, caps, figures, pi font)

Hujus difficillimæ absolutionis rarissimam laudem eximiè consecutus est Joachim Ibarra qui longe eminuit in splendidissima illa, et vere in omnibus regiâ, optimæ Salustii versionis Editione [...], quæ pariter stupendibus viris Hispanicarum, Latinarum, Hebraicarum, Phoenicia rumque literarum, necnon et artis *Typographiæ* peritissimis, prodiit Matriti, anno 1772, in fol. Et quid ab illa ingenios issimâ et acuratissi mâ gente. Quæ pretiosissimas Bibliothecas, et doctissimos earum catalogos habet, quid ad hispanicis musis omni disciplinarum et art-

E tudo isso porque, numa velha cidade alemã, alguem criara o processo facil de divulgar as ideias. depois foi a corrida vertiginosa da humanidade para as grandes invenções que tornaram pequeno o mundo e autorizam todas as esperanças. na base das conquistas maravilhosas do progresso, por detrás dos inventos que transformaram o mundo estão as pequenas e frágeis letras de Gutenberg.

Hahj*&a*

NATIONBUS DISPERGERET

STUPENDIBUS

Adinventionibus Dest

FTF Merlo Roman complete charcter set

abcdefghijklmnopqrstuvwxyzABCDEFGHIJKLMNOPQRS TUVWXYZ_1234567890,%‰!?&æœøßÆŒØ.:,;ABCDEFGHIJ KLMNOPQRSTUVWXYZ&ÆŒøfbfhfffifjfkflftffiffl&ſtðłþÐŁÞÐŁÞ° #ªº«»"‹›"'' (—)⁰¹²³⁴⁵⁶⁷⁸⁹⁄₀₁₂₃₄₅₆₇₈₉ (6) ½¼¾†‡*¡¿−¥€ƒ¢$©ı|‖ [@]™{·}āáâàäãåçčēéêèëğīíîìïñōóôòöõšūúûùüýÿž _1234567890ĀÁÂÀÄÃÅÇČĒÉÊÈËĞĪÍÎÌÏÑŌÓÔÒÖÕŠŪÚ ÛÙÜÝŸŽÁÂÀÄÃÅÇÉÊÈËÍÎÌÏÑÓÔÒÖÕÚÛÙÜŸ+−×÷<=>≠≤≥´ˆ`˜

Hujus diffcillimæ absolutionis rarissimam laudem eximiè consecutus est Joachim Ibarra qui longe eminuit in splendidissima illa, et vere in omnibus regiâ, optimæ Salustii versionis Editione [...], quæ pariter stupendibus viris Hispanicarum, Latinarum, Hebraicarum, Phoenicia rumque literarum, necnon et artis Typographiæ peritissimis, prodiit Matriti, anno 1772, in fol. Et quid ab illa ingenios issimâ et acuratissi mâ gente. Quæ pretiosissimas Bibliothecas, et doctissimos earum catalogos habet, quid ad hispanicis musis omni disciplinarum.

Chancillería

CRUZ

Sucedido en la ciudad de Lorca

Joaquim Ibarra 1772

FTF Merlo Italic complete charcter set

abcdefghijklmnopqrstuvwxyzABCDEFGHIJKLMNOPQRSTUV WXYZ1234567890,%‰!?GæœøßÆŒØ.:,;ABCDEFGHIJKLMNOP QRSTUVWXYZ&ÆŒØ&fhffiffiffjfkflftffflcłstðłþÐŁÞDLÞ°#ªº«»"‹›""'' (—)0123456789⁰⁄₀1234567890 (6)½¼¾†‡¡¿–¥€f¢$©1|//[@]&{·} āáàâäåçčēéèêëgīíìîïñōóòôöõšūúùûüýýž1234567890ĀÁÂÄÃÅ ÇČĒÉÈÊËĞĪÍÌÎÏÑŌÓÒÔÖÕŠŪÚÙÛÜÝŸŽÁÂÀÄÃÅÇÉÊÈËÍÎÌÏÑÓ ôồò̀ȍ́úûùüÿ+−×÷<=>≠≤±²´ˆˋ˜*

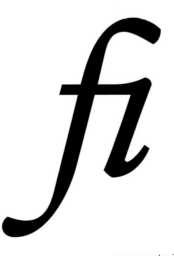

FTF Morgan Big

Mário Feliciano
2001

Big1 Regular, Big1 Oblique
Big1 Bold, Big1 Bold Oblique
Big2 Regular, Big2 Oblique
Big2 Bold, Big2 Bold Oblique
Big3 Regular, Big3 Oblique
Big3 Bold, Big3 Bold Oblique

BLOW

PI

OK

BEN

INVESTIGATE

GRAN

SOLAR

WIK

RUN FOR THE DOOR WHILE THEY SEARCH

STRONG

GUARDIANS OF THE UNIVERSE

POPULATION

MASTERMIND OF THE T-MEN

POWER-PACKED PAGES OF ADVENTURE

TWISTED BRAINS

PROFESSOR JEANS RIVER

NOW INTRODUCING THE SPACE CONQUERORS

INVENTION

FLYING SAUCERS

DRIVER

MILLION-DOLLAR

ftfinfo@secretonix.pt

ATOM

COSMIC SCIENTIST

INTRODUCING A NEW BUDGET OF ADVENTURE FANTASY AND FUN

SCREEN-SEARING STORY

DRAW ATTENTION TO THE LAVISH EXPENS

ADVENTURE

218E

THE BIG RUN

GRANGER

FT

FIELD

61058WE

SHOCK ENTERTAINMENT!

SOUNDS

WE1

AMPHIBASTRO

WHERE TEMPTATION

FTF Morgan Poster

Mário Feliciano
2001

Poster Regular, Poster Oblique
Poster Bold, Poster Bold Oblique
Poster Black, Poster Black Oblique

Feliciano

Mário Feliciano
2001

Regular (office, lining, caps, expert,
pi font, figures), Italic (office, lining,
caps, expert, pi font), Bold (office,
lining, caps, expert, pi font, figures),
Bold Italic (office, lining, caps, expert,
pi font)

1) Science instrument performance was nominal for all activities during this period. One frame of GS-4 data was recorded this week. The EDR backlog is 16 days.

Hafnz *afi*

2) There was one real-time schedule change made on 12/23 [DOY 358] when 4.9 hours of DSS-43 support substituted for DSS-45 released to NEAR. The total actual support for the period was 62.6 hours, of which 9.7 hours were large aperture coverage.

At some distance from the Sun, the supersonic solar wind will be held back from further expansion by the interstellar wind. The first feature to be encountered by a spacecraft as a result of this interstellar wind/solar wind interaction will be the termination shock, where the solar wind slows from supersonic to subsonic speed, and large changes in plasma flow direction and magnetic field orientation occur. Passage through the termination shock ends the termination shock phase and begins the heliosheath exploration phase. While the exact location of the termination shock is not known, it is very possible that Voyager 1 will complete the termination shock phase of the mission between the years 2001 and 2003 *when the spacecraft will be between 80 and 90 AU from the Sun. Most of the current estimates place the termination shock at around 85 ± 5 AU. After passage through the termination shock, the spacecraft will be operating in the heliosheath environment, which is still dominated by the Sun's magnetic field and particles contained in the solar wind.*

0123456789 High command transmissions

ABCDEFGHIJKLMNOPQRSTUVWXYZ123456

Three RTG units, electrically parallel-connected, are the central power sources for the mission module. Each RTG is made up of an isotopic heat source, a thermoelectric converter, a gas pressure venting system, temperature transducers, connectors, a heat rejecting CYLINDRICAL container, and bracketry. The RTGs are mounted in tandem (end-to-end) on a deployable boom as part **of the MM. The heat source radioisotopic fuel is Plutonium-238**

There are seven operating instruments on board each Voyager spacecraft, although the Plasma instrument on Voyager 1 is not returning useful data. Five of these instruments directly support the five science investigation teams.

These five instruments are:
MAG *Magnetic field investigation*
LECP *Low energy charged particle investigation*
PLS *Plasma investigation*
CRS *Cosmic ray investigation*
PWS *Plasma wave investigation*

Place verification operations 0123456789

Planet Earth

ftfinfo@secretonix.pt

Greetings to the Universe

The Voyager spacecraft will be the third and fourth human artifacts to escape entirely from the solar system. Pioneers 10 and 11, which preceded Voyager in outstripping the gravitational attraction of the Sun, both carried small metal plaques identifying their time and place of origin for the benefit of any other spacefarers that might find them in the distant future. With this example before them, NASA placed a more ambitious message aboard Voyager 1 and 2–a kind of time capsule, intended to communicate a story of our world to extraterrestrials. The Voyager message is carried by a phonograph record–a 12-inch goldplated copper disk containing sounds and images selected to portray the diversity of life and culture on Earth. The contents of the record were selected for NASA by a committee chaired by Carl Sagan of Cornell University. Dr. Sagan and his associates assembled 115 images and a variety of natural sounds, such as those made by surf, wind, and thunder; birds, whales, and other animals. To this, they added musical selections from different cultures and eras, spoken greetings from Earth-people in fifty-five languages, and printed messages from President Carter and U.N. Secretary-General Waldheim. Each record is encased in a protective aluminum jacket, together with a cartridge and a needle. Instructions, in symbolic language, explain the origin of the spacecraft, and indicate how the record is to be played. The 115 images are encoded

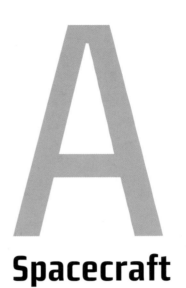

A
Spacecraft

FTF Morgan Sans Cond

Mário Feliciano
2001

Regular (office, lining, caps, expert, pi font, figures), Italic (office, lining, caps, expert, pi font), Bold (office, lining, caps, expert, pi font, figures), Bold Italic (office, lining, caps, expert, pi font)

Feliciano

ABILITY TO STORE *HGA* POINTING INFORMATION ON-BOARD

BACKUP MISSION LOAD DESCRIPTION

Flight system performance

RANGE, VELOCITY AND ROUND TRIP LIGHT TIME AS OF 12/29/00

Distance from the Sun (Km)	11,930,000,000	9,402,000,000
Distance from the Sun (Mi)	7,413,000,000	5,842,000,000
Distance from the Earth (Km)	12,039,000,000	9,533,000,000
Distance from the Earth (Mi)	7,481,000,000	5,923,000,000
Total Distance Traveled Since Launch (Km)	13,742,000,000	12,913,000,000
Total Distance Traveled Since Launch (Mi)	8,539,000,000	8,024,000,000
Velocity Relative to Sun (Km/sec)	17.259	15.768
Velocity Relative to Sun (Mi/hr)	38,606	35,271
Velocity Relative to Earth (Km/sec)	31.140	36.697
Velocity Relative to Earth (Mi/hr)	69,657	82,089
Round Trip Light Time (Hours:Minutes:Seconds)	22:18:34	17:39:58

The Voyager Interstellar Mission (VIM) has the potential for obtaining useful interplanetary—and possibly interstellar—fields, particles, and waves (FPW) science data until around the year 2020, when the spacecraft's ability to generate adequate electrical power for continued science instrument operation will come to an end. In order to capitalize on this lengthy data acquisition potential, it is imperative that the spacecraft have a continuing sequence of instructions for acquiring the desired science data, and that the spacecraft High Gain Antenna (HGA) remain boresighted on the Earth for continuous data transmission. Because of the long mission duration, and the likelihood of periodic spacecraft anomalies, it is also advantageous to continue the use of the onboard fault protection capability for automated responses to specific subsystem anomalies, and to provide an onboard sequence to continue spacecraft operation in the specific event of the future loss of command reception capability. All of these factors are considered in the VIM sequencing strategy. The

Mário Feliciano
2001

Tower One, Tower Two, Tower Three,
Tower Four

KGB

SQUADRON

ftfinfo@secretonix.pt

ROAMER
ACTION

Feliciano

FTF Rongel

Mário Feliciano
1999

Roman (osf, osf table, lining table,
expert, pi font, figures),
Italic (osf, osf table, lining table,
expert, pi font, figures)

Adinventionibus Dest

Na óptica de Simmel, nesta teoria é excluído de todo o sentido relativo à essência e ao valor da arte aquilo que não é totalmente interno àesfera estética. Há um enclausurar manifesto, uma tentativa fascizante de preservar a pureza estética

hujus difficillimæ absolutionis rarissimam laudem eximiè consecutus est Joachim Ibarra qui longe eminuit in splendidissima illa, et vere in omnibus regiâ, optimæ Salustii versionis Editione [...], quæ pariter stupendibus viris Hispanicarum, Latinarum, Hebraicarum, Phoeniciarumque literarum, necnon et artis Typographiæ peritissimis, prodiit Matriti, anno 1772, in fol. Et quid ab illa ingenios issimâ et acuratissimâ gente. Quæ pretiosissimas Bibliothecas, et doctissimos earum catalogos habet, quid ad hispanicis musis omni disciplinarum et artium genere sperandum sit, hoc illustrissimo exemplo abundè comprobavit.

NATIONBUS DISPERGERET

Hahj&*a*;

A B C D E F G H I J K L M N O P Q R S T U V W X Y Z &

Na óptica de Simmel, nesta teoria é excluído de todo
o sentido relativo à essência e ao valor da arte aquilo que não é
totalmente interno à esfera estética. Há um enclausurar manifesto,
uma tentativa fascizante de preservar a pureza estética

En este manuscrito tenemos
un exemplo sumamente persuasivo
de quán necesaria es la critica para
hacer juicio de los libros

A B C D E F G H I J K L M N O P Q R S T U V W X Y Z &

Bibliotheca

FTF Stella

Mário Feliciano
2000

Regular (osf, lining, osf table, lining table, expert figures, pi font), Italic (osf, lining, osf table, lining table, expert, pi font), Bold (osf, lining, osf table, lining table, expert figures, pi font), Bold Italic (osf, lining, osf table, lining table, expert, pi font)

There are approximately two billion children (persons under 18) in the world. However, since Santa does not visit children of Muslim, Hindu, Jewish or Buddhist religions, this reduces the workload for Christmas night to 15% of the total, or 378 million (according to the population reference bureau). At AN AVERAGE RATE OF 3.5 CHILDREN

There are approximately two billion *children (persons under 18) in the world. However, since Santa does not visit children of Muslim, Hindu, Jewish or Buddhist religions, this reduces the workload for Christmas night to 15% of the total, or 378 million (according to the population reference bureau). At an average rate of 3.5 CHILDREN PER HOUSEHOLD, THAT*

ABC

Santa Claus

Engineer's Perspective

The payload of the sleigh adds another interesting element. Assuming that each child gets nothing more than a medium-sized *Lego* set (two pounds), the sleigh is carrying over 500 thousand tons, not counting Santa himself. On land, a conventional REINDEER CAN PULL NO MORE THAN 300 POUNDS

THE PAYLOAD OF THE SLEIGH adds another interesting element. Assuming that each child gets nothing more than a medium-sized Lego *set (two pounds), the sleigh is carrying over 500 thousand tons, not counting Santa himself. On land, a conventional reindeer can pull no more than 300 pounds. Even granting that the flying reindeer could pull 10 times that amount, the job can't be done with eight or even nine of them; Santa would need 360,000 of them. This increases the payload, not counting the weight of the sleigh, another 54,000 tons, or roughly seven times the weight of the* Queen Elizabeth *(the ship, not the monarch).*

There are approximately two billion children (persons under 18) in the world. However, since Santa does not visit children of Muslim, Hindu, Jewish or Buddhist religions, this reduces the workload for Christmas night to 15% of the total, or 378 million (according to the population reference bureau). **AT AN AVERAGE RATE OF 3.5 CHILDREN**

There are approximately two billion *children (persons under 18) in the world. However, since Santa does not visit children of Muslim, Hindu, Jewish or Buddhist religions, this reduces the workload for Christmas night to 15% of the total, or 378 million (according to the population reference bureau). At an average rate of 3.5 CHILDREN PER HOUSEHOLD, THAT*

THE PAYLOAD OF THE SLEIGH adds another interesting element. Assuming that each child gets nothing more than a medium-sized *Lego* set (two pounds), the sleigh is carrying over 500 thousand tons, not counting Santa himself. On land, a conventional reindeer can pull no more than 300 pounds. Even granting that the flying reindeer could pull 10 times that amount, the job can't be done with eight or even nine of them; Santa would need 360,000 of them. This increases the payload, not counting the weight of the sleigh, another 54,000 tons, or roughly seven times the weight of the *Queen Elizabeth* (the ship, not the

Abefghist

Habcdefg*hijk***lmnop**

HUISHOUDELIJK

THE SPACECRAFT WILL BE BETWEEN

ABC

FORTIES

SEQUENCING

Como é seu habito, tantas vezes, Graham Greene escolheu

Æ

RESEARCH CONTROLS

Stan

Atmosphere

&

SHIPBUILDER

Engineering equipment

Civil engineering developers

DRAWING

Jornalista incomparável, um dos escritores mais

The incredible

Plaques kilométriques

METEOR

Em Londres os Serviços Secretos acreditam em tudo e Wormold é considerado

Feliciano

Since its inception in 1994, Galápagos Design Group continues to provide cost effective custom font technology solutions and creative type services for corporate identity and branding in numerous business sectors. Galápagos also continues to add new flavor to its unique type library.

Galápagos clients include many major font foundries, as well as original equipment manufacturers, independent software vendors, and design firms, such as:

Agilent Technologies, Apple, BP, DigitalVision, Eli Lilly, Hewlett Packard, Lockheed Martin, Microsoft, Qwest, Saatchi & Saatchi, and Wachovia Financial.

Galápagos Design — Font Technology and Design Solutions.

Contact: Larry Oppenberg or Mike Allen
Website: www. galapagosdesign.com
Telephone: 978 952 6200
Fax: 978 952 6260
email: info@galapagosdesign.com

George Ryan
2002

Burly and athletic, vigorous and strong, Robusto will add puissance to your project. The powerful build of each character portrays health and vitality, while the suave, curly tails add a seductive allure. Inspired by the lettering of Oz Cooper, George Ryan delivers another highly functional display type.

"Life will not be full and complete with me until I see the right type named 'Robusto'. I have awakened in the stilly night snickering at that name. I see a fat boy in a circus, a playful St. Bernard pup, an elephant, a Mack truck, or what have you... It should be a comic type".

Thoughts on Robusto — Oswald Cooper
from The Book of Oz Cooper

Galápagos

Bartholemé Open

Dennis Pasternak
2002

Bartholemé Open
Bartholemé SC Open

An award-winning classical design,
Bartholemé Open features a large
x-height, tightly curved counters, and
crisp serifs with tight bracketing.

SENATVS·POPVLVSQVE·ROMANVS

IMP·CAESARI·DIVI·NERVAE·F·NERVAE

TRAIANO·AVG·GERM·DACICO·PONTIF

·MAXIMO·TRIB·POT·

XVII·IMP·VI·COS·VI·P·P·ADDECLARAN

DVM·QVANTAE·ALTITVDINIS·MONS·ET

LOCVS·TANTIS·OPERIBVS·SIT·E·GESTVS

The base inscription on the Trajan Column
commemorating Trajan's victories over
King Decebalus in the Dacian wars of
the Danube·Carpathian territory.

978-952-6200

AÆBCDEFGHIJKLMNOØŒPQRSTUVWXYZ&aæb
cdeffiflghijklmnoøœpqrsßtuvwxyz $12345€67890
(.,:;?¿!¡...‹›«»“”‘’‚„) @*§†‡¶ ÅÇÉÏÔÑÙ åçéïôñù

Bartholemé Regular

Dennis Pasternak
2002

Bartholemé Regular
Bartholemé Medium
Bartholemé Bold
Bartholemé Extrabold

The four-weight semicondensed
Bartholemé family came into existence
as a family expansion based on the
designer's earlier concept, Bartholemé
Open. This hybrid family was inspired
by–and loosely based on–a number of
mid-twentieth-century type concepts
having Old Face or Modern influences.
Those inspirational type designs were
primarily designed for various propri-
etary photolettering technologies of
the times. Design qualities include a
large x-height, tightly curved counters,
and crisp serifs with tight bracketing.
This Bartholemé family was designed
for display use in titling and short
passages of text.

A letter is a designed area. It is a pattern made within a space. Its outlines have the effect of motion. It begins and ends. The things are true about the shapes of letters that are true about all designs that have pattern and motion. The pattern of a let ter may be graceful or it may be awkward, and the fact of its

A letter is a designed area. It is a pattern made within a space. Its outlines have the effect of motion. It begins and ends. The things are true about the shapes of letters that are true about all designs that have pattern and motion. The pattern of a let ter may be graceful or it may be awkward, and the fact of its

A letter is a designed area. It is a pattern made within a space. Its outlines have the effect of motion. It begins and ends. The things are true about the shapes of letters that are true about all designs that have pattern and motion. The pat tern of a letter may be graceful or it may be awkward, and

A letter is a designed area. It is a pattern made within a space. Its outlines have the effect of motion. It begins and ends. The things are true about the shapes of letters that are true about all designs that have pattern and motion. The pattern of a letter may be graceful or it may be awk

AÆBCDEFGHIJKLMNOØŒPQRSTUVWXYZ&aæb
cdeffiflghijklmnoøœpqrsßtuvwxyz $12345€67890
(.,:;?¿!¡...‹›«»“”‘’‚„) @§†‡¶ ÅÇÉÏÔÑÙ åçéïôñù*

Bartholemé Italic

Dennis Pasternak
2002

Bartholemé Italic
Bartholemé Medium Italic
Bartholemé Bold Italic
Bartholemé Extrabold Italic

Galápagos

A letter is a designed area. It is a pattern made within a space. Its outlines have the effect of motion. It begins and ends. The things are true about the shapes of letters that are true about all designs that have pattern and motion. The pattern of a let ter may be graceful or it may be awkward, and the fact of its

A letter is a designed area. It is a pattern made within a space. Its outlines have the effect of motion. It begins and ends. The things are true about the shapes of letters that are true about all designs that have pattern and motion. The pattern of a let ter may be graceful or it may be awkward, and the fact of its

A letter is a designed area. It is a pattern made within a space. Its outlines have the effect of motion. It begins and ends. The things are true about the shapes of letters that are true about all designs that have pattern and motion. The pat tern of a letter may be graceful or it may be awkward, and

A letter is a designed area. It is a pattern made within a space. Its outlines have the effect of motion. It begins and ends. The things are true about the shapes of letters that are true about all designs that have pattern and motion. The pattern of a letter may be graceful or it may be awk

McLemore

George Ryan
2002

McLemore Light
McLemore Light Italic
McLemore
McLemore Italic
McLemore Bold
McLemore Bold Italic
McLemore Black
McLemore Black Italic

¶ At a very young age, some children have a particular fascination with the colorful letters carved in the faces of wooden blocks. ¶ As they are *growing to adolescence, they are saturated with with letters of all types — animated letters, vibrant brush lettering, colorful signs and huge billboards.* ¶ Some older children start experimenting with drawing the letters they have in their active memory or in their own environment. *Some of these letters are primitive and others are very interesting.* ¶ **Some teens may attend an art school and others may work a job where working with letters is important.** *They are taught how letters are fit with one another to form fluid words.* ¶ **For some people, letter drawings become type, more refined while starting to understand the minutiæ** *of spa cing, curves and proportions of a well-design*

978-952-6200

AÆBCDEFGHIJKLMNOØŒPQRSTU VWXYZ&aæbcdeffifflghijklmnoøœpqr sßtuvwxyz $12345€67890 (.,:;?¿!¡…‹›«»

A letter is a designed area. It is a pattern made within a space. Its outlines have the effect of motion. It begins and ends. The things are true about the shapes of letters that are true about all designs that have pattern and motion. The

A letter is a designed area. It is a pattern made within a space. Its outlines have the effect of motion. It begins and ends. The things are true about the shapes of letters that are true about all designs that have pattern and motion. The

A letter is a designed area. It is a pattern made within a space. Its outlines have the effect of motion. It begins and ends. The things are true about the shapes of letters that are true about all designs that have pattern and motion. The

A letter is a designed area. It is a pattern made within a space. Its outlines have the effect of motion. It begins and ends. The things are true about the shapes of letters that are true about all designs that have pattern and motion. The

McLemore Regular

George Ryan
2002

McLemore Light
McLemore Regular
McLemore Bold
McLemore Black

The essence of this superior face is the slightly concave nature of the stems, arms, and serifs of each character. This creates a highly legible typeface with a graceful, natural presence on the page, and at larger point sizes, it's magical!

AÆBCDEFGHIJKLMNOØŒPQRSTUV WXYZ&aæbcdeffifflghijklmnoøœpqrsßtuv wxyz $12345€67890 (.,:;?¿!¡…‹›«»""''‚„) @

A letter is a designed area. It is a pattern made with in a space. Its outlines have the effect of motion. It be gins and ends. The things are true about the shapes of letters that are true about all designs that have pat tern and motion. The pattern of a letter may be crude

A letter is a designed area. It is a pattern made with in a space. Its outlines have the effect of motion. It begins and ends. The things are true about the shapes of letters that are true about all designs that have pat tern and motion. The pattern of a le

A letter is a designed area. It is a pattern made with in a space. Its outlines have the effect of motion. It begins and ends. The things are true about the shapes of letters that are true about all designs that have pattern and motion. The pattern of a letter may be

A letter is a designed area. It is a pattern made within a space. Its outlines have the effect of motion. It begins and ends. The things are true about the shapes of letters that are true about all designs that have pattern and motion. The

McLemore Italic

George Ryan
2002

McLemore Light Italic
McLemore Italic
McLemore Bold Italic
McLemore Black Italic

Galápagos

New Age

Alex Kaczun
2002

New Age Regular
New Age Italic

Chapter Eleven

¶ So I travelled, stopping ever and again, in gr eat strides of a thousand years or more, drawn on by the mystery of the earth's fate, watching with a strange fascination the sun grow larger and duller in the western sky, and the life of th e old earth ebb away. At last, more than thirty million years hence, the huge red-hot dome of the sun had come to obscure nearly a tenth pa rt of the darkling heavens. Then I stopped once more, for the crawling multitude of crabs had disappeared, and the red beach, save for its liv id green liverworts and lichens, seemed lifeless. And now it was flecked in white. A bitter cold assailed me.

excerpt from The Time Machine—*H.G.Wells*

AÆBCDEFGHIJKLMNOØŒPQRSTUVW XYZ&aæbcdeffifflghijklmnoøœpqrsßtuvw xyz $12345€67890 (.,:;?¿!¡...‹›«»""''‚„) @

A letter is a designed area. It is a pattern made within a space. Its outlines have the effect of mo tion. It begins and ends. The things are true about about the shapes of letters that are true about all

A letter is a designed area. It is a pattern made within a space. Its outlines have the effect of motion. It begins and ends. The things are true about the shapes of letters that are

New Age Regular

Alex Kaczun
2002

New Age Regular
New Age Bold

New Age: The dawn of a new age in typography. A sophisticated design with an air of class and distinction, New Age blends the readability of a serif typeface with the graphic impact of a sans serif. Numerous cursive elements add harmony, linking this typeface with the past. New Age–the best of both worlds.

AÆBCDEFGHIJKLMNOØŒPQRSTUVW XYZ&aæbcdeffifflghijklmnoøœpqrsßtuvwxy z $12345€67890 (.,:;?¿!¡...‹›«»""''‚„) @∫†*

A letter is a designed area. It is a pattern made within a space. Its outlines have the effect of motion. It begins and ends. The things are true about the shapes of letters that are true about all designs that have

A letter is a designed area. It is a pattern made within a space. Its outlines have the effect of motion. It begins and ends. The things are true about the shapes of letters that are true about

New Age Italic

Alex Kaczun
2002

New Age Italic
New Age Bold Italic

AÆBCDEFGHIJKLMNOØŒPQRSTUVWXYZ &aæbcdeffifflghijklmnoøœpqrsßtuvwxyz $12 345€67890 (.,:;?¿!¡...‹›«»""''‚„) @*∫†‡¶ ÅÇ

A letter is a designed area. It is a pattern made with in a space. Its outlines have the effect of motion. It begins and ends. The things are true about the shapes of letters that are true about all designs that have pat

A letter is a designed area. It is a pattern made with in a space. Its outlines have the effect of motion. It begins and ends. The things are true about the shapes of letters that are true about

New Age Condensed

Alex Kaczun
2002

New Age Condensed
New Age Bold Condensed

Galápagos

Culpepper Regular

George Ryan
2002

Culpepper Light
Culpepper Regular
Culpepper Extrabold

A Grecian urn inscribed by the artisan. A spiritual Pagan glyph carved in stone. A Celtic bracelet found in an excavation. All these images are brought to mind when Culpepper works its magic across the page. Developed by George Ryan, Culpepper is inspired by the work of Rudolph Koch. This new face is perfect for any artistic design, and will add a sense of antiquity to your work.

AÆBCDEFGHIJKLMNOØŒPQRSTUVWX
YZ&aæbcdeffifflghijklmnoøœpqrsßtuvwxy
z $12345€67890(.,:;?¿!¡…‹›«»""''„,) @*†‡§

A letter is a designed area. It is a pattern made within a space. Its outlines have the effect of motion. It begins and ends. The things are true about the shapes of letters that are true about all designs that have pattern and motion. The motion of a letter may be graceful or awkward, and the fact of its grace or awkwardness is apparent at once. Judgement upon these

A letter is a designed area. It is a pattern made within a space. Its outlines have the effect of motion. It begins and ends. The things are true about the shapes of letters that are true a bout all designs that have pattern and motion. The motion of a letter maybe graceful or awkward, and the fact of its grace or awkwardness is apparent at once.

A letter is a designed area. It is a pattern made within a space. Its outlines have the effect of motion. It begins and ends. The things are true about the shapes of letters that are true about all designs that have pattern and motion. The motion of a letter maybe graceful or awkward, and the fact of its grace or awk

Culpepper Regular SC

George Ryan
2002

Culpepper Light SC
Culpepper SC
Culpepper Extrabold SC

AÆBCDEFGHIJKLMNOØŒPQRSTUVW
XYZ&AÆBCDEFFIFLGHIJKLMNOØŒPQRSSST
UVWXYZ $12345€67890(.,:;?¿!¡…‹›«»""''„,)

A LETTER IS A DESIGNED AREA. IT IS A PATTERN MADE WITHIN A SPACE. ITS OUTLINES HAVE THE EFFECT OF MOTION. IT BEGINS AND ENDS. THE THINGS ARE TRUE ABOUT THE SHAPES OF LETTERS THAT ARE TRUE ABOUT ALL DESIGNS THAT HAVE PATTERN AND MOTION. THE MOTION OF A LETTER MAY BE GRACEFUL OR AWK WARD, AND THE FACT OF ITS GRACE

A LETTER IS A DESIGNED AREA. IT IS A PATTERN MADE WITHIN A SPACE. ITS OUTLINES HAVE THE EFFECT OF MOTION. IT BEGINS AND ENDS. THE THINGS ARE TRUE ABOUT THE SHAPES OF LETTERS THAT ARE TRUE A BOUT ALL DESIGNS THAT HAVE PATTERN AND MOTION. THE MOTION OF A LETTER MAYBE GRACEFUL OR AWK WARD, AND THE FACT OF ITS GRACE

A LETTER IS A DESIGNED AREA. IT IS A PATTERN MADE WITHIN A SPACE. ITS OUTLINES HAVE THE EFFECT OF MOTION. IT BEGINS AND ENDS. THE THINGS ARE TRUE ABOUT THE SHAPES OF LETTERS THAT ARE TRUE ABOUT ALL DESIGNS THAT HAVE PAT PATTERN AND MOTION. THE MO TION OF A LETTER MAYBE GRACE FUL OR AWKWARD, AND THE FACT

978-952-6200

ABCDEFGHIJKLMNOPQRSTUVWXYZ&abcdefgh
ijklmnopqrstuvwxyz $12345€67890 (.,:;?¿!¡...<>«»

A sleek flat panel color display

that has a smaller footprint to add more workspace and a high tech look to your home office.

Extreme Sans

Alex Kaczun
2002

A no-frills sans serif of the future, Extreme Sans features clean and simple lines, with no abrupt terminals. Character edges are rounded like high-tech routed parts of precise machinery. The overall look speaks of technology and innovation, and holds extreme possibilities for typographic expression today and tomorrow.

ABCDEFGHIJKL MNOPQRSTUVWXYZ&abcdefgh
ijklmnopqrstuvwxyz $12345€67890 (.,:;?¿!¡...<>«»

More gigabytes of storage space

let you create all types of multimedia projects without the worry of running out of disk space.

Extreme Sans Oblique

Alex Kaczun
2002

ABCDEFGHIJKLMNOPQRSTUVWXYZ&abcdefg
hijklmnopqrstuvwxyz $12345€67890 (.,:;?¿!¡...<>

Clean & simple lines, no abrupt

terminals. Character edges are rounded like high tech routed parts of precise machinery.

Extreme Sans Heavy

Alex Kaczun
2002

ABCDEFGHIJKLMNOPQRSTUVWXYZ&abcdefg
hijklmnopqrstuvwxyz $12345€67890 (.,:;?¿!¡...<>

The lightning-quick DSL speed

you have been waiting for. You can now download those huge sound and picture files in a f

Extreme Sans Heavy Obl

Alex Kaczun
2002

Galápagos

Dave Farey, Richard Dawson
2002

Tired of the functional monoline sans serif fonts? Ersatz has a style with vibrant roots in the Mediterranean climate of modern Spain. It's refreshing and lively. Basic constructions are simple and attractive, with its soft curves and kickbacks!

AÆBCDEFGHIJKLMNOØŒPQRSTUVWXYZ&aæb
cdeffiflghijklmnoøœpqrsßtuvwxyz $12345€678
90 (.,:;?¿!i…‹›«»""''",,) @*†‡§¶ ÅÇÉÏÔÑÙ åçéïôñ

Saucy Spanish flamencos

Vibrant Roots in the Mediterranean

Lively sans serif with soft curves & kickbacks

Unique biform letters mixing upper with lowercase elements

Dave Farey, Richard Dawson
2002

AÆBCDEFGHIJKLMNOØŒPQRSTUVWXYZ&a
æbcdeffiflghijklmnoøœpqrsßtuvwxyz $12345
€67890 (.,:;?¿!i…‹›«»""''",,) @*†‡§¶ ÅÇÉÏÔÑÙ

Designers who crave color

and sunlight create refreshing fonts

Listen carefully, you can hear the sharp gui

tars and soft tambourine sounds of exciting flamenco music

978-952-6200

AÆBCDEFGHIJKLMNOØŒPQRSTUVWXYZ
&aæbcdeffiflghijklmnoøœpqrsßtuvwxyz
$12345€67890(.,:;?¿!i…‹›«»""''‚„)@†‡§¶

Lower tax rates for home
owners that will affect future
town budgets for the next eight years.
This led to a fiery debate between the town council

Prop Ten

George Ryan
2002

A face with a twist! A slant on a classic style, this design features squared-off apexes, beveled t's, and dwarfed tails. This face offers designers the uniformity of a mono-spaced typeface with the legibility of a proportional one. Prop Ten delivered unequivocal clarity.

AÆBCDEFGHIJKLMNOØŒPQRSTUVWXYZ
&aæbcdeffiflghijklmnoøœpqrsßtuvwx
yz $12345€67890(.,:;?¿!i…‹›«»""''‚„)@

A stronger grassroots po
litical organization is making
a substantial difference in this year's
national election. It has changed the opinion of m

Prop Ten Bold

George Ryan
2002

Galápagos

Jorge

George Ryan
2002

Can you say "character"? A new cartoon face, Jorge (Hor-hay) brings words to life. Quirky and comical, Jorge will lighten the mood of your design with its wacky personality. Although the font was created in uppercase only, Jorge's four style variations add diversity and verve to the mix.

ABCDEFGHIJKLMNOPQRSTUVWXYZ& $12345€67890
{[(.,:;?¿!¡...<>«»""''',,,)]} @*§†‡¶ ©®™ ÅÇÉÏÑÔÙÆŒSS
WELCOME TO 4 STYLES OF ZANY FONTS
INSPIRED BY THE FARCICAL SATURDAY MORNING CARTOONS

Jorge Outline

George Ryan
2002

ABCDEFGHIJKLMNOPQRSTUVWXYZ& $12345€67890
{[(.,:;?¿!¡...<>«»""''',,,)]} @*§†‡¶ ©®™ ÅÇÉÏÑÔÙÆŒSS
OF THE FIFTIES. DO YOU REMEMBER
THE EXPRESSIONS OF THE COYOTE GETTING HIS LATEST ACME GIZMO?

Jorge Drop Shadow

George Ryan
2002

ABCDEFGHIJKLMNOPQRSTUVWXYZ& $12345€67
890 {[(.,:;?¿!¡...<>«»""''',,,)]} @*§†‡¶ ©®™ ÅÇÉÏÑÔÙ
WILEY NEVER DID GET TO CATCH HIS
NEMESIS, THE ELUSIVE ROADRUNNER, BUT ALWAYS SEEMED

Jorge Outline DS

George Ryan
2002

ABCDEFGHIJKLMNOPQRSTUVWXYZ& $12345€6
7890 {[(.,:;?¿!¡...<>«»""''',,,)]} @*§†‡¶ ©®™ ÅÇÉÏÑÔ
TO GET TOASTED, BLASTED TO BITS,
OR TAKE A NEVERENDING FREEFALL INTO A DEEP CANYON.

ABCDEFGHIJKLMNOPQRSTUVW
XYZ&abcdefghijklmnopqrstuvx
A three element
font inspired by classic theatre

Bing Inline

Dennis Pasternak
2002

Bing takes its inspiration from a combination of the classic cinema marquee and contemporary fabricated signage. The Bing family's versatility is what makes this typeface so stellar. Bing Script allows you to create a simple handwritten look on the page, while Bing Black can be used as a poster face to increase the visibility and punch of your message. Bing Inline combines the two faces to energize the prose in your project.

ABCDEFGHIJKLMNOPQRSTUV
WXYZ&abcdefghijklmnopqrst
marquees and fa
bricated contemporary signage

Bing Black

Dennis Pasternak
2002

ABCDEFGHIJKLMNOPQRSTUVWXYZ
&abcdefghijklmnopqrstuvwxyz $123
A script having roots
in irregular handblown tubular glass
used in traditional neon signs of the

Bing Script

Dennis Pasternak
2002

Galápagos

Dennis Pasternak
2002

Sleek and streetwise, Bisco is an expressive display face with irregular contours, giving weight and bounce. This design achieves high readability at all point sizes.

AÆBCDEFGHIJKLMNOØŒPQRSTUVWXYZ&AÆ
BCDEFFIFLGHIJKLMNOØŒPQRSSSTUVWXYZ $12345€6
7890 (.,:;?¿!¡…‹›«»""''„‚) @*†‡§¶ ÅÇÉÏÑÔÙ åç

GRAFITTI ARTISTS PROTEST!

LACK OF AVAILABLE SPACE ON REMAINING DOWNTOWN

BUILDINGS AND PUBLIC FIXTURES. A SPOKESPERSON FOR THE

GROUP STATED THE CITY COUNCIL'S IRRESPONSIBILITY IN PROVIDING ADEQUATE SPACE FOR FUTURE ENHANCEMENTS. THE PROTESTERS FEEL THEIR CREATIVITY IS BE

Alex Kaczun
2002

Handwriting with passion and flair, Swordtail is a freehand script with a swashbuckling style reminiscent of old Spain. There is an undeniable energy in the strokes, a rhythm and beat of a passionate hand.

AÆBCDEFGHIJKLMNOØŒPQRSTUV
WXYZ&aæbcdeffiflghijklmnoøœpqrsßt
uvwxyz $12345€67890 (.,?¿!¡…<>""""„‚) @

Buccaneers or Raiders

Eighteenth century pirates seizing gold and silver in their swashbuckling style on the high seas of the Caribbean. Ambushing and outrunning ships

978-952-6200

AÆBCDEFGHIJKLMNOØŒPQRST
UVWXYZ&aæbcdeffiflghijklmnoøœp
qrsßtuvwxyz $12345€67890 (.,:;?¿!¡…‹›

Off Broadway comedies made

a strong comeback this past year as reported

in entertainment's source of news, Variety magazine. It

has been reported the upturn in ticket sales is due to appearances by top
name stars, improved stage design, scripts, one-liners and overall appeal

Geis

George Ryan
2002

Curvaceous yet sleek, these well-developed characters create a nostalgic face with a contemporary feel. Bevelled ascenders and descenders combined with the gradient of thick-to-thin transitions give this typeface balance and rhythm, while the weight adds depth and grace.

Aa Bb Cc Dd Ee Ff Gg Hh Ii Jj Kk Ll
Mm Nn Oo Pp Qq Rr Ss Tt Uu Vv Ww Xx
Yy Zz & $12345€67890 (.,:;?¿!¡…‹›«» "",,,,)@

Sophisticated and stylish quill

inspired letterforms add a touch of class, at all point

sizes, in a formal or informal textual page setting. This script adds delicacy to the

the smaller point sizes required for invitations, or in specialized one-line titling usage.

Tiamaria

George Ryan
2002

Soft, sensual lines add subtle touches of the feminine in the form of a delicate script. The graceful Tiamaria adds a touch of class to the page.

Galápagos

Holland Fonts

Holland Fonts. Typefaces by Max Kisman.

...In the early 1980s, Max Kisman became the designer of a small, independent music magazine, *Vinyl*. This Amsterdam-based publication was set up very much as a response to the innovative British magazine, *The Face*. Responding to Neville Brody's radical designs for that magazine, Kisman began to experiment by creating new headline typefaces for each issue... (Emily King. New Faces: type design in the first decade of device-independent digital typesetting. 1987–1997. http://www.typotheque.com/articles/EK_PhD_chapter5.html)

Holland Fonts was founded in 2002.
95 Bolsa Avenue, Mill Valley, California, CA 94941, U.S.A.

www.hollandfonts.com / info@hollandfonts.com

BOEM

PAUKESLAG

daar ligt alles **PLAT**

O_____o

weer razen violen cello bassen koperen triangel

trommels **PAUKEN**

razen rennen razen rennen razen **RENNEN**

drama in volle slag hoeren slangen werpen zich op eerlijke

mannen het gezin wankelt de Fabriek wankelt

de eer wankelt ligt er

alle begrippen **VALLEN**

HALT!

MaxMix One

Max Kisman
1991

MaxMix One is a compilation of characters from various fonts for the FontFont
library and other custom alphabets
designed between 1985 and 1991.

"Boem Paukeslag" is a poem by Paul van
Ostaijen from the bundle *De Bezette
Stad* (The Occupied City), Berlin, 1920.

The remix of the poem using MaxMix
One was originally published as a poster
by *TYP/Typografisch Papier* in the
Netherlands in 1991.

Typefaces by Max Kisman,
available at FontFont.com are:
FF Scratch, FF Network, FF Cutout, FF
Fudoni, FF Rosetta, FF Jacque and FF
Vortex, published by FontShop
International, Germany.

Holland Fonts

Bebedot Black

Max Kisman
1998

Bebedot developed from doodles and scribbles in notebooks; irregular forms might very well contain a style for an alphabet.

ABCDEFGHIJKLMNOPQRSTUVWXYZabcdefghijklmnop
qrstuvwxyz0123456789$¢€£¥f-.,.:;...''""„,¡¿?!&ÂÇÉÎÑÒ

Significant
MODERN TYPE

Bebedot Blonde

Max Kisman
1998

Bebedot Blonde was first used in an intro spread in *Wired* magazine, designed by Max Kisman (#6.04, April 1998): *"To keep up you need the right answers. To get ahead you need the right questions."*
The name of this typeface was inspired by a women's clothing campaign on San Francisco's bus stands. The dot is for the com that never came.

ABCDEFGHIJKLMNOPQRSTUVWXYZabcdefghijklmnop
qrstuvwxyz0123456789$¢€£¥f-.,.:;...''""„,¡¿?!&ÂÇÉÎÑÒ

Lower case
CAPITAL LINE

Circuit Closed

Max Kisman
1997

A decorative tech typeface designed for use in station identities and animations for television.

ABCDEFGHIJKLMNOPQRSTUVWXYZabcdefghijklmnopq
rstuvwxyz0123456789$¢€£¥f-.,.:;...''""„,¡¿?!&ÂÇÉÎÑÒ

Alternatives
SHORT CUT ICONS

Circuit Open

Max Kisman
1997

The slight reference to the Westinghouse logo (designed by Paul Rand) was inspired by a dinner table created from a huge sign featuring that logo.

ABCDEFGHIJKLMNOPQRSTUVWXYZabcdefghijklmnopq
rstuvwxyz0123456789$¢€£¥f-.,.:;...''""„,¡¿?!&ÂÇÉÎÑÚ

Motherboard
EXPANSION CARD

Bfrika

Max Kisman
2001

Bfrika, an "Africa-inspired" typeface, was first used in *i-juici* magazine, the Typographic issue (#17, 2002, Durban, South Africa): "National Typographica." Its geometrical decorative design represents bold simplicity, directness, and rhythm. The name evolves from a text written for the spread in the magazine. The B replaces A. Bfrika. Africa be free.

BFRIKA . IHEARTHESOUNDO
FDRUMS . BEATINGONMYSKI
N . THEBASEDRIVESTHROUG
HMYBONES . ISHIVERFROMT
HESTRINGS . THERYTHMTAK
ESMEON . FOOTSTOMP . SCRE
AMANDSHOUTANDCLAP . SIN
GTHESONGOFSADNESS . SING
THESONGOFHOPE . THEBEAUT
YOFTHEDARKNESS . THEPURP
LESKYABOVE . VOICEOFSWEE
TNESS . VOICEOFANGER . VOI
CEOFNATURE . VOICEOFLOVE
. THEMINDMOVESWHENTHEBO
DYSTOPS . WISHINGTOBETHE
RE . DARKANDSTRONGANDYOU
NGANDDEEP . AFRIKABEFREE

ABCDEFGHIIJKLMNOPQRSTUV
WXYZABCDEFGHIJKLMNOPQR
STUVWXYZ1234567890?!!!¡¡!

Holland Fonts

Max Kisman
2001

Originally design in 1984 for a compilation CD of world music called *Mundenge* (the word for "youth dance" in Zairean dialect Kipende), this typeface took inspiration not only from the music itself but also from the hand-painted lettering of barbershop signs.

Modern music from Zaire is often played on instruments made out of utility objects, like the *ongong*: traditionally a calabash and an elephant tooth as blowpipe, now often a can with a plastic or metal blowpipe; the *kalinda*: a skin-covered 50-liter barrel with strings of rope; or *banjo*: a buffalo- or boa-skin-covered can with nylon strings.

Percussion instruments may vary from bottles, compact cassette boxes, and cooking pots to friction disks of cars and custom-made metal scrapers. Other popular instruments are self-made guitars, like the *likembe*–a thumb piano–and the *bass-likembe* with four metal lamellas, amplified by a washing tub, or a scraper made of two sardine cans with a spring in between and a car battery-powered megaphone.

ABCDEFGHIJKLMNOPQRSTUVWXYZABCDEFGHIJKLMNO
PQRSTUVWXYZ0123456789$¢€£¥§-„,¨;…'''""„¡¿?!&ÅÇ

MUNDENGE
BROUSSE-ROCK
FROM ZAIRE
'YOUTH DANCE'
ONGONG
KALINDA
BASS-LIKEMBE

info@hollandfonts.com

ABCDEFGHIJKLMNOPQRSTUVWXYZabcdefghijklmno
pqrstuvwxyz0123456789$¢€£¥ƒ-.,:;…''""",„¡¿?!&ÅÇÉÎÑÒ

LOOK Nevertheless IT'S TIME

Quickstep Regular

Max Kisman
2001

Quickstep was designed in 1994 for the twenty-fifth anniversary of SSP Printing Co. in Amsterdam, the Netherlands, a well-known print shop for the local design community.

ABCDEFGHIJKLMNOPQRSTUVWXYZabcdefghijklmno
pqrstuvwxyz0123456789$¢€£¥ƒ-.,:;…''""",„¡¿?!&ÅÇÉÎÑ

EYES Communicator SENSITIVE

Quickstep Bold

Max Kisman
1994

Quickstep Bold was used for an intro spread, designed by Max Kisman, of a Brian Eno quote in *Wired* magazine (#3.05.May 1995): *"The problem with computers is that they don't have enough Africa in them. What's pissing me off is that they use so little of my body."*

Quickstep's erratic manual appearance was the perfect complement to the paper cutout-style illustration.

ABCDEFGHIJKLMNOPQRSTUVWXYZabcdefghijklmnopq
rstuvwxyz0123456789$¢€£¥ƒ-.,:;…''""",„¡¿?!&ÅÇÉÎÑÒØ

BURN Mediterranean FIREPLACE

Quickstep Sans Regular

Max Kisman
2002

ABCDEFGHIJKLMNOPQRSTUVWXYZabcdefghijklmnopq
rstuvwxyz0123456789$¢€£¥ƒ-.,:;…''""",„¡¿?!&ÅÇÉÎÑÒ

SHOW Scandinavian EXHIBITION

Quickstep Sans Regular

Max Kisman
2002

Chip 01

Max Kisman
1996

Chip 01 was designed for use on a "high-tech" transparent telephone card for the Royal Dutch Telecommunications Company. The typeface gave the card its own identity with a technological reference.

ABCDEFGHIJKLMNOPQRSTUVWXYZabcde
fghijklmnopqrstuvwxyz0123456789

Mobile phoney

Chip 02

Max Kisman
2002

Chip 02 is an adapted version of its predecessor, Chip 01, and offers increased legibility.

ABCDEFGHIJKLMNOPQRSTUVWXYZabcde
fghijklmnopqrstuvwxyz0123456789

Long distance

Interlace Single

Max Kisman
1998

Interlace Single was inspired by video technology and designed for use on television station identities; it never quite made it.

ABCDEFGHIJKLMNOPQRSTUVWXYZabcdef
ghijklmnopqrstuvwxyz0123456789$¢€

Video projector

Interlace Double

Max Kisman
1998

ABCDEFGHIJKLMNOPQRSTUVWXYZabcdef
ghijklmnopqrstuvwxyz0123456789$¢€

Frequency rate

Tribe Mono

Max Kisman
2001

A "soft-tech" typeface design for *www.fontshop.com/tribe*, a short-lived online magazine about typography and graphic design.

ABCDEFGHIJKLMNOPQRSTUVWXYZabcde
fghijklmnopqrstuvwxyz0123456789?

Time zone clash

info@hollandfonts.com

ABCDEFGHIJKLMNOPQRSTUVWXYZabcdefghijklmnopqrstuv wxyz0123456789$-.,:;''""¡¿?!&ÅÇÉÎÑÖØÜåçéòøüŒæŒœ'"*/\

Sequence signal dip

Submarine Extra Light

Max Kisman
2003

Submarine originated from a type-face design developed for the web-site identity and logo of a small Dutch media production company bearing the same name.

ABCDEFGHIJKLMNOPQRSTUVWXYZabcdefghijklmnopqrstuv wxyz0123456789$-.,:;''""¡¿?!&ÅÇÉÎÑÖØÜåçéòøüŒæŒœ'"*/\

Periscope goes west

Submarine Light

Max Kisman
2003

ABCDEFGHIJKLMNOPQRSTUVWXYZabcdefghijklmnopqrstuv wxyz0123456789$-.,:;''""¡¿?!&ÅÇÉÎÑÖØÜåçéòøüŒæŒœ'"*/\

Sonar torpedo blasts

Submarine Regular

Max Kisman
2003

ABCDEFGHIJKLMNOPQRSTUVWXYZabcdefghijklmnopqrstuv wxyz0123456789$-.,:;''""¡¿?!&ÅÇÉÎÑÖØÜåçéòøüŒæŒœ'"*/\

Flying go submarine

Submarine Bold

Max Kisman
2003

ABCDEFGHIJKLMNOPQRSTUVWXYZabcdefghijklmnopqrstuvw xyz0123456789$-.,:;''""¡¿?!&ÅÇÉÎÑÖØÜåçéòøüŒæŒœ'"*/\

Depth deepest ocean

Submarine Extra Bold

Max Kisman
2003

Holland Fonts

ABCDEFGHIJKLMNOPQRSTUVWXYZabcdefghijklmnopqrstuvwxyz0123456789$¢€£¥ƒ-.,:
;…''""·¸¡¿?!8ÅÇÉÍÑÒ8Üåçéòøü ÆæŒœ"'*`˜/\|()[}[]¶§ß#@©®™ªº•+‹=›∑‰±µ

The port of San Francisco

THE GOLDEN GATE BRIDGE

Sunset at Tennessee Valley beach

Inspired by the unpretentious type
and lettering often seen in ports,
Pacific Standard Bold was originally
created as a poster typeface for the
Dutch *30th International Film
Festival Rotterdam* poster in 2001.

ABCDEFGHIJKLMNOPQRSTUVWXYZabcdefghijklmnopqrstuvwxyz0123456789$¢€£¥
ƒ-.,:;…""""·,¡¿?!8ÅÇÉÍÑÒ8Üåçéòøü ÆæŒœ"'*`˜/\|()[}[]¶§ß#@©®™ªº•+‹=›%‰±µ

Mt. Tamalpais and

HIGHWAY 1 NORTH

Sacramento River Runs

ABCDEFGHIJKLMNOPQRSTUVWXYZabcdefghijklmnopqrstuvwxyz0123456789$¢€£¥
ƒ-..:;…''""„,¡¿?!§ÅÇÉÎÑÒØÜåçéòøüÆæŒœ"'* ` ˜ /\|(){}[]¶§ß♯@©®™ªº•+<=>‰±µ

Hot dogs and short links

BREAKFAST SPECIALIST

Honk your horn 4 homegrown corn

ABCDEFGHIJKLMNOPQRSTUVWXYZabcdefghijklmnopqrstuvwxyz0123456789$¢€£¥
ƒ-..:;…''""„,¡¿?!§ÅÇÉÎÑÒØÜåçéòøüÆæŒœ"'* ` ˜/\|(){}[]¶§ß♯@©®™ªº•+<=>‰±µ

Crossroads ahead

COAST 2 COAST

Roadtrips and adventures

ABCDEFGHIJKLMNOPQRSTUVWXYZabcdefghijklmnopqrstuvwxyz0123456789$¢€£¥ƒ-.,:
;…'''""..¡¿?!8ÅÇÉÎÑÒØÜåçéòøüÆæŒœ"'*`˜/\|(){}[]¶§ß#@©®™ªº•+<=>%‰±µ

Jazzy swingers in Monterey

NORTH BEACH RESTAURANT

Whale migration Mendecino Coast

ABCDEFGHIJKLMNOPQRSTUVWXYZabcdefghijklmnopqrstuvwxyz0123456789$¢€£¥
ƒ-.,:;…""",,¡¿?!8ÅÇÉÎÑÒØÜåçéòøüÆæŒœ""*`˜/\|(){}[]¶§ß#@©®™ªº•+<=>%‰±

17-Mile Drive Big Sur

TWENTY9 PALMS, CA

The Joshua Tree Monument

ABCDEFGHIJKLMNOPQRSTUVWXYZabcdefghijklmnopqrstuvwxyz0123456789$¢£¥ƒ–.:
:...˙`´˜¨'"'..,¡¿?!8ÅÇÉÎÑÒØÜåçéòøü ÆæŒœ"˙*`˜/\|()()[]¶§#@©®™ªº•+<=>%‰±µ

Black birds over Bodega Bay
AND CALIFORNIA INCOGNITO
Summer Sunday BBQ at Rancho Nicasio

ABCDEFGHIJKLMNOPQRSTUVWXYZabcdefghijklmnopqrstuvwxyz0123456789$¢£ ¥
ƒ–.,:;...'"",,¡¿?!8ÅÇÉÎÑÒØÜåçéòøü ÆæŒœ""*`˜/\|()()[]¶§#@©®™ªº•+<=>%‰±µ

Point Reyes Station
SHUCKED OYSTERS
Redwoods and deer crossing

ABCDEFGHIJKLMNOPQRSTUVWXYZabcdefghijklmnopqrstuvwxyz0123456789$¢¥£ƒ–..:
:..`´˝˜"..¡¿?!8ÅÇÉÎÑØ0ÜåçéòøüÆæŒœ"'*`˜/\|(){}[]¶§ß#@©®™ªº•+<=>%‰±μ

The day breaks in the east

THE DISTANT HORIZON CLIPS

Portland, Oregon, and Seattle, Washington

ABCDEFGHIJKLMNOPQRSTUVWXYZabcdefghijklmnopqrstuvwxyz0123456789$¢¥£
ƒ–..,:;..."""„,¡¿?!8ÅÇÉÎÑØ0ÜåçéòøüÆæŒœ"'*`˜/\|(){}[]¶§ß#@©®™ªº•+<=>%‰±μ

Cruisin' the interstate

SNOW–COVERED TOP

Above the long and windy road

info@hollandfonts.com

Max Kisman
2002

Make your instant Christmas and winter holiday greeting cards with this Xbats picture font. Twenty-six regular (uppercase, A–Z) and twenty-six inverted (lowercase, a–z) images use the upcoming winter holiday season as a theme. Seven instant holiday messages (numerals, 1–5 and inverted 6–0 for English, ¡, !, ¿, and ? for Spanish) will make your greeting complete in any combination.

Holland Fonts

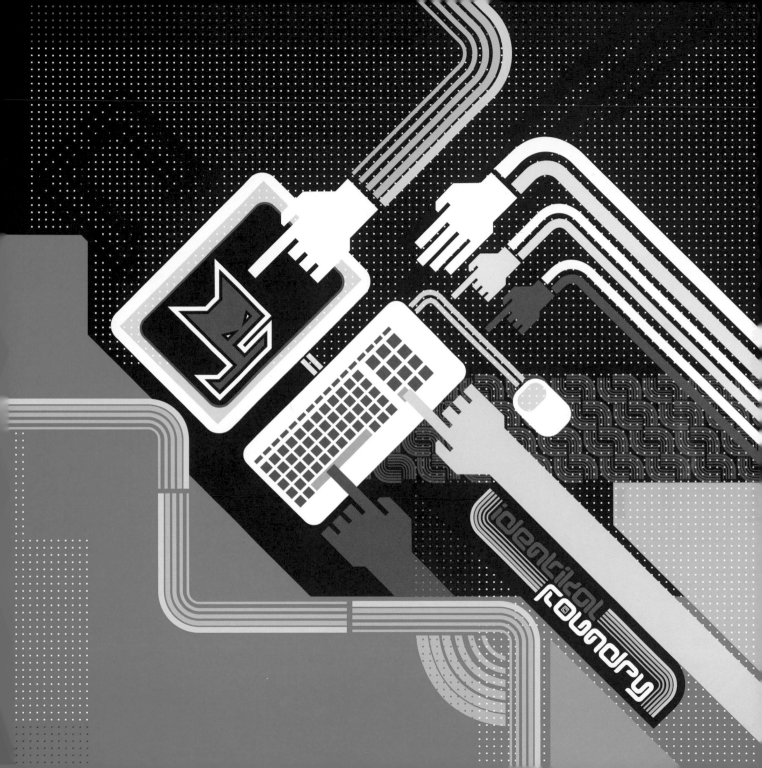

identikal foundry

AtomicType

Mailing Address:
Mill House
11 Nightingale Road
Horsham
RH12 2NW
ENGLAND

Sales Enquiries:
Tel: +44 (0) 1403 249 245
Fax: +44 (0) 1403 249 246
Email: paul@atomictype.co.uk
Web: atomictype.co.uk

Background:
AtomicType have represented exclusive font sales for the Identikal Foundry since 1998. There are over 50 separate font families available to purchase from the Identikal Foundry range, along with a whole host of collectable printed catalogs and information.

Contact Details:
Nick Hayes
Creative Director
The Identikal Corporation
Studio 5
The Oasis Buildings
Holloway Road
LONDON N7 6JN
ENGLAND

Tel: +44 (0) 20 7263 2129
Fax: +44 (0) 20 7272 1521
Mobile: +44 (0) 7957 497 569
Email: info@identikal.com
Web: www.identikal.com

Identikal Background:
The Identikal Corporation was founded by identical twins Adam & Nick Hayes whilst studying Graphic Communication at University in the mid-nineties. Since then, it has become recognised for combining an eclectic mixture of sound and vision, capable of producing unique work for any creative problem, from Graphic Design to Moving Image, Multimedia to Sound and Type Design.

Identikal have worked with clients all over the world, from Getty Images in America and Guinness in Eire, to the Drop Club in Hong Kong, whilst managing to keep a very impressive portfolio of work due to their striking and innovative style. They have developed a reputation that attracts some of the world's most desirable clients, such as Sony Computer Entertainment, Universal Music, Virgin, Ministry of Sound, EMAP publishing and many more.

Identikal are the team behind the cult success of the Identikal Foundry. They have created some of the hottest modern fonts of this new century, including worldwide collections of around 250 families. Publications including, *Maxim, Timeout, Dazed and Confused, Create, Mixmag, DJ Magazine, Wired* and many others have used Identikal typefaces throughout their pages. The fonts are also popular amongst various music acts such as, *Truesteppers, Shea Seger, Blue, Beverley Knight, Incognito, Shakira, Elisabeth Troy, MC Luck & DJ Neat,* to name but a few. Ad campaigns such as *PS2 The Third Place,* the launch of the *Nintendo Gameboy Advance,* and *Virgin Money* have also used fonts from the Identikal Foundry Collections. This has given Identikal a name in typography which many believe to be the strength and character behind the team.

If you would like to see more work from Identikal, you can check out the portfolio area on their site: **www.identikal.com.** Alternatively, contact them through email: **info@identikal.com.**

21st Century Typography

21st

Nick Hayes
1998

With its wide range of weights and numerous styles, the 21st typeface family was designed to represent the new century.

Identikal

21st Regular 15pt

AaBbCcDdEeFfGgHhIiJjKkLlMmNnOoPp
QqRrSsTtUuVvWwXxYyZz0123456789
<[{(/!?@£$¢¥%&ß::\)}]>

21st Black 9pt

21st century typography for the modern noughties digital designer. Seven weights with seven italics for a diversity of use in style and taste.

21st Bold 9pt

21st century typography for the modern noughties digital designer. Seven weights with seven italics for a diversity of use in style and taste.

21st Regular 9pt

21st century typography for the modern noughties digital designer. Seven weights with seven italics for a diversity of use in style and taste.

21st Fine 9pt

21st century typography for the modern noughties digital designer. Seven weights with seven italics for a diversity of use in style and taste.

21st Superfine 9pt

21st century typography for the modern noughties digital designer. Seven weights with seven italics for a diversity of use in style and taste.

21st Round Black 9pt

21st century typography for the modern noughties digital designer. Seven weights with seven italics for a diversity of use in style and taste.

21st Outline 9pt

21st century typography for the modern noughties digital designer. Seven weights with seven italics for a diversity of use in style and taste.

21st Black Italic 22pt

21st Italics
21st Black Italic

21st Fine & Superfine Italic 22pt

21st Fine Italic
21st Superfine Italic

21st Bold & Regular Italic 22pt

21st Bold Italic
21st Regular Italic

21st Round Black & Outline Italic 22pt

21st Round Black
21st Outline Italic

21st Black 22pt

21st Type Family
21st Black

21st Fine & Superfine 22pt

21st Fine
21st Superfine

21st Bold & Regular 22pt

21st Bold
21st Regular

21st Round Black & Outline 22pt

21st Round Black
21st Outline

Nick Hayes
1999

45 degrees has six variants within its family.

45 Degrees Light 15pt

AaBbCcDdEeFfGgHhIiJjKkLlMmNnOoPp
QqRrSsTtUuVvWwXxYyZz0123456789
≤<[{(/!?@£$¢€¥%&ßfifl:;*"'œœ†ø\)}]>≥

45 Degrees Regular 9pt

45 degrees is a typeface built up of horizontal and vertical lines with 45 degree angles. Its condensed look works well for headlines and logo arrangements for print.

45 Degrees Ultra Light 9pt

45 degrees is a typeface built up of horizontal and vertical lines with 45 degree angles. Its condensed look works well for headlines and logo arrangements for print.

45 Degrees Italics 17pt

45 degrees Regular Italic

45 degrees Light Italic

45 degrees Ultra Light Italic

Nick Hayes
2000

Angol has six variants within its family, including two styles, Round and Sharp.

Angol Assortment 44pt

AngolRoundSharp

Angol Round Black 19pt

AaBbCcDdEeFfGgHhIiJjKkLlMmNnOoPp
QqRrSsTtUuVvWwXxYyZz0123456789
≤<[{(/!?@£$¢€¥%&ßfifl:;*"'œœ†ø\)}]>≥

Angol Round Bold 14pt

The Angol typeface is a set of fonts designed for use in logotype and digital illustration projects.

Angol Round Regular 14pt

The Angol typeface is a set of fonts designed for use in logotype and digital illustration projects.

Angol Sharp Black 14pt

The Angol typeface is a set of fonts designed for use in logotype and digital illustration projects.

Angol Sharp Bold 14pt

The Angol typeface is a set of fonts designed for use in logotype and digital illustration projects.

Angol Sharp Regular 14pt

The Angol typeface is a set of fonts designed for use in logotype and digital illustration projects.

Nick Hayes
1999

Attac is a typeface family with eight variants.

Attac Regular 16pt

AaBbCcDdEeFfGgHhIiJjKkLlMmNnOoPp
QqRrSsTtUuVvWwXxYyZz0123456789
≤<[{(/!?@£$¢€¥%&ßfifl:;*"'œæ\)}]>≥

Attac Black 9pt

Attac is a typeface built up of eight different angles to form a family of fonts that look modern and stylish, yet keeping a classical legible flow to body copy and headlines.

Attac Bold 9pt

Attac is a typeface built up of eight different angles to form a family of fonts that look modern and stylish, yet keeping a classical legible flow to body copy and headlines.

Attac Semi-Bold 9pt

Attac is a typeface built up of eight different angles to form a family of fonts that look modern and stylish, yet keeping a classical legible flow to body copy and headlines.

Attac Black Italic 9pt

Attac is a typeface built up of eight different angles to form a family of fonts that look modern and stylish, yet keeping a classical legible flow to body copy and headlines.

Attac Bold Italic 9pt

Attac is a typeface built up of eight different angles to form a family of fonts that look modern and stylish, yet keeping a classical legible flow to body copy and headlines.

Attac Semi-Bold Italic 9pt

Attac is a typeface built up of eight different angles to form a family of fonts that look modern and stylish, yet keeping a classical legible flow to body copy and headlines.

Attac Regular Italic 9pt

Attac is a typeface built up of eight different angles to form a family of fonts that look modern and stylish, yet keeping a classical legible flow to body copy and headlines.

+44 (0) 1403 249 245

Click

Click Bold 30pt

AaBbCcDdEeFfGgHhIiJjKkLlMm
NnOoPpQqRrSsTtUuVvWwXxY
yZz1234567890‹[[{ఀ$£&!?}]]›

Click Regular 28pt

AaBbCcDdEeFfGgHhIiJjKkLlMmn
nOoPpQqRrSsTtUuVvWwXxYyZz

Click Light 28pt

AaBbCcDdEeFfGgHhIiJjKkLlMmn
nOoPpQqRrSsTtUuVvWwXxYyZz

Click Bold Italic 18pt
ClickBoldItalic

Click Regular Italic 18pt
ClickRegItalic

Click Light Italic 18pt
ClickLightItalic

Adam Hayes
2001

The Click typeface family is made up of six fonts.

Curvature

Curvature Black 25pt

AaBbCcDdEeFfGgHhIiJjKkLlMmNnOoPpQqRrSs
TtUuVvWwXxYyZz 1234567890 <[{%$£&}]>

Curvature Black Italic 16pt

AaBbCcDdEeFfGgHhIiJjKkLlMmNnOoPpQqRrSsTtUuVvWwXxYyZz

Curvature Bold 16pt
Identikal Curvature Bold TYPE

Curvature Bold Italic 16pt
IDENTIKAL Curvature Bold Italic

Curvature Regular 16pt
Identikal Curvature Regular TYPE

Curvature Regular Italic 16pt
IDENTIKAL Curvature Regular Italic

Curvature Fine 25pt

AaBbCcDdEeFfGgHhIiJjKkLlMmNnOoPpQqRrSs
TtUuVvWwXxYyZz 1234567890 <[{%$£&}]>

Curvature Fine Italic 16pt

AaBbCcDdEeFfGgHhIiJjKkLlMmNnOoPpQqRrSsTtUuVvWwXxYyZz

Curvature Rounded 16pt
Identikal Curvature Rounded

Curvature Rounded 16pt
Curvature Rounded Italic TYPE

Adam Hayes
1999

The Curvature family consists of ten typefaces.

Adam Hayes
2000

The Dieppe family consists of six type-faces.

Dieppe Bold 20pt

AaBbCcDdEeFfGgHhIiJjHkLlMmNnOoPpQqRrSs
TtUuVvWwHxYyZz 1234567890 <[{(@$&£)}]>

Dieppe Bold Oblique 12pt

AaBbCcDdEeFfGgHhIiJjHkLlMmNnOoPpQqRrSsTtUuVvWwHxYyZz1234567890

Dieppe Regular 20pt

AaBbCcDdEeFfGgHhIiJjHkLlMmNnOoPpQqRrSs
TtUuVvWwHxYyZz 1234567890 <[{(@$&£)}]>

Dieppe Regular Oblique 12pt

AaBbCcDdEeFfGgHhIiJjHkLlMmNnOoPpQqRrSsTtUuVvWwHxYyZz1234567890

Dieppe Light 20pt

AaBbCcDdEeFfGgHhIiJjHkLlMmNnOoPpQqRrSs
TtUuVvWwHxYyZz 1234567890 <[{(@$&£)}]>

Dieppe Light Oblique 12pt

AaBbCcDdEeFfGgHhIiJjHkLlMmNnOoPpQqRrSsTtUuVvWwHxYyZz1234567890

Adam Hayes
1999

The Distilla family consists of six type-faces. Distilla was formerly known as Formatt.

Distilla Bold 20pt

AaBbCcDdEeFfGgHhIiJjKkLlMmNnOoPpQqRrSs
TtUuVvWwXxYyZz 1234567890 <[{(@$&£)}]>

Distilla Bold Italic 12pt

AaBbCcDdEeFfGgHhIiJjKkLlMmNnOoPpQqRrSsTtUuVvWwXxYyZz123456

Distilla Regular 20pt

AaBbCcDdEeFfGgHhIiJjKkLlMmNnOoPpQqRrSs
TtUuVvWwXxYyZz 1234567890 <[{(@$&£)}]>

Distilla Regular Italic 12pt

AaBbCcDdEeFfGgHhIiJjKkLlMmNnOoPpQqRrSsTtUuVvWwXxYyZz123456

Distilla Light 20pt

AaBbCcDdEeFfGgHhIiJjKkLlMmNnOoPpQqRrSs
TtUuVvWwXxYyZz 1234567890 <[{(@$&£)}]>

Distilla Light Italic 12pt

AaBbCcDdEeFfGgHhIiJjKkLlMmNnOoPpQqRrSsTtUuVvWwXxYyZz123456

ID 01

ID 01 Left 27pt

AaBbCcDdEeFfGgHhIiJjKkLlMmNnOoPp
QqRrSsTtUuVvWwXxYyZz0123456789

Nick Hayes
2001

This typeface family has two styles available and is included on the font disc with this book.

ID 01 Left 56pt

ID01Left

ID 01Right 56pt

ID01Right

Kanal

Kanal Regular 15pt

AaBbCcDdEeFfGgHhIiJjKkLlMmNnOoPp
QqRrSsTtUuVvWwXxYyZz0123456789
<([{/?!£$&-_+=ß;:"|\]])> Kanal Regular

Kanal Ultra Light 9pt

The Kanal typeface is a monospaced font with condensed features suited to the publishing industry. Headlines as well as intro text flow finely over a longer line length.

Nick Hayes
1997

Kanal has eight variants within its font family.

Kanal Light 9pt

The Kanal typeface is a monospaced font with condensed features suited to the publishing industry. Headlines as well as intro text flow finely over a longer line length.

Kanal Normal 9pt

The Kanal typeface is a monospaced font with condensed features suited to the publishing industry. Headlines as well as intro text flow finely over a longer line length.

Kanal Ultra Light Italic 9pt

The Kanal typeface is a monospaced font with condensed features suited to the publishing industry. Headlines as well as intro text flow finely over a longer line length.

Kanal Light 9pt

The Kanal typeface is a monospaced font with condensed features suited to the publishing industry. Headlines as well as intro text flow finely over a longer line length.

Kanal Normal Italic 9pt

The Kanal typeface is a monospaced font with condensed features suited to the publishing industry. Headlines as well as intro text flow finely over a longer line length.

Kanal Light 9pt

The Kanal typeface is a monospaced font with condensed features suited to the publishing industry. Headlines as well as intro text flow finely over a longer line length.

Kneeon

Kneeon Regular 17pt

AaBbCcDdEeFfGgHhIiJjKkLlMmNnOoPp
QqRrSsTtUuVvWwXxYyZz0123456789
[([{!?ⁿ£$¢£¥&&ßfifl;:*"œæøøø]}]

Kneeon Regular 17pt

Kneeon typeface
CITY OF LIGHTS
Identikal Corp→

Nick Hayes
2001

Kneeon has eight variants within its font family. Its design has been based on the structure of neon typographic shapes.

Kneeon Bold 17pt

Kneeon typeface
CITY OF LIGHTS
Identikal Corp→

Kneeon Square 17pt

Kneeon typeface
CITY OF LIGHTS
Identikal Corp→

Kneeon Light 17pt

Kneeon typeface
CITY OF LIGHTS
Identikal Corp→

Kneeon Bold Italic 17pt

Kneeon typeface
CITY OF LIGHTS
Identikal Corp→

Kneeon Square Italic 17pt

Kneeon typeface
CITY OF LIGHTS
Identikal Corp→

Kneeon Light Italic 17pt

Kneeon typeface
CITY OF LIGHTS
Identikal Corp→

Monark

Adam Hayes
2000

The Monark family consists of eight typefaces.

Monark Black 20pt

AaBbCcDdEeFfGgHhIiJjKkLlMmNnOoPpQq
RrSsTtUuVvWwXxYyZz1234567890{(@$)}

Monark Black Italic 12pt

AaBbCcDdEeFfGgHhIiJjKkLlMmNnOoPpQqRrSsTtUuVvWwXxYyZz1234

Monark Bold 12pt

AaBbCcDdEeFfGgHhIiJjKkLlMmNnOoPpQqRrSsTtUuVvWwXxYyZz1234

Monark Bold Italic 12pt

AaBbCcDdEeFfGgHhIiJjKkLlMmNnOoPpQqRrSsTtUuVvWwXxYyZz1234

Monark Regular 12pt

AaBbCcDdEeFfGgHhIiJjKkLlMmNnOoPpQqRrSsTtUuVvWwXxYyZz1234

Monark Regular Italic 12pt

AaBbCcDdEeFfGgHhIiJjKkLlMmNnOoPpQqRrSsTtUuVvWwXxYyZz1234

Monark Light 20pt

AaBbCcDdEeFfGgHhIiJjKkLlMmNnOoPpQq
RrSsTtUuVvWwXxYyZz1234567890{(@$)}

Monark Light Italic 12pt

AaBbCcDdEeFfGgHhIiJjKkLlMmNnOoPpQqRrSsTtUuVvWwXxYyZz1234

Orbita

Nick Hayes
2002

The Orbita family consists of six typefaces.

Orbita Regular 26pt

AaBbCcDdEeFfGgHhIiJjKkLlMmNnOoPp
QqRrSsTtUuVvWwXxYyZz0123456789

Orbita Heavy 14p

AaBbCcDdEeFfGgHhIiJj
KkLlMmNnOoPpQqRrSs
TtUuVvWwXxYyZz0123

AaBbCcDdEeFfGgHhIiJj
KkLlMmNnOoPpQqRrSs
TtUuVvWwXxYyZz0123

Orbita Oblique Versions 20pt

HeavyOblique
RegularOblique
LightOblique

Phat

Adam Hayes
2000

The Phat family consists of six typefaces.

Phat Bold 20pt

AaBbCcDdEeFfGgHhIiJjKkLlMmNnOoPp
QqRrSsTtUuVvWwXxYyZz1234567890

Phat Bold Italic 12pt

PhatFont BoldItalic

Phat Regular Italic 12pt

PhatFont RegularItalic

Phat Regular 12pt

AaBbCcDdEeFf
GgHhIiJjKkLlMm
NnOoPpQqRrSs

Phat Light Italic 12pt

*AaBbCcDdEeFf
GgHhIiJjKkLlMm
NnOoPpQqRrSs*

Phat Light 12pt

AaBbCcDdEeFf
GgHhIiJjKkLlMm
NnOoPpQqRrSs

+44 (0) 1403 249 245

Phuture ODC

Adam Hayes
1998

The "Original" Phuture typeface was drawn up on the back of a sketchpad in 1993. It was then drawn electronically in 1995. More styles were added, as well as the ODC series.

Phuture ODC Ultra 30pt

AaBbCcDdEeFfGgHhIiJjKKLl
MmNnOoPpQqRrSsTtUuVvW
wXxYyZz1234567890⟨⟨⟨%?⟩⟩⟩

Phuture ODC Ultra Italic 12pt

AaBbCcDdEeFfGgHhIi
JjKKLlMmNnOoPpQqR
rSsTtUuVvWwXxYyZ

Phuture ODC Black 12pt

AaBbCcDdEeFfGgHhIi
JjKKLlMmNnOoPpQqRrS
sTtUuVvWwXxYyZz

Phuture ODC Black Italic 12pt

AaBbCcDdEeFfGgHhIi
JjKKLlMmNnOoPpQqRrS
sTtUuVvWwXxYyZz

Phuture Squared Closed

Adam Hayes
1995

Phuture Squared Closed contains six fonts within its family. The Phuture typeface family is a collection of twenty-eight fonts.

Phuture Squared Closed Bold 28pt

AaBbCcDdEeFfGgHhIiJjKKLlMmN
nOoPpQqRrSsTtUuVvWwXxYyZz

Phuture Squared Closed Plain 12pt

AaBbCcDdEeFfGgHhIiJj
KKLlMmNnOoPpQqRrSs

Phuture Squared Closed Italic 12pt

AaBbCcDdEeFfGgHhIiJj
KKLlMmNnOoPpQqRrSs

Phuture Squared Closed Fine 12pt

AaBbCcDdEeFfGgHhIiJj
KKLlMmNnOoPpQqRrSs

Phuture Squared Closed Outline 12pt

PHUTURE SQUARED CLOSED OUTLINE

Phuture Squared Closed A-Italic 12pt

PHUTURE SQUARED CLOSED A-ITALIC

Phuture Squared Open

Adam Hayes
1995

Phuture Squared Open contains six fonts within its family.

Phuture Squared Open Bold 12pt

PHUTURE SQUARED OPEN BOLD

Phuture Squared Open Plain 12pt

PHUTURE SQUARED OPEN PLAIN

Phuture Squared Open Fine 12pt

PHUTURE SQUARED OPEN FINE

Phuture Squared Open A-Italic 12pt

PHUTURE SQUARED OPEN A-ITALIC

Phuture Squared Open Outline 12pt

PHUTURE SQUARED OPEN OUTLINE

Phuture Squared Open Italic 12pt

PHUTURE SQUARED OPEN ITALIC

Phuture Rounded Open

Adam Hayes
1995

Phuture Rounded Open contains six fonts within its family. The Phuture font family is seen as one of our most original and inspiring typefaces.

Phuture Rounded Open Bold 28pt

AaBbCcDdEeFfGgXhIiJjKKLlMm
NnOoPpQqRrSsTtUuWwXxYyZz

Phuture Rounded Open Plain 12pt

AaBbCcDdEeFfGgHhIiJj
KKLlMmNnOoPpQqRrSs

Phuture Rounded Open Italic 12pt

AaBbCcDdEeFfGgHhIiJj
KKLlMmNnOoPpQqRrSs

Phuture Rounded Open Fine 12pt

AaBbCcDdEeFfGgHhIiJj
KKLlMmNnOoPpQqRrSs

Phuture Rounded Open Outline 12pt

PHUTURE ROUNDED OPEN OUTLINE

Phuture Rounded Open A-Italic 12pt

PHUTURE ROUND CLOSED A-ITALIC

Phuture Rounded Closed

Adam Hayes
1995

Phuture Rounded Closed contains six fonts within its family.

Phuture Rounded Closed Bold 12pt

PHUTURE ROUNDED CLOSED BOLD

Phuture Rounded Closed Plain 12pt

PHUTURE ROUNDED CLOSED PLAIN

Phuture Rounded Closed Fine 12pt

PHUTURE ROUNDED CLOSED FINE

Phuture Rounded Closed A-Italic 12pt

PHUTURE ROUNDED CLOSED A-ITALIC

Phuture Rounded Closed Outline 12pt

PHUTURE ROUNDED CLOSED OUTLINE

Phuture Rounded Closed Italic 12pt

PHUTURE ROUNDED CLOSED ITALIC

Plotta

Adam Hayes
1998

The Plotta family consists of six typefaces.

Plotta Bold 20pt

AaBbCcDdEeFfGgHhIiJjKkLlMmNnOoPpQqRr
SsTtUuVvWwXxYyZz1234567890 <((@$£))>

Plotta Bold Italic 12pt

AaBbCcDdEeFfGgHhIiJjKkLlMmNnOoPpQqRrSsTtUuVvWwXxYyZz

Plotta Bold 20pt

AaBbCcDdEeFfGgHhIiJjKkLlMmNnOoPpQqRr
SsTtUuVvWwXxYyZz1234567890 <((@$£))>

Plotta Regular Italic 12pt

AaBbCcDdEeFfGgHhIiJjKkLlMmNnOoPpQqRrSsTtUuVvWwXxYyZz

Plotta Light 20pt

AaBbCcDdEeFfGgHhIiJjKkLlMmNnOoPpQqRr
SsTtUuVvWwXxYyZz1234567890 <((@$£))>

Plotta Light Italic 12pt

AaBbCcDdEeFfGgHhIiJjKkLlMmNnOoPpQqRrSsTtUuVvWwXxYyZz

Podium

Adam Hayes
1999

Podium was originally drawn up for a V.I.P. club called Drop, base in Hong Kong. We had so many inquiries about it that we decided to make it into a font family. The Podium family consists of six typefaces.

Podium Bold 20pt

AaBbCcDdEeFfGgHhIiJjKkLlMmNnOoPpQq
RrSsTtUuVvWwXxYyZz1234567890(({&$})

Podium Bold Italic 12pt

AaBbCcDdEeFfGgHhIiJjKkLlMmNnOoPpQqRrSsTtUuVvWwXxYyZz

Podium Regular 20pt

AaBbCcDdEeFfGgHhIiJjKkLlMmNnOoPpQq
RrSsTtUuVvWwXxYyZz1234567890(({&$})

Podium Regular Italic 12pt

AaBbCcDdEeFfGgHhIiJjKkLlMmNnOoPpQqRrSsTtUuVvWwXxYyZz

Podium Light 20pt

AaBbCcDdEeFfGgHhIiJjKkLlMmNnOoPpQq
RrSsTtUuVvWwXxYyZz1234567890(({&$})

Podium Light Italic 12pt

AaBbCcDdEeFfGgHhIiJjKkLlMmNnOoPpQqRrSsTtUuVvWwXxYyZz

+44 (0) 1403 249 245

Reaction Heavy 20pt

AaBbCcDdEeFfGgHhIiJjKkLlMmNnOoPpQqRr SsTtUuVvWwXxYyZz1234567890 ‹‹((@$£))›

Reaction Heavy Italic 12pt

AaBbCcDdEeFfGgHhIiJjKkLlMmNnOoPpQqRrSsTtUuVvWwXxYyZz

Reaction Ultra 12pt

AaBbCcDdEeFfGgHhIiJjKkLlMmNnOoPpQqRrSsTtUuVvWwXxYyZz

Reaction Ultra Italic 12pt

AaBbCcDdEeFfGgHhIiJjKkLlMmNnOoPpQqRrSsTtUuVvWwXxYyZz

Reaction Bold Italic 12pt

AaBbCcDdEeFfGgHhIiJjKkLlMmNnOoPpQqRrSsTtUuVvWwXxYyZz

Reaction Bold Italic 12pt

AaBbCcDdEeFfGgHhIiJjKkLlMmNnOoPpQqRrSsTtUuVvWwXxYyZz

Reaction Regular Italic 12pt

AaBbCcDdEeFfGgHhIiJjKkLlMmNnOoPpQqRrSsTtUuVvWwXxYyZz

Reaction Regular Italic 12pt

AaBbCcDdEeFfGgHhIiJjKkLlMmNnOoPpQqRrSsTtUuVvWwXxYyZz

Reaction Fine Italic 12pt

AaBbCcDdEeFfGgHhIiJjKkLlMmNnOoPpQqRrSsTtUuVvWwXxYyZz

Reaction Fine Italic 12pt

AaBbCcDdEeFfGgHhIiJjKkLlMmNnOoPpQqRrSsTtUuVvWwXxYyZz

Reaction

Adam Hayes
2000

The Reaction typeface family is made up of ten fonts.

Rebirth Ultra 18pt

AaBbCcDdEeFfGgHhIiJjKkLlMmNnOoPp QqRrSsTtUuVvWwXxYyZz1234567890

Rebirth Ultra Italic 12pt

AaBbCcDdEeFfGgHhIiJjKkLlMmNnOoPpQqRrSsTtUuVvWw

Rebirth Black 12pt

AaBbCcDdEeFfGgHhIiJjKkLlMmNnOoPpQqRrSsTtUuVvWw

Rebirth Black Italic 12pt

AaBbCcDdEeFfGgHhIiJjKkLlMmNnOoPpQqRrSsTtUuVvWw

Rebirth Regular 12pt

AaBbCcDdEeFfGgHhIiJjKkLlMmNnOoPpQqRrSsTtUuVvWw

Rebirth Regular Italic 12pt

AaBbCcDdEeFfGgHhIiJjKkLlMmNnOoPpQqRrSsTtUuVvWw

Rebirth Fine 18pt

AaBbCcDdEeFfGgHhIiJjKkLlMmNnOoPp QqRrSsTtUuVvWwXxYyZz1234567890

Rebirth Fine Italic 12pt

AaBbCcDdEeFfGgHhIiJjKkLlMmNnOoPpQqRrSsTtUuVvWw

Rebirth

Adam Hayes
1999

The Rebirth family consists of eight typefaces.

Identikal

The Revalo family consists of a Modern version, which is rounded, and a Classic version, which has flat edges. This collection of fonts has been specifically designed for the publishing industry and corporate identity design teams.

Various Revalo Modern Weights at 54pt

Revalo™ **Modern** Font Family

Revalo Modern Regular 24pt

AaBbCcDdEeFfGgHhIiJjKkLlMmNnOoPp
QqRrSsTtUuVvWwXxYyZz0123456789
‹‹[{(/!?@£$¢€¥%&ßfifl:;*"œæ†ø\)}]›‹

Revalo Modern Black 10pt

The Revalo Modern Classic font family has been crafted with the Modern Digital Designer in mind. The classic version has a sharp formal look to its characteristics, whereas the Modern version oozes style and definition.

Revalo Modern Bold 10pt

The Revalo Modern Classic font family has been crafted with the Modern Digital Designer in mind. The classic version has a sharp formal look to its characteristics, whereas the Modern version oozes style and definition.

Revalo Modern Light 10pt

The Revalo Modern Classic font family has been crafted with the Modern Digital Designer in mind. The classic version has a sharp formal look to its characteristics, whereas the Modern version oozes style and definition.

Revalo Modern Thin 10pt

The Revalo Modern Classic font family has been crafted with the Modern Digital Designer in mind. The classic version has a sharp formal look to its characteristics, whereas the Modern version oozes style and definition.

Revalo Modern Italics 22pt

Modern Black Italic

Modern Bold Italic

Modern Bold Italic

Modern Black Italic

Modern Regular Italic

Revalo™ Modern Family

Various Revalo Classic Weights at 54pt

Revalo™ **Classic** Font Family

Revalo Classic Regular 24pt

AaBbCcDdEeFfGgHhIiJjKkLlMmNnOoPp
QqRrSsTtUuVvWwXxYyZz0123456789
‹‹[{(/!?@£$¢€¥%&ßfifl:;*"œæ†ø\)}]›‹

Revalo Classic Black 10pt

The Revalo Modern Classic font family has been crafted with the Modern Digital Designer in mind. The classic version has a sharp formal look to its characteristics, whereas the Modern version oozes style and definition.

Revalo Classic Bold 10pt

The Revalo Modern Classic font family has been crafted with the Modern Digital Designer in mind. The classic version has a sharp formal look to its characteristics, whereas the Modern version oozes style and definition.

Revalo Classic Light 10pt

The Revalo Modern Classic font family has been crafted with the Modern Digital Designer in mind. The classic version has a sharp formal look to its characteristics, whereas the Modern version oozes style and definition.

Revalo Classic Thin 10pt

The Revalo Modern Classic font family has been crafted with the Modern Digital Designer in mind. The classic version has a sharp formal look to its characteristics, whereas the Modern version oozes style and definition.

Revalo Classic Italics 22pt

Classic Black Italic

Classic Light Italic

Classic Bold Italic

Classic Thin Italic

Classic Regular Italic

Revalo™ Classic Family

+44 (0) 1403 249 245

Robustik Bold 20pt

AaBbCcDdEeFfGgHhIiJjKkLlMmNnOoPp
QqRrSsTtUuVvWwXxYyZz1234567890

Robustik Bold Oblique 12pt

AaBbCcDdEeFfGgHhIiJjKkLlMmNnOoPpQqRrSsTtUuVvWwXxYyZz

Robustik Regular 20pt

AaBbCcDdEeFfGgHhIiJjKkLlMmNnOoPp
QqRrSsTtUuVvWwXxYyZz1234567890

Robustik Regular Oblique 12pt

AaBbCcDdEeFfGgHhIiJjKkLlMmNnOoPpQqRrSsTtUuVvWwXxYyZz

Robustik Light 20pt

AaBbCcDdEeFfGgHhIiJjKkLlMmNnOoPp
QqRrSsTtUuVvWwXxYyZz1234567890

Robustik Bold Light 12pt

AaBbCcDdEeFfGgHhIiJjKkLlMmNnOoPpQqRrSsTtUuVvWwXxYyZz

Seize Regular 25pt

AaBbCcDdEeFfGgHhIiJjKkLlMmNnOoPpQqRrSs
TtUuVvWwXxYyZz1234567890<[{(@$&£)}]>

Seize Regular 18pt

AaBbCcDdEeFfGgHhIiJjKkLlMmNnOoPpQqRrSsTtUuVvWwXxYyZz

Seize Light & Seize Light italic

AaBbCcDdEeFfGgHhIi
JjKkLlMmNnOoPpQqRr
SsTtUuVvWwXxYyZz

Identikal Seize Light Italic

Seize Bold & Seize Bold Italic 25pt

AaBbCcDdEeFfGgHhIi
JjKkLlMmNnOoPpQqRr
SsTtUuVvWwXxYyZz

Identikal Seize Light Italic

Seize Regular 25pt

AaBbCcDdEeFfGgHhIiJjKkLlMmNnOoPpQqRrSs
TtUuVvWwXxYyZz1234567890<[{(@$&£)}]>

Seize Regular 18pt

AaBbCcDdEeFfGgHhIiJjKkLlMmNnOoPpQqRrSsTtUuVvWwXxYyZz

Robustik

Adam Hayes
2001

The Robustik typeface family is made up of six fonts.

Seize

Nick Hayes
2000

The Seize family consists of eight typefaces.

Sharp was originally drawn up as a logotype for Salt Records, back in 1998. A year later, we decided to turn it into a typeface family. It has now become one of our most used fonts, and is great for illustration and logo work.

RaBbcCDdEeFfGgHhIi
JjKkLlMmNnOoPpQqR
rSsTtUuVvWwXxYyZz
1234567890 <[[@\$&]]>

Sharp Ultra Italic 20pt

Identikal present: Sharp Ultra Italic

Sharp Bold

Adam Hayes
1999

RaBbcCDdEeFfGgHhIiJjKkLlMmN
nOoPpQqRrSsTtUuVvWwXxYyZz

Sharp Bold Italic 18pt

Identikal present: Sharp Bold Italic

Sharp Regular

Adam Hayes
1999

RaBbcCDdEeFfGgHhIiJjKkLlMmN
nOoPpQqRrSsTtUuVvWwXxYyZz

Sharp Regular Italic 18pt

Identikal present: Sharp Regular Italic

Sharp Light

Adam Hayes
1999

RaBbcCDdEeFfGgHhIiJjKkLlMmN
nOoPpQqRrSsTtUuVvWwXxYyZz

Sharp Light Italic 18pt

Identikal present: Sharp Light Italic

Sharp Bold 20p

<[[@?!\$&]]>

Sharp Regular 20pt

<[[@?!\$&]]>

Sharp Light 20pt

<[[@?!\$&]]>

+44 (0) 1403 249 245

Stak Bold 26pt

AaBbCcCDEeFfGgHhIiJjKkLlMm
NnOoPpQqRrSsTtUuVvWwXxYyZz
0123456789<([!@£$%&*|€?†¥®])>

Stak Bold Italic 26pt

AaBbCcCDEeFfGgHhIiJjKkLlMm
NnOoPpQqRrSsTtUuVvWwXxYyZz
0123456789<([!@£$%&*|€?†¥®])>

Stak Light 16pt

AaBbCcCDEeFfG
GHhIiJjKkLlMm
NnOoPpQqRrSsT
TUuVvWwXxYyZz

Stak Light Italic 16pt

AaBbCcCDEeFfG
GHhIiJjKkLlMm
NnOoPpQqRrSsT
TUuVvWwXxYyZz

Stak Regular 16pt

AaBbCcCDEeFfG
GHhIiJjKkLlMm
NnOoPpQqRrSsT
TUuVvWwXxYyZz

IDENTIKAL Stak italic regular

Stak

Nick Hayes
2001

Stak consists of six typefaces.

Trak Black 26pt

AaBbCcDdEeFfGgHhIiJjKkLlMmNnOoPpQ
qRrSsTtUuVvWwXxYyZz1234567890

Trak Black 14pt

AaBbCcDdEeFfGgHhIiJjKkLlMmNnOoPpQqRrSsTtUuVvWwXxYyZz1234567

Trak Fine 26pt

AaBbCcDdEeFfGgHhIiJjKkLlMmNnOoPpQ
qRrSsTtUuVvWwXxYyZz1234567890

Trak Fine Italic 14pt

AaBbCcDdEeFfGgHhIiJjKkLlMmNnOoPpQqRrSsTtUuVvWwXxYyZz1234567

Trak

Adam Hayes
1999

Trak consists of ten typefaces.

Trak Semi Bold 14pt

AaBbCcDdEeFfGgHhIiJj
KkLlMmNnOoPpQqRrSs
TtUuVvWwXxYyZz123

Trak Semi Bold Italic 14pt

AaBbCcDdEeFfGgHhIiJj
KkLlMmNnOoPpQqRrSs
TtUuVvWwXxYyZz123

Trak Regular 14pt

AaBbCcDdEeFfGgHhIiJj
KkLlMmNnOoPpQqRrSs
TtUuVvWwXxYyZz123

Trak Regular Italic 14pt

AaBbCcDdEeFfGgHhIiJj
KkLlMmNnOoPpQqRrSs
TtUuVvWwXxYyZz123

Trak Bold 14pt

AaBbCcDdEeFfGgHhIiJj
KkLlMmNnOoPpQqRrSs
TtUuVvWwXxYyZz123

Trak Bold Italic 14pt

AaBbCcDdEeFfGgHhIiJj
KkLlMmNnOoPpQqRrSs
TtUuVvWwXxYyZz123

Tremble

Adam Hayes
1999

The Tremble family consists of eight typefaces.

Tremble Ultra 20pt

AaBbCcDdEeFfGgHhIiJjKkLlMmNnOoPpQqRrSsTt
UuVvWwXxYyZz 1234567890 ‹[{(@/^¿&£?!"":\\$)}]›

Tremble Ultra Italic 12pt

AaBbCcDdEeFfGgHhIiJjKkLlMmNnOoPpQqRrSsTtUuVvWwXxYyZz1234567

Tremble Bold 13pt

AaBbCcDdEeFfGgHhIiJj
KkLlMmNnOoPpQqRrSs
TtUuVvWwXxYyZz1234

Tremble Bold Italic 13pt

AaBbCcDdEeFfGgHhIiJj
KkLlMmNnOoPpQqRrSs
TtUuVvWwXxYyZz1234

Tremble Regular 13pt

AaBbCcDdEeFfGgHhIiJj
KkLlMmNnOoPpQqRrSs
TtUuVvWwXxYyZz1234

Tremble Regular Italic 13pt

AaBbCcDdEeFfGgHhIiJj
KkLlMmNnOoPpQqRrSs
TtUuVvWwXxYyZz1234

Tremble Light 13pt

AaBbCcDdEeFfGgHhIiJj
KkLlMmNnOoPpQqRrSs
TtUuVvWwXxYyZz1234

Tremble Light Italic 13pt

AaBbCcDdEeFfGgHhIiJj
KkLlMmNnOoPpQqRrSs
TtUuVvWwXxYyZz1234

UNDA Series

Nick Hayes
1998

UNDA Series consists of fifteen typefaces. The original concept of UNDA was to offer a variety of effects within one set of fonts.

UNDA Series Square 35pt

AaBbCcDdEeFfGgHhIiJjKkLlMmN
nOoPpQqRrSsTtUuVvWwXxYyZz

UNDA Series Circle 35pt

AaBbCcDdEeFfGgHhIiJjKkLlMmN
nOoPpQqRrSsTtUuVvWwXxYyZz

UNDA Series Triangle 35pt

AaBbCcDdEeFfGgHhIiJjKkLlMmN
nOoPpQqRrSsTtUuVvWwXxYyZz

UNDA Series Vertical 35pt

AaBbCcDdEeFfGgHhIiJjKkLlMmN
nOoPpQqRrSsTtUuVvWwXxYyZz

UNDA Series Horizontal 35pt

AaBbCcDdEeFfGgHhIiJjKkLlMmN
nOoPpQqRrSsTtUuVvWwXxYyZz

UNDA Angle 30pt

AaBbCcDdEeFfGgHhIiJjKkLlMmNnOoPpQ
qRrSsTtUuVvWwXxYyZz0123456789

UNDA Angle Italic 18pt

AaBbCcDdEeFfGgHh
IiJjKkLlMmNnOoPpQq
RrSsTtUuVvWwXxYy

UNDA Angle Fine 18pt

AaBbCcDdEeFfGgHh
IiJjKkLlMmNnOoPpQq
RrSsTtUuVvWwXxYy

UNDA Angle Fine Italic 18pt

AaBbCcDdEeFfGgHh
IiJjKkLlMmNnOoPpQq
RrSsTtUuVvWwXxYy

UNDA Bitmap 18pt

AaBbCcDdEeFfGgHh
IiJjKkLlMmNnOoPpQq
RrSsTtUuVvWwXxYy

UNDA Bitmap Italic 18pt

AaBbCcDdEeFfGgHh
IiJjKkLlMmNnOoPpQq
RrSsTtUuVvWwXxYy

UNDA Bitmap Fine 18pt

AaBbCcDdEeFfGgHh
IiJjKkLlMmNnOoPpQq
RrSsTtUuVvWwXxYy

UNDA Bitmap Fine Italic 18pt

AaBbCcDdEeFfGgHh
IiJjKkLlMmNnOoPpQq
RrSsTtUuVvWwXxYy

UNDA Outline 18pt

AaBbCcDdEeFfGgHh
IiJjKkLlMmNnOoPpQq
RrSsTtUuVvWwXxYy

UNDA Outline Italic 18pt

AaBbCcDdEeFfGgHh
IiJjKkLlMmNnOoPpQq
RrSsTtUuVvWwXxYy

UNDA Series (cont).

Nick Hayes
1998

UNDA Series consists of fifteen typefaces. The original concept of UNDA was to offer a variety of effects within one set of fonts.

Identikal

Wired Black 20pt

AaBbCcDdEeFfGgHhIiJjKkLlMmNnOoPpQqRrSs
TtUuVvWwXxYyZz1234567890 ‹([{%£&?!$}])›

Wired Black Italic 11pt

AaBbCcDdEeFfGgHhIiJjKkLlMmNnOoPpQqRrSsTtUuVvWwXxYyZz

Wired Regular 11pt

AaBbCcDdEeFfGgHhIiJjKkLlMm

Wired Regular Italic 11pt

AaBbCcDdEeFfGgHhIiJjKkLlMm

Wired Light Italic 11pt

AaBbCcDdEeFfGgHhIiJjKkLlMm

Wired Light Italic 11pt

AaBbCcDdEeFfGgHhIiJjKkLlMm

Wired Serif 11pt

AaBbCcDdEeFfGgHhIiJjKkLlMm

Wired Serif Italic 11pt

AaBbCcDdEeFfGgHhIiJjKkLlMm

Wired

Adam Hayes
1999

Wired is a family of eight typefaces.

Zero Open Regular 22pt

AaBbCcDdEeFfGgHhIiJjKkLlMmNnOoPpQ
qRrSsTtUuVvWwXxYyZz1234567890

Zero Open Bold 19pt

Zero Open Bold

Zero Open Regular 19pt

Zero Open

Zero Open Fine 19pt

Zero Open Fine

Zero Closed Bold 19pt

Zero Closed Bold

Zero Closed Regular 19pt

Zero Closed

Zero Closed Fine 19pt

Zero Closed Fine

Zero

Nick Hayes
2000

Zero consists of six typefaces.

ingoFonts

Fonts Ⓟ and Ⓒ by Ingo Zimmermann
since 1994

Ingo Zimmermann _____ *1967 son of a graphic designer _____ graffiti, then studied graphic design, typography, and calligraphy, as well as photography _____
exhibitions _____ work for numerous magazines, preferring own typefaces _____

ingoFonts
Fonts ℗ and © by Ingo Zimmermann
since 1994

www.ingo-zimmermann.de

At ingoFonts all fonts can be downloaded.
Gratis. Free.
Here's the catch: The files offered here to
download contain only a reduced font.
That means, the font only consists of uppercase
and lowercase from A to Z, or rather, a to z.
The complete font, including numbers, umlauts,
punctuation, and especially ligatures, is only
available with your order and your cash.

Kreitmayrstraße 30/30a
86165 Augsburg (Germany)
info@ingo-zimmermann.de

Anatole France

Anatole France

Aa Bb Cc Dd Ee Ff Gg Hh Ii Jj Kk Ll Mm Nn

ABCDEFGHIJKLMN
OPQRSTUVWXYZ

abcdefffiflghijklmn
opqrstßuvvvvwxyz

0123456789

&/'!¿?—————— „"""''

Anatole France

Ingo Zimmermann
1997

Bold, decorative poster type in
the style of Art Deco.

An old portfolio of script patterns
from the 1920s or 1930s includes
among its pages a handwritten poster
script, very typical for the 1920s. To
begin with, there is the emphasized
decorative character, which stands
out due to stressing the stems. Next,
the attempt to portray the character
forms with the help of a few–but
always recurring–basic elements is
driven to the limits. Theoretically
speaking, that which should have led
to a contrived, geometrically deter-
mined type obtains a likeable and
pleasant look through the ductus of
the manually guided brush.

A few fonts already exist that
have been drawn in accordance
with the exact same principles.
But these are just drawn–only
drawn. Anatole France retains the
hand script character, in spite of
its stringent composition.

ingoFonts

Charpentier Renaissance

Ingo Zimmermann
1996

Very readable Antiqua typeface in
three styles: Renaissance, Baroque,
and Classicism.

Charpentier is the Antiqua form of
the san serif Graz2006 (the very
first ingoFont). The uppercase of
Charpentier is developed from Roman
monumental lettering; the lowercase is
modeled on the Caroligian minuscule.

Charpentier Renaissance

ABCDEFGHIJKLMNOPQRSTUVWXYZ
abbecchckdeffffiflftghijklllmmmnnuoppæqrrasffchfiffftß
ttitzuunrvwxyz 0123456789 & / ! ? - - — . , : ; „ " » « ( )

Charpentier Baroque

Ingo Zimmermann
1996

Charpentier Baroque

ABCDEFGHIJKLMNOPQRSTUVWXYZ
abcdeffiflghijklmnopqrsßtuvwxyz
O123456789 & / ! ? - - — . , : ; „ " » « ( )

Charpentier Classicistique

Ingo Zimmermann
1996

Charpentier Classicistique

ABCDEFGHIJKLMNOPQRSTUVWXYZ
abcdeffiflghijklmnopqrsßtuvwxyz
O123456789 & / ! ? - - — . , : ; „ " » « ( )

Charpentier Classicistique Italique

ABCDEFGHIJKLMNOPQRSTUVWXYZ
abcdeffiflghijklmnopqrsßtuvwxyz
0123456789 & / ! ? - - — . , : ; „ " » « ( )

info@ingo-zimmermann.de

DeFonte Léger

ABCDEFGHIJKLMNOPQRSTUVWXYZ
abcdeffiflghijklmnopqrsßtuvwxyz
0123456789 / ! ? - – — . , : ; „ " » « ( )

DeFonte Normale

ABCDEFGHIJKLMNOPQRSTUVWXYZ
abcdeffiflghijklmnopqrsßtuvwxyz
0123456789 / ! ? - – — . , : ; „ " » « ( )

DeFonte DemiGras

ABCDEFGHIJKLMNOPQRSTUVWXYZ
abcdeffiflghijklmnopqrsßtuvwxyz
0123456789 / ! ? - – — . , : ; „ " » « ( )

DeFonte Gros

ABCDEFGHIJKLMNOPQRSTUVWXYZ
abcdeffiflghijklmnopqrsßtuvwxyz
123 5 7 / ! ? - – — . , : ; „ ( )

DeFonte

Ingo Zimmermann
1995

Variation of Helvetica according to the "blur" principle.

The underlying typeface is based on Helvetica, the only true run-of-the-mill typeface of the twentieth century. The distorted principle used simulated the photographic effect of halation and/or overexposure. The light typestyle, DeFonte Léger, nearly breaks on the thin points, whereas on those points where the lines meet or cross, dark spots remain. The characters are "nibbled at" from the inner and outer brightness. On the normal and semibold typestyles, DeFonte Normale and DeFonte Demi Gras, the effect is limited almost exclusively to the end strokes and corners, which appear to be strongly rounded off. The bold version, DeFont Gros, is especially attractive. As a result of "overexposure," counters (internal spaces) are closed in, and characters become blurred and turn into spots; new characteristic forms are created that are astoundingly legible.

ingoFonts

Déformé

Ingo Zimmermann
1995

Deconstructivist variation on the Clarendon style.

Déformé was born out of the distortion of the time-honored Clarendon letter-forms, in which the stems and thin strokes have been reversed. Thus, a typeface was created that will remind some readers of a Western typeface, and others of the ordinary typeface of a typewriter. Actually, it is still a robust Clarendon that has survived its disfigurement quite well. Déformé, like its "mother," is easily legible, in spite of the inherent emphasis that one is not used to seeing.

Déformé

ABCDEFGHIJKLMNOPQRSTUVWXYZ
abcdeffifflghijklmnopqrsßtuvwxyz
0123456789 &/!?--—.,:;„"»«()

DeKunst

Ingo Zimmermann
1995

Deconstructivist initials; each character in two variations.

Typefaces are defined by vectors—contours descriptive of the inner and outer form of the letter—and their filled-in sections. DeKunst was created by distorting and overlapping vectorized lines and shapes. Nearly similar forms and reflections lend an ornamental effect to some of the characters. Geometrical gimmicks sometimes remind one of Kurt Schwitters's compositions. Incidental amorphous forms call to mind the paintings and sculptures of Hans Arp or Alexander Calder.

info@ingo-zimmermann.de

DePixel Illeqlule

ABCDEFGHIJKLMNOPQRSTUVWXYZ

abcdderfffrcghijklmnoparsßtuvwxyz

0123456789 /|?---

.,;;„'"×«()

Die ILLEGIBLE DEPIXEL entscand aus der Übertreibung des Pixeleffekts. Wie andere Screenfonts auch ist sie aus einzelnen Pixeln aufgebaut. Nur beträgt die Versalhöhe lediglich 5 Pixel, die n-Höhe gar nur 4 Pixel. Dazu zeigt sie den aus dem Web bekannten Effekt einer zu kleinen Schriftdarstellung, der Texte nahezu unleserlich erscheinen lässt.

DePixel

Ingo Zimmermann
1999

Simulation of a pixel typeface made up of not enough pixels.

Illegible DePixel was developed from the exaggeration of the pixel effect on Apple's renowned Geneva. As with all screen fonts, it simulates the composition of individual pixels. Only here, the cap height amounts to only 5 pixels, and the x-height a mere 4 pixels. Furthermore, this typeface shows the well-known effect found on the Web of a font design that is too small and makes texts appear almost illegible.

ingoFonts

Deutsche Schrift Callwey

abcdefghijklmnopqrstuvwxyz

abcduffifflgfijklmnopqrßtuvwxyz --.,;;„"

Diese Schrift erscheint auf einem Blatt einer Schreibmustermappe des Callwey-Verlags aus den zwanziger oder dreißiger Jahren. Sie ist dort als „Deutsche Schrift" bezeichnet. Die sogenannte Deutsche Schrift ist eine im neunzehnten Jahrhundert entstandene Schreibschrift. Nach ihrem Erfinder kennt man sie auch unter dem Namen „Sütterlinschrift".

Deutsche Schrift Callwey

Ingo Zimmermann
1998

So-called Deutsche Schreibschrift (German handwriting), according to a sample from ca. 1920 or 1930.

Deutsche Schrift is a script type that appeared in the nineteenth century, and is also called "Sütterlinschrift," after its creator. An example of the typeface appears in a portfolio of script samples from the Callwey-Verlag from the '20s or '30s. In that example, the script is called Deutsche Schrift.

Ingo Zimmermann
1998

Sans serif headline font; characters are also available in alternative forms.

The characters of Die Überschrift range between the narrow boundaries of cap height and baseline. No ascender or descender breaks through the range. The legibility is ensured, particularly by the classic Roman proportions and the greatest possible distinction in the letterforms. The uppercase letters of Die Überschrift were originally designed as a headline font for the magazine *motion*. Their versatility and flexibility, even with deformity and distortion, made them a favorite for *motion* layouts. In order to open up a wider spectrum of utilization for this letter type, minuscules were also conceived with time, adding to the original, exclusively uppercase, typeface.

>>Josef
>>Josefov

DIE ÜBERSCHRIFT ELEGANT

AΛBBCCDDEFGGHIIJKLMMNOPQRRSTUVWWXYZ
O123456789 /!?-–——.,:;„" " "»«()

DIE ÜBERSCHRIFT Normal

AΛBBCCDDEFGGHIIJKLMMNOPQRRSTUVWWXYZ
abccħdkdefffifflgghijklmnopqrsßtuvwxyz
O123456789 /!?-–——.,:;„" " "»«()

DIE ÜBERSCHRIFT Gequetscht

AΛBBCCDDEFGGHIIJKLMMNOPQRRSTUVWWXYZ
abccħdkdefffiflghijklmnopqrsßtuvwxyz
O123456789 /!?-–——.,:;„" " "»«()

DIE ÜBERSCHRIFT Halbfett

AΛBBCCDDEFGGHIIJKLMMNOPQRRSTUVWWXYZ
abcdefffiflghijklmnopqrsßtuvwxyz
O123456789 /!?-–——.,:;„" " "»«()

info@ingo-zimmermann.de

Faber Eins/Zwei Normal

ABCDEFGHIJKLMNOPQRSTUVWXYZ
aabcdeεfffiflfiflgghijkllmnopqrrsʃßttuuvwxyz 0123456789 /!?--—.,:;„""»«()

Faber Eins/Zwei Schmal Normal

ABCDEFGHIJKLMNOPQRSTUVWXYZ
aabcdeεfffiflgghijkllmnopqrrsʃßttuuvwxyz 0123456789 /!?--—.,:;„""»«()

Faber Eins/Zwei Breit Normal

ABCDEFGHIJKLMNOPQRSTUVWXYZ
abcdeεfffiflfiflgghijkllmnopqrrsʃßttuuvwxyz 0123456789 /!?--—.,:;„""»«()

Faber Eins Normal Kursiv

ABCDEFGHIJKLMNOPQRSTUVWXYZ
abcdeffiflghijklmnopqrsʃßtuuvwxyz 0123456789 / !?--—.,:;„"»«()

Faber Eins/Zwei Kräftig

ABCDEFGHIJKLMNOPQRSTUVWXYZ
aabcdeεfffiflffiflgghijkllmnopqrrsʃßttuuvwxyz 0123456789 /!?--—.,:;„""»«()

Faber Eins/Zwei Halbfett

ABCDEFGHIJKLMNOPQRSTUVWXYZ
aabcdeεfffiflgghijkllmnopqrrsʃßttuuvwxyz 0123456789 /!?--—.,:;„""»«()

Faber Eins/Zwei Fett

ABCDEFGHIJKLMNOPQRSTUVWXYZ
aabcdeεfffiflgghijkllmnopqrrsʃßttuuvwxyz 0123456789 /!?--—.,:;„""»«()

Faber Eins/Zwei

Ingo Zimmermann
1996

Easily legible sans serif type; many letters are also available in alternative styles.

Faber Eins (one) is actually two fonts. Its capital letters are directly derived from the Roman Capitalis Monumentalis. The minuscules combine modern perception with traditional forms. There are two types of some of the minuscules: a standard design in a Gill Sans style, and a more abstract variant in conformity with medieval uncials of the letters a, e, f, g, l, r, t, and u. Faber Eins and Faber Zwei (two) differ only in the standard assignment of the characters on the keyboard: in the case of Faber Eins, the standard forms represent the standard assignment, whereas Faber Zwei represents the uncials.

Display characters are Faber Eins/Zwei Halbfett (bold) and Fett (black). The circular interiors in some of its letterforms lend a special character to Faber Eins Fett.

››Faber Drei

ingoFonts

Faber Drei

Ingo Zimmermann
1998

Roman variant of Faber Drei.

Faber Drei (Faber Three) is the Roman typeface that was born out of the sans serif design Faber Eins (Faber One). The proportions are nearly identical to those of Faber Eins, which means two things: The capitals are based on the classical example of the Roman Monumental Lettering, and the lowercase characters originated in the written Carolingian minuscule. In comparison, Faber Drei has heavy–although very short–serifs. The character of contrasting strokes is not very pronounced; therefore, this font is closely related to the first Roman typefaces from the fifteen century. The Kursiv also has very reserved serifs, which are quite appealing to the modern reading habits.

<<Faber Eins/Zwei

Faber Drei Normal

ABCDEFGHIJKLMNOPQRRSTUVWXYZ
abcchckdefffiflftghijklmmmnopqrsßttuvwxyz
0123456789 /!?&-−—.,:;„ ""«»«()

Die »Faber Drei« hat ihren Ursprung in der serifenlosen »Faber Eins«, deren Antiquaversion sie ist. Die Proportionen sind nahezu mit denen der »Faber Eins« identisch. Die Versalien orientieren sich am klassischen Vorbild der Römischen Capitalis Monumentalis, die Minuskeln haben ihren Ursprung in der geschriebenen Karolingischen Minuskel. Die »Faber Drei« hat vergleichsweise kräftige, wenn auch sehr kurze Serifen. Der Wechselzug-Charakter ist nicht sehr stark ausgeprägt. Damit steht sie in der Nähe der allerersten Antiquas aus dem

Faber Drei Kursiv

ABCDEFGHIJKLMNOPQRRSTUVWXYZ
abcchckdeffffiflftghijklmmmnopqrsſßtttuvwxyz
0123456789 /!?&-−—.,:;„ ""«»«()

15. Jahrhundert. Ihren charakteristischen Ausdruck erhält sie durch die offenen Formen von CDGOQ und bcdeopq. Aber auch die Spitzen von AMNVWZ sind typisch für die »Faber Drei«. Die relativ langen Ober- und Unterlängen verhelfen der Schrift zu sehr prägnanten Wortbildern. Die »Faber Drei« ist eine sehr gut lesbare Mengensatzschrift, die auch in sehr grosser Anwendung reizvolle Details bietet. Die Verwendung der Ligaturen ergibt ein geschlosseneres Satzbild, kann aber auch zu einer willkommenen Störung der Sehgewohnheit führen. Ganz in Tradition der

Faber Drei Kräftig

ABCDEFGHIJKLMNOPQRSTUVWXYZ
abcchckdeffffiflftghijklmnopqrsßtuvwxyz
0123456789 /!?&-−—.,:;„ ""«»«()

ersten Kursivschriften steht die »Faber Drei Kursiv«. Ihre Formen ergeben ein geschlossenes fließendes Satzbild. Dabei behält sie die charakteristischen offenen Einzelformen der geraden »Faber Drei«. Auch die Kursiv hat sehr zurückhaltende Serifen, was den modernen Lesegewohnheiten sehr entgegenkommt. Für die negative Anwendungen steht die »Faber Drei Kräftig« zur Verfügung. Ihre kräftigeren Striche verschaffen ihr ein sichereres Auftreten. Als Auszeichnungsschrift zur »Faber Drei Normal« ist sie jedoch zu schwach. Die »Faber Drei« ist eine

info@ingo-zimmermann.de

Faber Fraktur Normal

ABCDEFGHIJKLMNOPQRSTUVWXYZ

abcchckddeffffifistoghijkelllmmmnopqrsliMtktuvowxyz 0123456789 / !?=--.,:;„"»«()

Faber Fraktur Kurrent

ABCDEFGHIJKLMNOPQRSTUVWXYZ

abcchckdefghijkelllll mmmnopqrsßktuvwxyz 0123456789 / !?=--.,:;„"»«()

Faber Fraktur Halbfett

ABCDEFGHIJKLMNOPQRSTUVWXYZ

abcchckdefffffistghijkelllmmmnopqrsliMtktuvwxyz 0123456789 / !?=--.,:;„"»«()

ʃFaber Gotik Text

ABCDEFGHIJKLMNOPQRSTUVWXYZ

abcchckdefffffifistghijklmnopqrsßtttuvwxyz 0123456789 / !?---.,:;„"»«○

Faber Gotik Gothic

ABCDEFGHIJKLMNOPQRSTUVWXYZ

abcchckdefffffifistghijklmnopqrsßtttuvwxyz 0123456789 / !?---.,:;„"»«○

ʃFABER GOTIK CAPITALS

ABCDEFGHIJKLMNOPQRSTUVWXYZ

ABCDEFGHIJKLMNOPQRSTUVWXYZ 0123456789 / !?---.,:;„"»«○

Faber Fraktur

Ingo Zimmermann
1994

An easy-to-read modern Fraktur without flourish.

Faber Fraktur omits the frills that often make typefaces difficult to read. This font also features the repetition of a few similar basic type forms. At the same time, the typical contrasting strokes of a historical handwritten Fraktur are retained. All characters are reduced to their basic skeletons. The fanciness and manifold breaks (or fractures) typical of blackletter typefaces are reduced considerably, to a few instances. Faber Fraktur does not appear nearly so foreign and archaic as the old broken fonts. Alternative forms are available for the characters d, g, k, s, x, and l. Typical for a blackletter typeface: the long s, which is replaced only at the end of a word or syllable by the round s.

Faber Gotik

Ingo Zimmermann
2002

Contrived Gothic, according to modern form principles, in three variations.

Faber Gotik is reminiscent of Gutenberg, who created the first moveable block letters 555 years ago. The characters are composed of squares, which are lined up straight or in a more or less slanted manner. The principle of breaking applied here is analogous to the historical model. Even the form of the characters is based on the model from the Middle Ages.

In Faber Gotik Text, the historical form is most loyally retained, whereas Faber Gotik Gothic is almost a contrived modern typeface. Somewhat unusual, Faber Gotik Capitals is a Gothic cap font.

ingoFonts

Fixogum

Ingo Zimmermann
1998

A capital letter typeface written freely with a tub of *Fixogum*.

Who can forget the green tube that was always present on any graphic artist's table? *Fixogum* is an adhesive that is removable and leaves no traces of its use, because the dried glue can be rubbed away with your fingers. All lay-outs were glued with Fixogum until the Apple Macintosh was introduced. In the hand of the calligrapher, this green tube resulted–in a roundabout way–in the creation of the typeface Fixogum. Fixogum is composed of capitals only; however, they are joined in such a peculiar way that a typeface that is more or less fluent is produced. The forms are archaic and represent a basic script. Fixogum results in a pleasantly structured typeface. The rows appear to be closed. As a whole, Fixogum is some-what reminiscent of graffiti handwriting, which might have something to do with the writer's past.

info@ingo-zimmermann.de

Josef Leicht

AΛBBCDEFGGHIIJKLMMNOPQRRSTUVWWXYZ
abcchckddefffiflgghijkllmnopqrsßßtuvwxyz
0123456789 /!?--—.,:;„""" "»«()

Josef Normal

AΛBBCDEFGGHIIJKLMMNOPQRRSTUVWWXYZ
abcchckddefffiflgghijkllmnopqrsßßtuvwxyz
0123456789 /!?--—.,:;„""" "»«()

Josef Kursiv

AΛBBCDEFGGHIIJKLMMNOPQRRSTUVWWXYZ
abcchckddefffiflgghijkllmnopqrsßßtuvwxyz
0123456789 /!?--—.,:;„""" "»«()

Josef Halbfett

AΛBBCDEFGGHIIJKLMMNOPQRRSTUVWWXYZ
abcddefffiflghijkllmnopqrsßßtuvwxyz
0123456789 /!?--—.,:;„""" "»«()

Josef Fett

AΛBBCDEFGGHIIJKLMMNOPQRRSTUVWWXYZ
abcddefffiflghijkllmnopqrsßßtuvwxyz
0123456789 /!?--—.,:;„""" "»«()

Josef

Ingo Zimmermann
2000

A sans serif body type developed from
Die Überschrift.
In memory of Josef Zimmermann,
1912-2000.

Josef evolved out of Die Überschrift.
Josef uses the capitals from Die Überschrift, whereas the finer points of the
minuscules have been revised so that
the result is an excellent readable
body type. Josef extenders go far
beyond those of Die Überschrift, as the
ascenders and descenders are notice-
ably longer than the H-height.
Classical and modern type forms are
united in Josef. Going against the
typographical trend, a and g are modern, but the alternative classical form
is also available as an optional keyboard layout. Other characters also
have two variations. Rigid, rational
forms have been draw for d, f, j, and l,
as well as playful versions. Together
with the familiar variations of the
capitals in Die Überschrift, a number
of combinations are possible.

‹‹Die Überschrift
››Josefov

ingoFonts

Josefov

Ingo Zimmermann
2003

Slab serif variation of the sans serif Josef.

Strictly speaking, Josefov is not a Roman typeface, in spite of its serifs. The sans serif Josef, the underlying typeface, was decorated with heavy, rectangular serifs. The serifs merge into the stems rounded, but the stems and hairlines themselves also run together in a rounded form. On the round characters, the serifs are attached horizontally, against all traditions, whereas the double-sided serifs reflect examples of the ascenders of some early printers of the fifteenth century.

‹‹Die Überschrift
››Josefov

Josefov Leicht
ABCDEFGHIJKLMNOPQRSTUVWXYZ
abcchckdeffiflghijklmnopqrsßtuvwxyz
0123456789 /!?--—.,:;„""""»«()

Josefov Normal
ABCDEFGHIJKLMNOPQRSTUVWXYZ
abcchckdeffiflghijklmnopqrsßtuvwxyz
0123456789 /!?--—.,:;„""""»«()

Josefov Halbfett
ABCDEFGHIJKLMNOPQRSTUVWXYZ
abcchckdeffiflghijklmnopqrsßtuvwxyz
0123456789 /!?--—.,:;„""""»«()

Klex

Ingo Zimmermann
1996

A calligraphic alphabet in bold/light brushstrokes.

Actually, a typeface like this one should be written with a wide brush; this one was written with a thick, pointed brush. Thus were created the round or misshapen ends of the stems, and the sometimes excessively pointed ends of the hairlines. For each character of Klex, the large brush was dipped in the ink anew. Using this method, the forms turned out very soft, in spite of their geometrical rigidity. The individual characters are heavy, simple, and monumental, so that they are also suitable as initials.

info@ingo-zimmermann.de

Maier's Nr. 8 Mager

ABCDEFGHIJKLMNOPQRSTUVWXYZ
abcchckdDefffffflghijklmnopqrsßttttzuvwxyz
0123456789 /!?=-—.,:;j „„ "" »«()

Maier's Nr. 8 Halbfett

ABCDEFGHIJKLMNOPQRSTUVWXYZ
abcchckdDefff fiflghijklmnopqrsßttttzuvwxyz
0123456789 /!?=-—.,:;j „ "" »«()

Maier's Nr. 21 Mager

ABCDEFGHIJKLMNOPQRSTUVWXYZ
ABCDEFGHIJKLMNOPQRSTUVWXYZ
abcdefff fiflghijklmnopqrsfsttttuvwxyz
0123456789 /!?=-—.,:;j „ "" »«()

Maier's Nr. 21 Normal

ABCDEFGHIJKLMNOPQRSTUVWXYZ
ABCDEFGHIJKLMNOPQRSTUVWXYZ
abcdefff fiflghijklmnopqrsfsttttuvwxyz
0123456789 /!?=-—.,:;j „ "" »«()

Maier's Nr. 8

Ingo Zimmermann
2002

A sketched "script for technicians" from ca. 1900; very geometrical, rigid forms characterized by typical signs of Jugendstil/Art Nouveau.

A magazine from ca. 1900 carries the title *Schriftensammlung für Techniker: Verkleinerte Schriften der wichtigsten Alphabete* (Collection of scripts for technical specialists: reduced scripts of the most important alphabets), by Karl O. Maier. It served as the model for technical professionals in which, at that time, the captions of drawings were still done by hand. The high degree of abstraction in Maier's Nr. 8 presents a strange effect to those who know the age of the original. In comparison, many of today's so-called ultramodern types suddenly look quite old-fashioned.

Maier's Nr. 21

Ingo Zimmermann
2002

A sketched "script for technicians" from ca. 1900; very geometrical, rigid forms characterized by typical signs of Jugendstil/Art Nouveau.

Worthy of note are the Art Nouveau forms of Maier's Nr. 21 that were characteristic around the turn of the twentieth century. The characters of the original model have been scanned, digitized, and greatly magnified. In the process, special attention was also given to keep the "messy" edges, typical of handwritten scripts, effectively noticeable in the digitized form. In this way, this "technical" typeface maintains a handmade flavor.

ingoFonts

Schwabacher DR

Ingo Zimmermann
1998

Heavy, broken Script;
Rudolf Koch's first print
from 1909.

Heavy, broken script; Rudolf Koch's first
print from 1909.

On an old page full of script examples
from the 1930s, this script is described
as "Schwabacher (used by the Deutsche
Reichsbahn)." As a matter of fact, it is
the first print of the Offenbach script
master Rudolf Koch, who came out with
this script in 1909. At that time, it was
given the name Neudeutsche (New
German). Later, it became very popular
under the name Koch-Schrift, and was
at times the official script of the
Deutsche Reichsbahn (German National
Railway).

Schwabacher der Deutschen Reichsbahn

ABCDEFGHIJKLMN
OPQRSTUVWXYZ
abcchckdefffffffififlftghijklmno
pqrsßsiss stßtttitttzuvwxyz
0123456789
/!?=–—.,:;„" » « ()

info@ingo-zimmermann.de

Wendelin Normal

ABCDEFGHIJKLMNOPQRSTUVWXYZ abbecchckdfteffffififlftghijkl
mmmnruoppeqrrasßttiuvwxyz 0123456789 /!?-—.,:;„""»«()

Wendelin Normal Kapitälchen

ABCDEFGHIJKLMNOPQRSTUVWXYZ
ABCDEFGHIJKLMNOPQRSTUVWXYZ 0123456789 /!?-—.,:;„""»«()

Wendelin Normal Kursiv

ABCDEFGHIJKLMNOPQRSTUVWXYZ abbecchckdfteffffififlftghijkl
mmmnruoppeqrrasßttiuvwxyz 0123456789 /!?-—.,:;„""»«()

Wendelin Kräftig

ABCDEFGHIJKLMNOPQRSTUVWXYZ abbecchckdfteffffififlftghijkl
mmmnruoppeqrrasßttiuvwxyz 0123456789 /!?-—.,:;„""»«()

Wendelin Halbfett Kursiv

ABCDEFGHIJKLMNOPQRSTUVWXYZ abbecchckdfteffffififlftghijkl
mmmnruoppeqrrasßttiuvwxyz 0123456789 /!?-—.,:;„""»«()

Wendelin Fett

ABCDEFGHIJKLMNOPQRSTUVWXYZ abcdeffiflghijkl
mnopqrsßtuvwxyz 0123456789 /!?-—.,:;„""»«()

Wendelin Fett Kursiv

ABCDEFGHIJKLMNOPQRSTUVWXYZ abcdeffiflghijkl
mmmnopqrsßtuvwxyz 0123456789 /!?——.,:;„""»«()

Wendelin Breitfett

ABCDEFGHIJKLMNOPQRSTUVWXYZ abcdeffiflghijkl
mnopqrsßtuvwxyz 0123456789 /!?-—.,:;„""»«()

Wendelin

Ingo Zimmermann
1996

Easy-to-read modern sans serif.

Originally, Wendelin was created as a body type for the magazine *motion*. With time, this type continued to be elaborated on and further developed. Wendelin Normal brings Franklin Gothic very much to mind. All other versions, especially Kursiv, are new creations, in some cases with quite unusual details.

ingoFonts

DELUXE TYPE FOR THE POST-ATOMIC AGE...

Jukebox, created by Jason Walcott in 2003, began as an independent type foundry in 2000 under the name "JAW Fonts". Jason became interested in type and typography while studying Illustration and Graphic Design at Kean College of New Jersey. After graduating in 1997, he moved to Southern California, where Jukebox is now located. Jason's original designs are often inspired by the whimsical and ingenious designs of hand lettering, found in retro signage, old movie titles, television, and even product labels. Many of these sources serve as the starting point for the development of full typefaces. The Jukebox library also includes a small selection of digital revivals based on older photolettering/metal typefaces. Jason continues to develop new fonts, and Jukebox strives to supply designers and anyone interested in type with fresh and inventive faces.

Jukebox type is available through Veer.com. All Jukebox fonts are available for both Mac and PC, in PostScript and TrueType formats, and contain full accented character sets and kerning pairs.

Jukebox
1116 North Spaulding Ave. Unit D
West Hollywood, CA 90046
Phone: 323·650·2740   email: jasonwalcott@earthlink.net
Web: www.JAWarts.com
to purchase Jukebox type, please visit www.veer.com

Special Thanks to my father, Andrew, my grandparents, Mary and John,
and my mother, Ann, whose continued generosity and support
have made Jukebox possible.   —Jason Walcott
I dedicate this section to my dear, departed grandfather, John W. Walcott "Pappah". 1921-2003

ABCDEFGHIJKLMNOPQRSTUVWXYZ
abcdefghijklmnopqrstuvwxyz 1234567890 ÁáÊêÑñ &€$
Too Much of a Good Thing is Never Enough!

Acroterion JF

Jason Walcott
2002

An elegant, high-class script, digitally revived from an older photo/letterpress face.

ABCDEFGHIJKLMNOPQRSTUVWXYZ
abcdefghijklmnopqrstuvwxyz 1234567890 ÁáÊêÑñ ¥€$
Don't underestimate the Power of Laughter.

Adage Script JF

Jason Walcott
2002

A warm, "down home" script font, digitally revived from an older photo/letterpress face.

ABCDEFGHIJKLMNOPQRSTUVWXYZ
abcdefghijklmnopqrstuvwxyz 1234567890 ÁáÊêÑñ &€$
I scaled the Matterhorn and danced the Polka.

Alpengeist JF

Jason Walcott
2001

A blackletter face with an old-world feel. Perfect for a fairy tale, a horror novel, or even personalizing your alpenhorn.

ABCDEFGHIJKLMNOPQRSTUVWXYZ
abcdefghijklmnopqrstuvwxyz 1234567890 ÁáÊêÑñ &€$
Merry Christmas and Happy New Year!

Annabelle JF

Jason Walcott
2002

A flowing script font named after the designer's mother.

Jukebox

Blairesque JF

Jason Walcott
2001-2002

A family of three typefaces and one dingbat font, designed to be used together or separately. The dingbat font contains an alternate set of numerals. This type family is dedicated to the child in all of us.

Blairesque JF-Curly

ABCDEFGHIJKLMNOPQRSTUVWXYZ AMRT
abcdefghijklmnopqrstuvwxyz yg 1234567890 ÁáÊêÑñ &€$

Blairesque JF-Festive

ABCDEFGHIJKLMNOPQRSTUVWXYZ llff Th
abcdefghijklmnopqrstuvwxyz 1234567890 ÁáÊêÑñ &€$

Blairesque JF-Gothic

ABCDEFGHIJKLMNOPQRSTUVWXYZ
abcdefghijklmnopqrstuvwxyz 1234567890 ÁáÊêÑñ &€$

Blairesque JF-Happy Grams

1234567890

Blairesque Curly

Jason Walcott
2001

When in Rome, eat some Spaghetti!
The Many Faces of Paris

Blairesque Festive

Jason Walcott
2002

I Sailed around the World.
The Big Book of Children's Stories

138   323-650-2740

International Summit cancelled for Beach Party!

Do you know the way home?

Blairesque Gothic

Jason Walcott
2001

Blairesque Happy Grams

Jason Walcott
2001

Jukebox

Boxer Script JF

Jason Walcott
2001

A heavy script face reminiscent of machine-cut automobile lettering of the 1940s and 1950s.

ABCDEFGHIJKLMNOPQRSTUVWXYZ
abcdefghijklmnopqrstuvwxyz 1234567890 ÁáÊêÑñ &€$
fauu

Antique Car Shows on Television.

Bronson Gothic JF

Jason Walcott
2002

A heavy industrial-style font named after a dear friend of the designer.

ABCDEFGHIJKLMNOPQRSTUVWXYZ
abcdefghijklmnopqrstuvwxyz 1234567890 ÁáÊêÑñ &€$

A Cruise to Alaska is best in June?

Buena Park JF

Jason Walcott
2001

This Clarendon-style face has subtle flourishes.

ABCDEFGHIJKLMNOPQRSTUVWXYZ
abcdefghijklmnopqrstuvwxyz 1234567890 ÁáÊêÑñ &€$

He got lost in Wichita, Kansas.

Cavetto JF-Roman

Jason Walcott
2002

This Modern-style family consists of three faces: roman, italic, and italic alternate.

ABCDEFGHIJKLMNOPQRSTUVWXYZ
abcdefghijklmnopqrstuvwxyz 1234567890 ÁáÊêÑñ &€$

The quick Brown Fox jumps over the Lazy Dog. 9 pt.
The quick Brown Fox jumps over the Lazy Dog. 10 pt.
The quick Brown Fox jumps over the Lazy Dog. 12 pt.
The quick Brown Fox jumps over the Lazy Dog. 14 pt.

Cavetto Italic

ABCDEFGHIJKLMNOPQRSTUVWXYZ
abcdefghijklmnopqrstuvwxyz 1234567890 ÁáÊêÑñ &€$

Cavetto Italic Alternate

ABCDEFGHIJKLMNOPQRSTUVWXYZ
d, fg hklmnry 1234567890 &
A A K K M R R Ih C V W &

Summer Clouds Roll By

Summer Clouds Roll By

ABCDEFGHIJKLMNOPQRSTUVWXYZ
abcdefghijklmnopqrstuvwxyz 1234567890 ÁáÊêÑñ &€$

The Year of the Dragon is here!

ABCDEFGHIJKLMNOPQ
RSTUVWXYZ
abcdefghijklmnopqrstuvwxyz 1234567890 ÁáÊêÑñ 8 €$

Join us for an Evening at the Opera House

Cavetto JF-Italic/Alt.

Jason Walcott
2002

The italic and italic alternate variants of the Cavetto family.

Charade JF

Jason Walcott
2001

A whimsical font that's full of fun and charm.

Debonair JF

Jason Walcott
2000-2001

An elegant script digitally revived from an older photo/letterpress face.

Jukebox

Fairy Tale JF

Jason Walcott
2000

An "almost-but-not-quite" blackletter face, inspired by a popular fairy tale.

ABCDEFGHIJKLMNOPQRSTUVWXYZ
abcdefghijklmnopqrstuvwxyz 1234567890 ÁáÊêÑñ & €$

The Prince and Princess lived happily ever after.

Fenway Park JF

Jason Walcott
2001

This athletic-style script font, useful for a variety of applications, has proved to be one of Jukebox's most popular.

ABCDEFGHIJKLMNOPQRSTUVWXYZ
abcdefghijklmnopqrstuvwxyz 1234567890 ÁáÊêÑñ & €$

Take Me Out To The Ballgame!

Friki Tiki JF

Jason Walcott
2001

Inspired by a popular tiki-themed attraction, this font says "Aloha."

ABCDEFGHIJKLMNOPQRSTUVWXYZ THTI
ABCDEFGHIJKLMNOPQRSTUVWXYZ THTaFrFa
1234567890 ÁáÊêÑÑ &€$

WHEN YOU GO TO HAWAII, YOU MIGHT GET LEI'D...

Gypsy Switch JF

Jason Walcott
2002

A fun and light typeface, useful for a variety of purposes.

ABCDEFGHIJKLMNOPQRSTUVWXYZ
abcdefghijklmnopqrstuvwxyz 1234567890 ÁáÊêÑñ &€$

I had Fun playing my Xylophones.

ABCDEFGHIJKLMNOPQRSTUVWXYZ

abcdefghijklmnopqrstuvwxyz 1234567890 ÁáÈêÑñ ¿€$

Once Upon a Time in Las Vegas...

Holiday Times JF

Jason Walcott
2000

A festive and fun font, so named because it was inspired by a beloved Christmas source.

ABCDEFGHIJKLMNOPQRSTUVWXYZ

abcdefghijklmnopqrstuvwxyz 1234567890 ÁáÈêÑñ &€$

Congratulations on your Wedding Day!

Jeffriana JF

Jason Walcott
2001

A handwriting-style script font, named after a dear friend of the designer.

Kon Tiki Aloha

ABCDEFGHIJKLMNOPQRSTUVWXYZ

ABCDEFGHIJKLMNOPQRSTUVWXYZ 1234567890 ÁáÉÊÑÑ &€$

Kon Tiki Aloha Ligatures

TA EB CK ND EN FA FO FE FU FI KO LI AM ON OÃ OP OR RE SE TH TU TE TI TR LY TY
AT CA TCE DEA FRG ANGA KK KKE LOMANT OOEP NARA TS TOADEDMEES
UT VO WA VIRY ZOUT ERKALS VE VAKO ANLE LA LUST RUMOO BA BI BUB

WELCOME TO THE POLYNESIAN TRADERS

WELCOME TO THE POLYNESIAN TRADERS

Kon Tiki JF-Aloha/Ligs.

Jason Walcott
2002

The Kon Tiki font family was inspired by the Polynesian kitch of the 1950s and 1960s. It consists of seven typefaces with full character sets and one alternate ligature font.

Jukebox

Kon Tiki JF-Enchanted

Jason Walcott
2002

ABCDEFGHIJKLMNOPQRSTUVWXYZ
abcdefghijklmnopqrstuvwxyz 1234567890 ÚáÊêÑñ &€$

Take an Exciting Cruise and go Surfing!

Kon Tiki JF-Hula

Jason Walcott
2002

ABCDEFGHIJKLMNOPQRSTUVWXYZ
1234567890 ÁÁÊÊÑÑ &€$

PALM TREES LOOK BEST AT THE BEACH.

Kon Tiki JF-Kona

Jason Walcott
2002

ABCDEFGHIJKLMNOPQRSTUVWXYZ
abcdefghijklmnopqrstuvwxyz
1234567890 ÁáÊêÑñ &€$

Tiki Joe says, "Buy my Pineapples!"

Kon Tiki JF-Lanai

Jason Walcott
2002

ABCDEFGHIJKLMNOPQRSTUVWXYZ
1234567890 ÁÁÊÊÑÑ &€$

WELCOME TO KAUAI ISLAND

Kon Tiki JF-Lounge

Jason Walcott
2002

ABCDEFGHIJKLMNOPQRRSTUVWXY3

abcdefghijklmnopqrstuvwxyz 1234567890 ÁáÊêÑñ &€$

Dine at the famous Tahitian Lanai!

Kon Tiki JF-Trader

Jason Walcott
2002

ABCDEFGHIJKLMNOPQRSTUVWXYZ

abcdefghijklmnopqrstuvwxyz 1234567890 ÁáÊêÑñ &€$

Climb the slopes of Mauna Loa.

Manual Script JF

Jason Walcott
2002

A calligraphic script face based on a hand-lettered alphabet in a "how-to" book about calligraphy.

ABCDEFGHIJKLMNOPQRSTUVWXYZ U

abcdefghijklmnopqrstuvwxyz asvw

1234567890 ÁáÊêÑñ &€$

Thank You for all your kindness.

Mary Helen JF

Jason Walcott
2002

Free-flowing and light, this font is named after the designer's paternal grandmother.

ABCDEFGHIJKLMNOPQRSTUVWXYZ

abcdefghijklmnopqrstuvwxyz 1234567890 ÁáÊêÑñ &€$

A W Ye llrs creror

Call me when you get back to North Carolina...

Jukebox

Opulence JF

Jason Walcott
2002

An elegant copperplate script, digitally revived from an older photo/letterpress face.

ABCDEFGHIJKL MNOP2RSTUVWXYZ
abcdefghijklmnopqrstuvwxyz 1234567890 ÁáÊêÑñ &€$

You are cordially invited to the Embassy Ball.

Peregroy JF

Jason Walcott
2001

An upright script face that combines handwritten and calligraphic qualities.

ABCDEFGHIJKLMNOPQRSTUVWXYZ
abcdefghijklmnopqrstuvwxyz 1234567890 ÁáÊêÑñ &€$

Delicious candy is a must for Halloween!

Primrose JF

Jason Walcott
2002

An unusual demi-formal script, digitally revived from an older photo/letterpress face.

ABCDEFGHIJKLMNOPQRSTUVWXYZ
abcdefghijklmnopqrstuvwxyz 1234567890 ÁáÊêÑñ &€$

Never leave home without Clean Underwear.

Rambler Script JF

Jason Walcott
2002

This upbeat script font was inspired by a hand-lettered car ad from the 1950s.

ABCDEFGHIJKLMNOPQRSTUVWXYZ
abcdefghijklmnopqrstuvwxyz 1234567890 ÁáÊêÑñ &€$

Let's go for a Spin in my Astro Jets!

Randolph JF

Jason Walcott
2002

A heavy engravers-style family consisting of a roman, italic, and two swash variants. Named for the designer's hometown in New Jersey.

Randolph JF-Regular

ABCDEFGHIJKLMNOPQRSTUVWXYZ
abcdefghijklmnopqrstuvwxyz 1234567890 ÁáÊêÑñ &€$

Randolph JF-Italic

ABCDEFGHIJKLMNOPQRSTUVWXYZ
abcdefghijklmnopqrstuvwxyz 1234567890 ÁáÊêÑñ &€$

Randolph JF-Swash

ABCDEFGHIJKLMNOPQRSTUVWXY
fhkmnrvw ÁÊÑñ & KRTh rivíwi

Randolph JF-Swash Italic

ABCDEFGHIJKLMNOPQRSTUVWXY
fhkmnrvw ÁÊÑñ & KRTh rivíwi

Regular and Swash

Where are all the Flowers?

Italic and Swash Italic

Where are all the Flowers?

Retro Repro JF

Jason Walcott
2002

A new version of an old typeface called Repro Script, originally designed by Jerry Mullen in 1953.

ABCDEFGHIJKLMNOPQRSTUVWXYZ
abcdefghijklmnopqrstuvwxyz 1234567890 ÁáÊêÑñ &€$

"Quality and Customer Satisfaction" is our Motto!

Jukebox

Saharan JF

Jason Walcott
2001

Inspired by some hotel signage, this font is perfect for any Vegas, desert, or Arabian theme. Or use it on vanity plates for your camel.

ABCDEFGHIJKLMNOPQRSTUVWXYZ
1234567890 ÁáÊêÑñ &€$

ELVIS HAS ENTERED THE BUILDING.

Scriptorama JF-Hostess

Jason Walcott
2002

The Scriptorama family consists of three script faces that can be used separately or together. They celebrate the hand-lettered signage of days gone by.

The Hostess variant is reminiscent of 1960s style and class.

ABCDEFGHIJKLMNOPQRSTUVWXYZ
abcdefghijklmnopqrstuvwxyz 1234567890 ÁáÊêÑñ &€$

The Art and Style of Hollywood

Scriptorama JF-Markdown

Jason Walcott
2002

The Markdown variant is done in the style of hand-painted window lettering.

ABCDEFGHIJKLMNOPQRSTUVWXYZ
1234567890 ÁáÊêÑñ &€$

HUGE SALE ON FACTORY-DIRECT SOFAS!

Scriptorama JF-Tradeshow

Jason Walcott
2002

The Tradeshow variant captures the charm of hand-painted signs from the 1950s.

ABCDEFGHIJKLMNOPQRSTUVWXYZ
abcdefghijklmnopqrstuvwxyz 1234567890 ÁáÊêÑñ &€$

Amish Craft Fair in September

323-650-2740

ABCDEFGHIJKLMNOPQRSTUVWXYZ
abcdefghijklmnopqrstuvwxyz 1234567890 ÁáÊêÑñ &€$

Friends Are The Family We Choose For Ourselves.

Shirley Script JF

Jason Walcott
2003

A casual script font with a touch of flair. Named after a dear friend of the designer.

ABCDEFGHIJKLMNOPQRSTUVWXYZ
abcdefghijklmnopqrstuvwxyz 1234567890 ÁáÊêÑñ &€$

California Sunshine is Good for Everyone.

Southland JF

Jason Walcott
2002

A unique typeface with heavy contrast and dynamic flourishes. Based on a hand-lettered alphabet.

Spaulding Sans Regular

ABCDEFGHIJKLMNOPQRSTUVWXYZ
abcdefghijklmnopqrstuvwxyz 1234567890 ÁáÊêÑñ & € $

Spaulding Sans Italic

ABCDEFGHIJKLMNOPQRSTUVWXYZ
abcdefghijklmnopqrstuvwxyz 1234567890 ÁáÊêÑñ &€$

The quick Brown Fox jumps over the Lazy Dog. 12 pt Regular
The quick Brown Fox jumps over the Lazy Dog. 14 pt Regular

The quick Brown Fox jumps over the Lazy Dog. 12 pt Italic
The quick Brown Fox jumps over the Lazy Dog. 14 pt Italic

Spaulding Sans JF

Jason Walcott
2001

The Spaulding Sans family is a sans serif design with Venetian proportions.

Jukebox

Stanzie JF

Jason Walcott
2000

A script face with a hand-lettered feel, digitally revived from an older photo/letterpress face.

ABCDEFGHIJKLMNOPQRSTUVWXYZ
abcdefghijklmnopqrstuvwxyz 1234567890 ÁáÊêÑñ &€$

Please don't feed the Type Designers.

Valentina JF

Jason Walcott
2001

A lighthearted script font with a slightly retro feel. Named after one of the designer's dearest friends.

ABCDEFGHIJKLMNOPQRSTUVWXYZ
abcdefghijklmnopqrstuvwxyz 1234567890 ÁáÊêÑñ &€$

A Trip to Seattle Uncovers Hilarious Family Secret!

Varsity Script JF

Jason Walcott
2001

This font is reminiscent of the hand-embroidered lettering on athletic jerseys.

ABCDEFGHIJKLMNOPQRSTUVWXYZ
abcdefghijklmnopqrstuvwxyz 1234567890 ÁáÊêÑñ &€$

Little League Team wins the big game on Friday!

Viceroy JF

Jason Walcott
2000-2002

A heavier yet elegant script font, digitally revived from an older photo/letterpress face.

ABCDEFGHIJKLMNOPQRSTUVWXYZ
abcdefghijklmnopqrstuvwxyz 1234567890 ÁáÊêÑñ & €$ Tderxz

An Evening of Classical Music at Carnegie Hall

Walcott Gothic

Jason Walcott
2001

The Walcott Gothic family consists of three styles that celebrate the golden age of Hollywood.

Walcott Gothic Fountain

ABCDEFGHIJKLMNOPQRSTUVWXYZ
ABCDEFGHIJKLMNOPQRSTUVWXYZ 1234567890 ÁÁÊÊÑñ &€$

Walcott Gothic Hollywood

ABCDEFGHIJKLMNOPQRSTUVWXYZ
ABCDEFGHIJKLMNOPQRSTUVWXYZ 1234567890 ÁÁÊÊÑñ &€$

Walcott Gothic Sunset

ABCDEFGHIJKLMNOPQRSTUVWXYZ
ABCDEFGHIJKLMNOPQRSTUVWXYZ 1234567890 ÁÁÊÊÑñ &€$

IT'S AN HONOR JUST TO BE NOMINATED.

It's an honor just to be nominated.

IT'S AN HONOR JUST TO BE NOMINATED.

Jukebox

ABCDEFGHIJKLMNOPQRSTUVWXYZ
abcdefghijklmnopqrstuvwxyz
1234567890 ÁáÊêÑñ ¢€$

"I am Wonder the Wonderboy!"

mvbfonts.com

ABCDEFGHIJKLMNOPQRSTUVWXYZ&ÆŒ
abcdefghijklmnopqrstuvwxyz æœfiflß 1234567890 ?!
ABCDEFGHIJKLMNOPQRSTUVWXY&Z

ABCDEFGHIJKLMNOPQRSTUVWXYZ&ÆŒ
abcdefghijklmnopqrstuvwxyz æœfiflß 1234567890 ?!

The quick brown fox jumps over a lazy dog pack my box
with five dozen liquor jugs jaded zombies acted quaintly

The quick brown fox jumps over a lazy dog pack my box with five
dozen liquor jugs jaded zombies acted quaintly but kept driving

MVB Verdigris™

Mark van Bronkhorst
2003

A new text family inspired by six-teenth-century typefaces of French punchcutters Robert Granjon (roman) and Pierre Haultin (italic).

Release scheduled for summer 2003 will include Roman, Italic, Small Caps, Bold, Bold Italic, and Extras for all weights.

We promptly judged antique ivory buckl es for the next prize. How razorback jum ping frogs can level six piqued gymnasts Sixty zippers were quickly picked from th e woven jute bag. Crazy Fredericka boug ht many very exquisite opal jewels. Jump by vow of quick, lazy strength in Oxford Pack my box with five dozen liquor jugs. J ackdaws love my big sphinx of quartz. Wa ltz nymph, for quick jigs vex bud. The qu ick brown fox jumps over a lazy dog. Pack

We promptly judged antique ivory buckles for t he next prize. How razorback jumping frogs ca n level six piqued gymnasts. Sixty zippers were quickly picked from the woven jute bag. Crazy Fredericka bought many very exquisite opal je wels. Jump by vow of quick, lazy strength in Ox ford. Pack my box with five dozen liquor jugs. J ackdaws love my big sphinx of quartz. Waltz nymph, for quick jigs vex bud. The quick brow n fox jumps over a lazy dog. Pack my box with five dozen liquor jugs. Jaded zombies acted qua

WE PROMPTLY JUDGED ANTIQUE IVORY BUCKLES FOR THE NEXT PRIZE. HOW R AZORBACK JUMPING FROGS CAN LEVEL SIX PIQUED GYMNASTS. SIXTY ZIPPERS WERE QUICKLY PICKED FROM THE WOV EN JUTE BAG. CRAZY FREDERICKA BOUG HT MANY VERY EXQUISITE OPAL JEWELS JUMP BY VOW OF QUICK, LAZY STRENGT H IN OXFORD. PACK MY BOX WITH FIVE DOZEN LIQUOR JUGS. JACKDAWS LOVE M Y BIG SPHINX OF QUARTZ. WALTZ, NYMP

Verdigris

starz
@do3*
rgeck
s.com
Quep>

info@mvbfonts.com

ABCDEFGHIJKLMNOPQRS
TUVWXY&Zabcdefghijk
lmnopqrstuvwxyz@123
4567890 The quick br
own fox jumps over a
lazy dog pack my box

ABCDEFGHIJKLMNOPQRS
TUVWXY&Zabcdefghijk
lmnopqrstuvwxyz@123
4567890 The quick br
own fox jumps over a
lazy dog pack my box

ABCDEFGHIJKLMNOPQRS
TUVWXY&Zabcdefghijk
lmnopqrstuvwxyz@123
4567890 The quick br
own fox jumps over a
lazy dog pack my box

ABCDEFGHIJKLMNOPQRS
TUVWXY&Zabcdefghijk
lmnopqrstuvwxyz@123
4567890 The quick br
own fox jumps over a
lazy dog pack my box

ABCDEFGHIJKLMNOPQRS
TUVWXY&Zabcdefghijk
lmnopqrstuvwxyz@123
4567890 The quick br
own fox jumps over a
lazy dog pack my box

ABCDEFGHIJKLMNOPQRS
TUVWXY&Zabcdefghijk
lmnopqrstuvwxyz@123
4567890 The quick br
own fox jumps over a
lazy dog pack my box

Sarge
Sarge
Sarge
Sarge
Sarge
Sarge

MVB Fantabular™

Akemi Aoki
2002

Regular
Regular Italic
Medium
Medium Italic
Bold
Bold Italic

ABCDEFGHIJKLMNOPQRS
TUVWXY&Zabcdefghijk
lmnopqrstuvwxyz@123
4567890 The quick br
own fox jumps over a
lazy dog pack my box

ABCDEFGHIJKLMNOPQRS
TUVWXY&Zabcdefghijk
lmnopqrstuvwxyz@123
4567890 The quick br
own fox jumps over a
lazy dog pack my box

ABCDEFGHIJKLMNOPQRS
TUVWXY&Zabcdefghijk
lmnopqrstuvwxyz@123
4567890 The quick br
own fox jumps over a
lazy dog pack my box

ABCDEFGHIJKLMNOPQRS
TUVWXY&Zabcdefghijk
lmnopqrstuvwxyz@123
4567890 The quick br
own fox jumps over a
lazy dog pack my box

ABCDEFGHIJKLMNOPQRS
TUVWXY&Zabcdefghijk
lmnopqrstuvwxyz@123
4567890 The quick br
own fox jumps over a
lazy dog pack my box

ABCDEFGHIJKLMNOPQRS
TUVWXY&Zabcdefghijk
lmnopqrstuvwxyz@123
4567890 The quick br
own fox jumps over a
lazy dog pack my box

Sarge
Sarge
Sarge
Sarge
Sarge
Sarge

MVB Fantabular™ Sans

Akemi Aoki
2002

Regular
Regular Italic
Medium
Medium Italic
Bold
Bold Italic

MVB Fonts

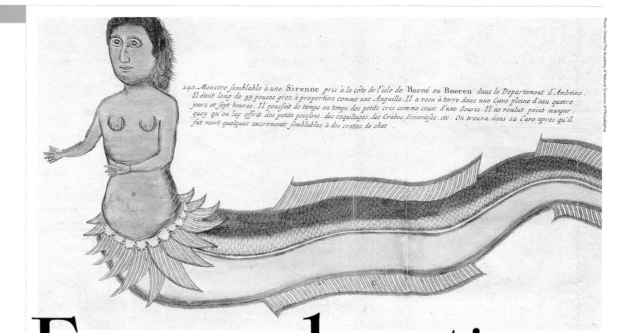

240. *Monstre semblable à une Sirenne pris à la côte de l'isle de Borné ou Boeren dans le Departement d'Amboine. Il étoit long de 59. pouces gros à proportion comme une Anguille. Il a vecu à terre dans une Cuve pleine d'eau quatre jours et sept heures. Il poussoit de temps en temps des petits cris comme ceux d'une Souris. Il ne voulut point manger quoy qu'on luy offrit des petits poissons, des coquillages, des Crabes, Ecrevisses etc. On trouva dans sa Cuve apres qu'il fut mort quelques excrements semblables à des crottes de chat.*

Engraved captions

in an old **&** *and weird* natural history **I** book inspired Alan Greene and Mark van Bronkhorst to develop MVB SIRENNE. Louis Renard's *Poissons, Ecrevisses et Crabes* (1719) claimed that a Sirenne (mermaid) had been captured and observed in a tub of water for four days and seven hours before expiring.

GIVEN AMPLE TIME TO VIEW THE SPECIMEN, Samuel Fallours (the artist whose illustrations were the basis for Renard's book) made the drawing of the mermaid, after which the engraved image (above) was made for publication. The caption with the image reads: *"A Monster resembling a Sirenne caught on the coast of the island of Borné or Boeren [Buru] in the Province of Ambon. It was fifty-nine inches long, and of an eel-like proportion. It lived on shore in a tank of water for four days and seven hours. It uttered occasional cries similar to those of a mouse. It would not eat, although it was offered small fishes, molluscs, crabs, crayfishes, etc. After its death, a few feces similar to those of a cat were found in its tank."* One might wonder: did Fallours have something sexy in his tub, or was the whole story—right down to the catlike droppings—merely a tall tale?

MVB Sirenne offers four optical sizes: '*Six*' for small print (used here), '*Text*' (for text like that at left), '*Eighteen*' for text & display, and '*Seventy-Two*' for initials and very large settings.

A 40-page Specimen Book of MVB Sirenne tells the complete story of the mermaid and is available from MVB Fonts while supplies last. Email *info@mvbfonts.com* to request a copy.

ABCDEFGHIJKLMNOPQRSTUVWXYZ&ÆŒ1234567890
A B C D E F G H I J K L M N O P Q R S T U V W X Y Z & Æ Œ
abcdefghijklmnopqrstuvwxyzßfffiflffiffl1234567890
( ) [ ] { } ? ! @ # $ ¢ ƒ £ ¥ % * ¼ ½ ¾ ⅛ ⅜ ⅝ ⅞ ⅓ ⅔ . , a b d e i l m n o r s t

ABCDEFGHIJKLMNOPQRSTUVWXYZ&ÆŒ1234567890
abcdefghijklmnopqrstuvwxyzßfffififfiffl1234567890
( ) [ ] { } ? ! @ # $ ¢ ƒ £ € * ¼ ½ ¾ ⅛ ⅜ ⅝ ⅞ ⅓ ⅔ . , a b d e i l m n o r s t*

MONSTRE SEMBLABLE À UNE SIRENNE pris à la côte de l'isle de Borné ou Boeren dans le Departement d'Amboine. Il étoit long de 59 pouces gros à proportion comme une Anguille. Il a vecu à terre dans une Cuve pleine d'eau quatre jours et sept heures. Il poussoit de *temps en temps des petits cris comme ceux d'une Souris. Il ne voulut point manger quoy qu'on luy offrit des petits poissons, des coquillages, des Crabes, Ecrevisses, etc. On trouva dans sa Cuve apres qu'il fut mort quelques excrements semblables à des crottes de chat.*

MVB Sirenne™ Six

Alan Greene
2002

Roman OSF and TF
Roman Small Caps
Roman Extras
Italic OSF and TF
Italic Extras

ABCDEFGHIJKLMNOPQRS
TUVWXYZ&ÆŒ1234567890

ABCDEFGHIJKLMNOPQRSTUVWXYZ&ÆŒ

abcdefghijklmnopqrstuvwxyzßfffififfiffl1234567890

( ) [ ] { } ? ! @ # $ ¢ ƒ £ € ¥ % * ¼ ½ ¾ ⅛ ⅜ ⅝ ⅞ ⅓ ⅔ . , a b d e i l m n o r s t

A A B B C C D D E E F F G G H I J K L M M N N O P P
Q R R S S T U U V V W X X Y Z & Æ Œ 1 2 3 4 5 6 7 8 9 0
abcdefghijklmnopqrstuvwxyzßfffififfiffl1234567890
*( ) [ ] { } ? ! @ # $ ¢ ƒ £ € ¥ % * ¼ ½ ¾ ⅛ ⅜ ⅝ ⅞ ⅓ ⅔ . , a b d e i l m n o r s t*

ABCDEFGHIJKLMNOPQRSTUVWXYZ&1234567890
abcdefghijklmnopqrstuvwxyz?!@$¢ƒ£¥1234567890

ABCDEFGHIJKLMNOPQRSTUVWXYZ&1234567890
abcdefghijklmnopqrstuvwxyz?!@$¢ƒ£¥1234567890

MVB Sirenne™ Text

Alan Greene
2002

Roman OSF and TF
Roman Small Caps
Roman Extras
Italic OSF and TF
Italic Swash
Italic Extras
Bold OSF and TF
Bold Extras
Bold Italic OSF and TF
Bold Italic Extras

Monstre semblable à une Sirenne pris à la côte de l'isle de Borné ou Boeren d ans le Departement d'Amboine. Il étoit long de 59 pouces gros à proportion comme une Anguille. Il a vecu à terre dans une Cuve pleine d'eau quatre jou rs et sept heures. Il poussoit de temps en temps des petits cris comme ceux d'une Souris. Il ne voulut point man ger quoy qu'on luy offrit des petits poi

Monstre semblable à une Sirenne pris à la côte de l'isle de Borné ou Boeren da ns le Departement d'Amboine. Il étoit l ong de 59 pouces gros à proportion com me une Anguille. Il a vecu à terre dans une Cuve pleine d'eau quatre jours et se pt heures. Il poussoit de temps en temps des petits cris comme ceux d'une Souris. Il ne voulut point manger quoy qu'on luy offrit des petits poissons, des coquil

Monstre semblable à une Sirenne pr is à la côte de l'isle de Borné ou Boe ren dans le Departement d'Amboine. Il étoit long de 59 pouces gros à pro portion comme une Anguille. Il a ve *cu à terre dans une Cuve pleine d'e au quatre jours et sept heures. Il pousso it de temps en temps des petits cris co mme ceux d'une Souris. Il ne voulut p oint manger quoy qu'on luy offrit des*

MVB Sirenne™ Display

Alan Greene
2002

Eighteen Roman
Eighteen Roman Small Caps
Eighteen Roman Extras
Eighteen Italic
Eighteen Italic Swash
Eighteen Italic Extras

ABCDEFGHIJKLMNOPQRSTUVWXYZ&ÆŒ

ABCDEFGHIJKLMNOPQRSTUVWXYZ&ÆŒI234567890

abcdefghijklmnopqrstuvwxyz ß ff fi fl ffi ffl

()[]{}?!@#$¢ƒ£€¥%*¼½¾⅛⅜⅝⅞⅓⅔.,ᵃᵇᵈᵉⁱˡᵐⁿᵒʳˢᵗ

AABBCCDDEFFGGHIJKLMMNNOPP

QRRSSTUVVWXXYZ&ÆŒ1234567890

abcdefghijklmnopqrstuvwxyz ß ff fi fl ffi ffl

*()[]{}?!@#$¢ƒ£€¥%*¼½¾⅛⅜⅝⅞⅓⅔.,ᵃᵇᵈᵉⁱˡᵐⁿᵒʳˢᵗ*

MVB Sirenne Eighteen

MVB Sirenne Seventy-Two Swash Italic

MONSTRE semblable à une Sirenne pris à la côte de l'isle de Borné ou Boeren dans le Departement d'Amboine. Il étoit long de 59 pouces gros à proportion comme une Anguille. Il a vecu à terre dans une Cuve pleine d'eau quatre *jours et sept heures. Il poussoit de temps en temps des petits cris comme ceux d'une Souris. Il ne voulut point manger quoy qu'on luy offrit des petits poissons, des coquillages, des Crabes, Ecrevisses, etc. On trouva dans sa Cuve apres qu'il fut mort quelques excrements semblables à des crottes de chat.*

MVB Sirenne Eighteen

SIRENNE

Regulation 215

Maestro Jones

PEASANT GIRL

OBLITERATES

Bartholomew's

Safflower Queen

MVB Sirenne™ Display

Alan Greene
2002

Seventy-Two Roman
Seventy-Two Roman Small Caps
Seventy-Two Roman Extras
Seventy-Two Italic
Seventy-Two Italic Swash
Seventy-Two Italic Extras

MVB Sirenne Seventy-Two

MVB Fonts

Akemi Aoki
2003

My daily friend.

info@mvbfonts.com

MVB Grenadine™

Akemi Aoki
2003

Regular
Regular Italic
Medium
Medium Italic
Bold
Bold Italic
Extra Bold
Extra Bold Italic
Black
Black Italic
Ultra
Ultra Italic

ABCD   GHIJ KLMNOPQR TU W YZ C
abcdefghijklmnopqrstuvwxyz1234567890?!
Ultra

ABCDEFGHIJKLMNOPQRSTUVWXYZ&ÆŒ
abcdefghijklmnopqrstuvwxyz1234567890?!@
Ultra Italic

ABCDEFGHIJKLMNOPQRSTUVWXYZ&ÆŒ
abcdefghijklmnopqrstuvwxyz1234567890?!@$
Black

ABCDEFGHIJKLMNOPQRSTUVWXYZ&ÆŒ
abcdefghijklmnopqrstuvwxyz1234567890?!@$¢
Black Italic

ABCDEFGHIJKLMNOPQRSTUVWXYZ&ÆŒ
abcdefghijklmnopqrstuvwxyz1234567890?!@$¢
Extra Bold

ABCDEFGHIJKLMNOPQRSTUVWXYZ&ÆŒ
abcdefghijklmnopqrstuvwxyz1234567890?!@$¢£
Extra Bold Italic

ABCDEFGHIJKLMNOPQRSTUVWXYZ&ÆŒ
abcdefghijklmnopqrstuvwxyz1234567890?!@$¢£
Bold

ABCDEFGHIJKLMNOPQRSTUVWXYZ&ÆŒ
abcdefghijklmnopqrstuvwxyz1234567890?!@$¢£¥
Bold Italic

ABCDEFGHIJKLMNOPQRSTUVWXYZ&ÆŒ
abcdefghijklmnopqrstuvwxyz1234567890?!@$¢£¥
Medium

ABCDEFGHIJKLMNOPQRSTUVWXYZ&ÆŒ
abcdefghijklmnopqrstuvwxyz1234567890?!@$¢£¥€
Medium Italic

ABCDEFGHIJKLMNOPQRSTUVWXYZ&ÆŒ
abcdefghijklmnopqrstuvwxyz1234567890?!@$¢£¥€
Regular

ABCDEFGHIJKLMNOPQRSTUVWXYZ&ÆŒ
abcdefghijklmnopqrstuvwxyz1234567890?!@$¢£¥€
Italic

MVB Fonts

MVB Peccadillo™

Holly Goldsmith & Alan Greene
2002

Eight
Eight Alternates
Twenty-Four
Twenty-Four Alternates
Ninety-Six
Ninety-Six Alternates

MVB Peccadillo Ninety-Six us a revival of a nineteenth-century metal typeface. Holly Goldsmith digitized the face, retaining the distortions caused by worn type and letterpress splat. The Eight and Twenty-Four sizes were then adapted by Alan Greene.

ABGHMQRS&
abefghimrstv

ABCDEFGHIJKLMNO
PQRSTUVWXYZ&ÆŒ
1234567890 ᴬⁿᴰ C°⸳ $⸺¢£€
abcdefghijklmnopq
rstuvwxyzﬀﬁﬂﬄﬃ?!

ABCDEFGHIJKLMNOPQRSTUVWXYZ&ÆŒ
1234567890§ C°·$¢¥£€@#%*{}[]()
abcdefghijklmnopqrstuvwxyzﬀﬁﬂﬄﬃ?!
The quick brown fox jumps over a lazy dog. Pack
my box with five dozen liquor jugs. Crazy Frede
ricka bought many very exquisite opal jewels. J

MVB Bovine™

Mark van Bronkhorst
1993

Regular
Round

BOVINE
BOVINE

ABCDEFGHIJ
KLMNOPQR
STUVWXY&Z
1234567890

MVB Magnesium™

Mark van Bronkhorst
1992 & 2003

Regular
Condensed (new)

NO PARKING
GO AWAY
ESTATE SALE
DISCOTHEQUE

ABCDEFGHIJ
KLMNOPQR
STUVWXY&Z
1234567890
ABCDEFGHIJKL
MNOPQRSTUVX
Y&Z1234567890

ABCDEFGHIJKLMNOPQRS
TUVWXYZÆŒ&1234567890
ABCDEFGHIJKLMNOPQRSTUVWXYZ
abcdefghijklmnopqrstuvwxyzæœ
fffiflffiffflß$¢¥ƒ€£@?!1234567890
ABCDEFGHIJKLMNOPQRSTUV
WXYZ&abcdefghijklmnopqrstuvwxyz?!
Semibold Bold Inline Adornado

WE PROMPTLY JUDGED antique ivory buckles for the next prize How razorback jumping frogs c an level six piqued gymnasts Six ty zippers were quickly picked f rom the woven jute bag. Crazy F redericka bought many very exq uisite opal jewels. *Jump by vow of qu ick, lazy strength in Oxford. Pack m y box with five dozen liquor jugs. Jac kdaws love my big sphinx of quartz Waltz nymph, for quick jigs vex bud. The quick brown fox jumps over a la zy dog. Pack my box with five dozen*

MVB Celestia™ Antiqua

Mark van Bronkhorst
1993-1996

Roman
Roman Small Caps
Italic
Semibold
Bold
Inline
Adornado
Ornaments

ABCDEFGHIJKLMN
abcdefghijklmnopqrstuvwxyz1234567890
OPQRSTUVWXY&Z

Sprinkling Rain Wondrous

MVB Chanson d'Amour™

Kanna Aoki
1995

ABCDEFGHIJKLMNO
PQRSTUVWXYZ&ÆŒ
ABCDEFGHIJKLMNOPQRSTUVWXY&Z
abcdefghijklmnopqrstuvwxyzfiflß?!
ABCDEFGHIJKLMNOPQRS
TUVWXYZÆŒ&abcdefghijklmno
pqrstuvwxyzfififlß1234567890$¢¥£@

WE PROMPTLY JUDGED antique iv ory buckles for the next prize. Ho w razorback jumping frogs can lev el six piqued gymnasts. Sixty zip pers were quickly picked from the woven jute bag. Crazy Fredericka bought many very exquisite opal je wels. *Jump by vow of quick, lazy stre ngth in Oxford. Pack my box with five dozen liquor jugs. Jackdaws love my bi g sphinx of quartz. Waltz nymph, for q uick jigs vex bud. The quick brown fox jumps over a lazy dog. Pack my box wi*

MVB Gryphius™

Otto Trace
2003

Roman
Roman Small Caps
Italic
Italic Alternates

Old type used by printer Sebastianus Gryphius in the early sixteenth century.

MVB Fonts

MVB Hotsy Totsy™

Akemi Aoki
1996 & 2002

Roman
Semibold
Bold
Ultra (new)
Hi-Lite
Rocksie

ABCDEFGHIJ
KLMNOPQRS
TUVWXY&Z
1234567890%
abcdefghijkl
mnopqrstuvw
xyz₩¢¥ƒ€£@

Semibold

Hotsy

Semibold

sy

Rocksie

Totsy

Hi-Lite

sy

Dogfood
Parsnips

Ultra

Rumproast
Liverwurst

Bold

Tortilla chips
Frozen dessert

Semibold

Spreadable cheese
Disposable diapers

Roman

ABCDEFGHIJKLMNOP
QRSTUVWXYZ&1234567890
abcdefghijklmnopqrstuvwxyz
ABCDEFGHIJKLMNOP
QRSTUVWXYZ&1234567890
abcdefghijklmnopqrstuvwxyz

Café Mimi
Chocolate
Fancy Teas
Saxophones
Floribunda
Beauteous

MVB Café Mimi™

Kanna Aoki
1996 & 2003

Regular
Bold (new)

ABCDEFGHIJKLMNOPQRSTUV
abcdefghijklmnopqrstuvwxyz
ABCDEFGHIJKLMNOPQRSTUVWXYZ
abcdefghijklmnopqrstuvwxyz?!@$¢*

Dear Bob
Sweetheart
Cudgel Rat

MVB Emmascript™

Kanna Aoki
1996 & 2002

Regular
Bold (new)

ABCDEFGHIJKLMNO
PQRSTUVWXYZ&123
4567890 0123456789 O
abcdefghijklmnopqrstuvwxyz
ABCDEFGHIJKLMNOPQRSTUV
🌀 ☀ ⚙ 🐦 🐈 🏰 🐌 👠 👑 🎵

Greymantle
HOLIDAY
Elfin shoes
Dental work
Persnickety

MVB Greymantle™

Kanna Aoki
1993

Regular
Extras

MVB Fonts

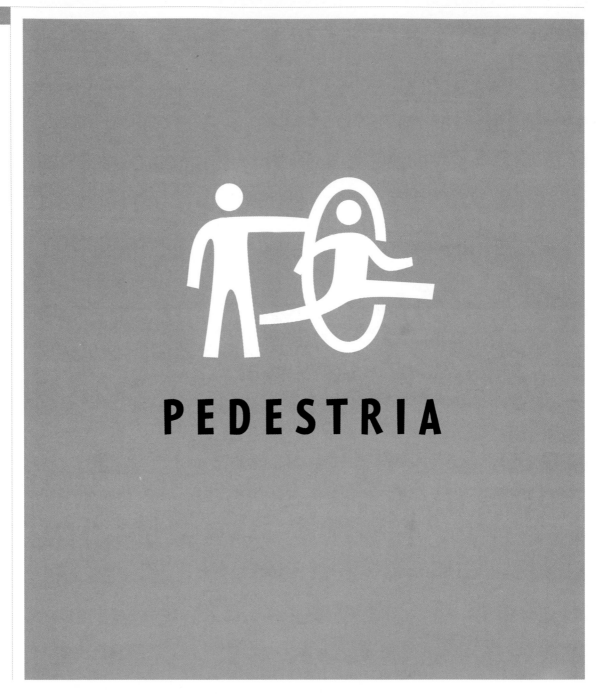

ABCDEFGHIJKLMNOPQRSTUVWXY&Z
abcdefghijklmnopqrstuvwxyz1234567890
The quick brown fox jumps over a lazy dog pack

ABCDEFGHIJKLMNOPQRSTUVWXY&Z
abcdefghijklmnopqrstuvwxyz1234567890
My box with five dozen liquor jugs jaded zombies

ABCDEFGHIJKLMNOPQRSTUVWXY&Z
abcdefghijklmnopqrstuvwxyz1234567890
Acted quaintly but kept driving their oxen forwa

ABCDEFGHIJKLMNOPQRSTUVWXY&Z
abcdefghijklmnopqrstuvwxyz1234567890
Waltz, nymph, for quick jigs vex Bud jump by vow

ABCDEFGHIJKLMNOPQRSTUVWXY&Z
abcdefghijklmnopqrstuvwxyz1234567890
Of quick, lazy strength in Oxford how razorback

ABCDEFGHIJKLMNOPQRSTUVWXY&Z
abcdefghijklmnopqrstuvwxyz1234567890
Jumping frogs can level six piqued gymnasts Pack

Akemi Aoki
2002

Regular
Regular Italic
Medium
Medium Italic
Bold
Bold Italic
Pict One
Pict Two

MVB Fonts

NEUFVILLE DIGITAL
FUNDICIÓN TIPOGRÁFICA NEUFVILLE
BAUERSCHE GIESSEREI
LUDWIG & MAYER
FONDERIE TYPOGRAPHIQUE FRANÇAISE
FUNDICIÓN TIPOGRÁFICA NACIONAL

NEUFVILLE ®
DIGITAL

CLASSIC AND MODERN ORIGINAL TYPEFACES

The rich heritage of famous foundries is united in Neufville, which took over their assets in the seventies of the former century. In 1997, Neufville Digital was born as a collaboration between FT Bauer from Barcelona and Visualogik from the Netherlands. The main goal of Neufville Digital is to make this heritage available to the digital world, as well as publishing contemporary and new type designs.

The newest font fabrication technology is being used to ensure the highest level of digital quality. All fonts comply with the latest versions of current standards. Full-featured OpenType fonts, containing swashed and alternate characters, have been planned for release.

Full Latin character support - including Central European, Baltic and Turkish - is available for most of our text and display fonts. For some of them, even Greek and Cyrillic glyphs have been designed. Extended glyph sets also include genuine small caps, old style figures, and alternates.

Custom typography to suit your needs is available upon request: special glyphs, symbols, logos, extended character sets, on screen improvement, delta hinting, unusual formats, and printer support. Custom font licenses and license models can be tailored to fit your situation.

Your house style can benefit from our corporate type offerings; please feel free to ask for information.

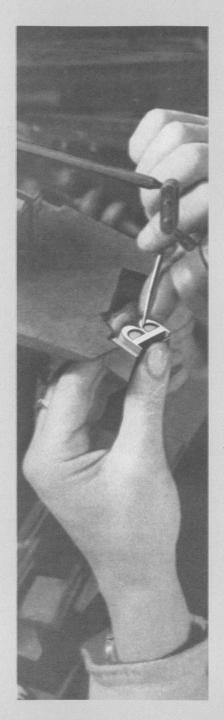

Neufville Digital fonts are available from selected font stores and directly from:

Main distributor:

Fundición Tipográfica Bauer, SL
Calle Selva de Mar, 50
E-08019 BARCELONA
España
tel.: +34 93 308 45 45
fax: +34 93 308 21 14
email: bauer@neufville.com

Manufacturer and main distributor:

Visualogik Technology & Design bv
Sint Janssingel 38   P.O. Box 1953
NL-5200 BZ 's-HERTOGENBOSCH
The Netherlands
tel.: +31 73 613 27 47
fax: +31 73 614 77 14
email: visualogik@neufville.com

Internet sales:

MyFonts
www.myfonts.com

NEUFVILLE ®
DIGITAL

www.neufville.com

Light

abcdefghijklmopqrstuvwxyz
ABCDEFGHIJKLMNOPQRSTUVWXYZ
0123456789
([{&·:;.,!?¿¡*%}]) €$¢£¥ƒ fifl

Futura ND

Paul Renner
1928

BAUER CLASSICS

Character sets supported:
- Windows Latin 1 · MacRoman
- Turkish · CE · Baltic

Features:
- Old style figures
- Genuine small caps
- Alternate characters

Unicode v3.0 compliant

Light Oblique

abcdefghijklmopqrstuvwxyz
ABCDEFGHIJKLMNOPQRSTUVWXYZ
0123456789
([{&·:;.,!?¿¡%}]) €$¢£¥ƒ fifl*

Futura ND

Paul Renner
1930

BAUER CLASSICS

Book Oblique

abcdefghijklmopqrstuvwxyz
ABCDEFGHIJKLMNOPQRSTUVWXYZ
0123456789
([{&·:;.,!?¿¡%}]) €$¢£¥ƒ fifl*

Futura ND

Paul Renner
1939

BAUER CLASSICS

Light

Ce matin-là, j'étais très en retard pour aller à l'école, et j'avais grand-peur d'être grondé, d'autant que M. Hamel nous avait dit qu'il nous interrogerait sur les participes, et je n'en savais pas le premier mot.
Un moment, l'idée me vint de manquer la classe et de prendre ma course à travers champs. Le temps était si chaud, si clair! On entendait les merles siffler à la lisière du bois, et dans le pré Rippert, derrière la scierie, les Prussiens qui faisaient l'exercice. Tout cela me tentait bien plus que la règle des

Light Oblique

Ce matin-là, j'étais très en retard pour aller à l'école, et j'avais grand-peur d'être grondé, d'autant que M. Hamel nous avait dit qu'il nous interrogerait sur les participes, et je n'en savais pas le premier mot.
Un moment, l'idée me vint de manquer la classe et de prendre ma course à travers champs. Le temps était si chaud, si clair! On entendait les merles siffler à la lisière du bois, et dans le pré Rippert, derrière la scierie, les Prussiens qui faisaient l'exercice. Tout cela me tentait bien plus que la règle des

Book Oblique

Ce matin-là, j'étais très en retard pour aller à l'école, et j'avais grand-peur d'être grondé, d'autant que M. Hamel nous avait dit qu'il nous interrogerait sur les partici-pes, et je n'en savais pas le premier mot.
Un moment, l'idée me vint de manquer la classe et de prendre ma course à travers champs. Le temps était si chaud, si clair! On entendait les merles siffler à la lisière du bois, et dans le pré Rippert, derrière la scierie, les Prussiens qui faisaient l'exercice. Tout cela me tentait bien plus que la règle

Futura ND

Paul Renner
1930 - 1939

BAUER CLASSICS

Futura ND

Paul Renner
1932

BAUER CLASSICS

Character sets supported:
·Windows Latin 1 · MacRoman
·Turkish · CE · Baltic

Features:
·Old style figures
·Genuine small caps
·Alternate characters

Unicode v3.0 compliant

Book

abcdefghijklmopqrstuvwxyz
ABCDEFGHIJKLMNOPQRSTUVWXYZ
0123456789
([{&:;.,!?¿¡*%}]) €$¢£¥ƒ fifl MMa

Futura ND

Paul Renner
1928

BAUER CLASSICS

Medium

abcdefghijklmopqrstuvwxyz
ABCDEFGHIJKLMNOPQRSTUVWXYZ
0123456789
([{&:;.,!?¿¡*%}]) €$¢£¥ƒ fifl

Futura ND

Paul Renner
1930

BAUER CLASSICS

Medium Oblique

abcdefghijklmopqrstuvwxyz
ABCDEFGHIJKLMNOPQRSTUVWXYZ
0123456789
([{&:;.,!?¿¡%}]) €$¢£¥ƒ fifl*

Futura ND

Paul Renner
1928 - 1932

BAUER CLASSICS

Book

Ce matin-là, j'étais très en retard pour aller à l'école, et j'avais grand-peur d'être grondé, d'autant que M. Hamel nous avait dit qu'il nous interrogerait sur les participes, et je n'en savais pas le premier mot. Un moment, l'idée me vint de manquer la classe et de prendre ma course à travers champs. Le temps était si chaud, si clair! On entendait les merles siffler à la lisière du bois, et dans le pré Rippert, derrière la scierie, les Prussiens qui faisaient l'exercice. Tout cela me tentait bien plus que la règle

Medium

Ce matin-là, j'étais très en retard pour aller à l'école, et j'avais grand-peur d'être grondé, d'autant que M. Hamel nous avait dit qu'il nous interrogerait sur les participes, et je n'en savais pas le premier mot.
Un moment, l'idée me vint de manquer la classe et de prendre ma course à travers champs. Le temps était si chaud, si clair! On entendait les merles siffler à la lisière du bois, et dans le pré Rippert, derrière la scierie, les Prussiens qui faisaient l'exer-

Medium Oblique

Ce matin-là, j'étais très en retard pour aller à l'école, et j'avais grand-peur d'être grondé, d'autant que M. Hamel nous avait dit qu'il nous interrogerait sur les participes, et je n'en savais pas le premier mot.
Un moment, l'idée me vint de manquer la classe et de prendre ma course à travers champs. Le temps était si chaud, si clair! On entendait les merles siffler à la lisière du bois, et dans le pré Rippert, derrière la scierie, les Prussiens qui faisaient l'exer-

Demibold

abcdefghijklmopqrstuvwxyz
ABCDEFGHIJKLMNOPQRSTUVWXYZ
0123456789
([{&:;.,!?¿¡*%}]) €$¢£¥ƒ fifl

Futura ND

Paul Renner
1930

BAUER CLASSICS

Character sets supported:
·Windows Latin 1 · MacRoman
·Turkish · CE · Baltic

Features:
·Old style figures
·Genuine small caps
·Alternate characters

Unicode v3.0 compliant

Demibold Oblique

abcdefghijklmopqrstuvwxyz
ABCDEFGHIJKLMNOPQRSTUVWXYZ
0123456789
([{&:;.,!?¿¡*%}]) €$¢£¥ƒ fifl

Futura ND

Paul Renner
1930

BAUER CLASSICS

Bold Oblique

abcdefghijklmopqrstuvwxyz
ABCDEFGHIJKLMNOPQRSTUVWXYZ
0123456789
([{&:;.,!?¿¡*%}]) €$¢£¥ƒ fifl

Futura ND

Paul Renner
1928

BAUER CLASSICS

Demibold

Ce matin-là, j'étais très en retard pour aller à l'école, et j'avais grand-peur d'être grondé, d'autant que M. Hamel nous avait dit qu'il nous interrogerait sur les participes, et je n'en savais pas le premier mot.
Un moment, l'idée me vint de manquer la classe et de prendre ma course à travers champs. Le temps était si chaud, si clair! On entendait les merles siffler à la lisière du bois, et dans le pré Rippert, derrière la scierie, les

Demibold Oblique

Ce matin-là, j'étais très en retard pour aller à l'école, et j'avais grand-peur d'être grondé, d'autant que M. Hamel avait dit qu'il nous interrogerait sur les participes, et je n'en savais pas le premier mot.
Un moment, l'idée me vint de manquer la classe et de prendre ma course à travers champs. Le temps était si chaud, si clair! On entendait les merles siffler à la lisière du bois, et dans le pré Rippert, derrière la scierie, les Prussiens qui faisaient

Bold Oblique

Ce matin-là, j'étais très en retard pour aller à l'école, et j'avais grand-peur d'être grondé, d'autant que M. Hamel nous avait dit qu'il nous interrogerait sur les partici-pes, et je n'en savais pas le premier mot.
Un moment, l'idée me vint de man-quer la classe et de prendre ma course à travers champs. Le temps était si chaud, si clair! On entendait les merles siffler à la lisière du

Futura ND

Paul Renner
1928 - 1930

BAUER CLASSICS

Futura ND

Paul Renner
1928

BAUER CLASSICS

Character sets supported:
·Windows Latin 1 · MacRoman
·Turkish · CE · Baltic

Features:
·Old style figures
·Genuine small caps
·Alternate characters

Unicode v3.0 compliant

Bold

abcdefghijklmopqrstuvwxyz
ABCDEFGHIJKLMNOPQRSTUVWXYZ
0123456789
([{&:;.,!?¿¡*%}]) €$¢£¥ƒ fifl

Futura ND

Paul Renner
1936

BAUER CLASSICS

ExtraBold

abcdefghijklmopqrstuvwxyz
ABCDEFGHIJKLMNOPQRSTUVWXYZ
0123456789
([{&:;.,!?¿¡*%}]) €$¢£¥ƒ fifl

Futura ND

Paul Renner
1930

BAUER CLASSICS

ExtraBold Oblique

abcdefghijklmopqrstuvwxyz
ABCDEFGHIJKLMNOPQRSTUVWXYZ
0123456789
([{&:;.,!?¿¡*%}]) €$¢£¥ƒ fifl

Futura ND

Paul Renner
1928 - 1936

BAUER CLASSICS

Bold

Ce matin-là, j'étais très en retard pour aller à l'école, et j'avais grand-peur d'être grondé, d'autant que M. Hamel nous avait dit qu'il nous interrogerait sur les participes, et je n'en savais pas le premier mot.
Un moment, l'idée me vint de manquer la classe et de prendre ma course à travers champs. Le temps était si chaud, si clair! On entendait les merles siffler à la lisière du bois,

ExtraBold

Ce matin-là, j'étais très en retard pour aller à l'école, et j'avais grand-peur d'être grondé, d'autant que M. Hamel nous avait dit qu'il nous interrogerait sur les participes, et je n'en savais pas le premier mot. Un moment, l'idée me vint de manquer la classe et de prendre ma course à travers champs. Le temps était si chaud, si clair! On entendait les merles siffler à la

ExtraBold Oblique

Ce matin-là, j'étais très en retard pour aller à l'école, et j'avais grand-peur d'être grondé, d'autant que M. Hamel nous avait dit qu'il nous interrogerait sur les participes, et je n'en savais pas le premier mot. Un moment, l'idée me vint de manquer la classe et de prendre ma course à travers champs. Le temps était si chaud, si clair! On entendait les merles siffler à la

SCOsF Light

ABCDEFGHIJKLMOPQRSTUVWXYZ
UVWXYZ   0123456789

ABCDEFGHIJKLMNOPQRST
([{&:;.,!?¿¡*%}]) €$¢£¥ƒ

Futura ND

Paul Renner
1928 - 1930

BAUER CLASSICS

Character sets supported:
·Windows Latin 1 · MacRoman
·Turkish · CE · Baltic

Features:
·Old style figures
·Genuine small caps
·Alternate characters

Unicode v3.0 compliant

SCOsF Light Oblique

ABCDEFGHIJKLMOPQRSTUVWXYZ
UVWXYZ   0123456789

ABCDEFGHIJKLMNOPQRST
([{&:;.,!?¿¡*%}]) €$¢£¥ƒ

SCOsF Book

ABCDEFGHIJKLMOPQRSTUVWXYZ
UVWXYZ   0123456789

ABCDEFGHIJKLMNOPQRST
([{&:;.,!?¿¡*%}]) €$¢£¥ƒ

Futura ND

Paul Renner
1932 - 1939

BAUER CLASSICS

SCOsF Book Oblique

ABCDEFGHIJKLMOPQRSTUVWXYZ
UVWXYZ   0123456789

ABCDEFGHIJKLMNOPQRST
([{&:;.,!?¿¡*%}]) €$¢£¥ƒ

SCOsF Medium

ABCDEFGHIJKLMOPQRSTUVWXYZ
UVWXYZ   0123456789

ABCDEFGHIJKLMNOPQRST
([{&:;.,!?¿¡*%}]) €$¢£¥ƒ

Futura ND

Paul Renner
1930

BAUER CLASSICS

SCOsF Medium Oblique

ABCDEFGHIJKLMOPQRSTUVWXYZ
UVWXYZ   0123456789

ABCDEFGHIJKLMNOPQRST
([{&:;.,!?¿¡*%}]) €$¢£¥ƒ

SCOsF Bold

ABCDEFGHIJKLMOPQRSTUVWXYZ
RSTUVWXYZ 0123456789 ([{&:;.,!?¿¡*%}]) €$¢£¥ƒ

ABCDEFGHIJKLMNOPQ

Futura ND

Paul Renner
1928

BAUER CLASSICS

SCOsF Bold Oblique

ABCDEFGHIJKLMOPQRSTUVWXYZ
RSTUVWXYZ 0123456789 ([{&:;.,!?¿¡*%}]) €$¢£¥ƒ

ABCDEFGHIJKLMNOPQ

Paul Renner
1950

BAUER CLASSICS

Character sets supported:
·Windows Latin 1 · MacRoman
·Turkish · CE · Baltic

Features:
·Old style figures
·Genuine small caps
·Alternate characters

Unicode v3.0 compliant

Cn Light

abcdefghijklmopqrstuvwxyz ABCDEFGHIJKLMNOPQRSTUV
WXYZ 0123456789 ([{&:;.,!?¿¡*%}]) €$¢£¥ƒ fi fl

Ce matin-là, j'étais très en retard pour aller à l'école, et j'avais grand-peur d'être grondé, d'autant que M. Hamel nous avait dit qu'il nous interrogerait sur les participes, et je n'en savais pas le premier mot. Un moment, l'idée me vint de manquer la classe et de prendre ma course à travers champs. LE TEMPS ÉTAIT SI CHAUD, SI CLAIR! On entendait les merles siffler à la lisière du bois, et dans le pré Rippert, derrière la scierie, les Prussiens qui faisaient l'exercice. Tout cela me tentait bien plus que la règle des participes; mais j'eus la force de résister, et je courus bien vite vers l'école.

Cn Light Oblique

*abcdefghijklmopqrstuvwxyz ABCDEFGHIJKLMNOPQRSTUV
WXYZ 0123456789 ([{&:;.,!?¿¡*%}]) €$¢£¥ƒ fi fl*

Paul Renner
1936

BAUER CLASSICS

Cn Medium

abcdefghijklmopqrstuvwxyz ABCDEFGHIJKLMNOPQRST
UVWXYZ 0123456789 ([{&:;.,!?¿¡*%}]) €$¢£¥ƒ fi fl

Ce matin-là, j'étais très en retard pour aller à l'école, et j'avais grand-peur d'être grondé, d'autant que M. Hamel nous avait dit qu'il nous interrogerait sur les participes, et je n'en savais pas le premier mot. Un moment, l'idée me vint de manquer la classe et de prendre ma course à travers champs. LE TEMPS ÉTAIT SI CHAUD, SI CLAIR! On entendait les merles siffler à la lisière du bois, et dans le pré Rippert, derrière la scierie, les Prussiens qui faisaient l'exercice. Tout cela me tentait bien plus que la règle des participes; mais j'eus la force de résister, et je courus bien vite vers

Cn Medium Oblique

*abcdefghijklmopqrstuvwxyz ABCDEFGHIJKLMNOPQRST
UVWXYZ 0123456789 ([{&:;.,!?¿¡*%}]) €$¢£¥ƒ fi fl*

Paul Renner
1930

BAUER CLASSICS

Cn Bold

**abcdefghijklmopqrstuvwxyz ABCDEFGHIJKLMNOPQRSTUV
WXYZ 0123456789 ([{&:;.,!?¿¡*%}]) €$¢£¥ƒ fi fl**

Cn Bold Oblique

***abcdefghijklmopqrstuvwxyz ABCDEFGHIJKLMNOPQRSTUV
WXYZ 0123456789 ([{&:;.,!?¿¡*%}]) €$¢£¥ƒ fi fl***

Paul Renner
1936

BAUER CLASSICS

Cn ExtraBold

**abcdefghijklmopqrstuvwxyz ABCDEFGHIJKLMNOPQRSTUV
WXYZ 0123456789 ([{&:;.,!?¿¡*%}]) €$¢£¥ƒ fi fl**

Cn ExtraBold Oblique

***abcdefghijklmopqrstuvwxyz ABCDEFGHIJKLMNOPQRSTUV
WXYZ 0123456789 ([{&:;.,!?¿¡*%}]) €$¢£¥ƒ fi fl***

sales@neufville.com

Ce matin-là, j'étais très en retard pour aller à l'école, et j'avais grand-peur d'être grondé, d'autant que M. Hamel nous avait dit qu'il nous interrogerait sur les participes, et je n'en savais pas le premier mot. Un moment, l'idée me vint de manquer la classe et de prendre ma course à travers champs. Le temps était si chaud, si clair! On entendait les merles siffler à la lisière du bois, et dans le pré Rippert, derrière la scierie, les Prussiens qui faisaient l'exercice. Tout cela me

Cn SCOsF Light
ABCDEFGHIJKLMOPQRSTUVWXYZ ABCDEFGHIJKLMNOPQRST
UVWXYZ   0123456789   ([{&:;.,!?¿¡*%}]) €$¢£¥ƒ

Cn SCOsF Light Oblique
ABCDEFGHIJKLMOPQRSTUVWXYZ ABCDEFGHIJKLMNOPQRST
UVWXYZ   0123456789   ([{&:;.,!?¿¡*%}]) €$¢£¥ƒ

Futura ND Condensed

Paul Renner
1950
BAUER CLASSICS

Character sets supported:
·Windows Latin 1 · MacRoman
·Turkish · CE · Baltic

Features·
·Old style figures
·Genuine small caps
·Alternate characters

Unicode v3.0 compliant

Ce matin-là, j'étais très en retard pour aller à l'école, et j'avais grand-peur d'être grondé, d'autant que M. Hamel nous avait dit qu'il nous inter-rogerait sur les participes, et je n'en savais pas le premier mot. Un moment, l'idée me vint de man-quer la classe et de prendre ma course à travers champs. Le temps était si chaud, si clair! On entendait les merles siffler à la lisière du bois,

Cn SCOsF Medium
ABCDEFGHIJKLMOPQRSTUVWXYZ ABCDEFGHIJKLMNOPQRST
UVWXYZ   0123456789   ([{&:;.,!?¿¡*%}]) €$¢£¥ƒ

Cn SCOsF Medium Oblique
ABCDEFGHIJKLMOPQRSTUVWXYZ ABCDEFGHIJKLMNOPQRST
UVWXYZ   0123456789   ([{&:;.,!?¿¡*%}]) €$¢£¥ƒ

Futura ND Condensed

Paul Renner
1936
BAUER CLASSICS

Cn SCOsF Bold
ABCDEFGHIJKLMOPQRSTUVWXYZ ABCDEFGHIJKLMNOPQRST
UVWXYZ   0123456789   ([{&:;.,!?¿¡*%}]) €$¢£¥ƒ

Cn SCOsF Bold Oblique
ABCDEFGHIJKLMOPQRSTUVWXYZ ABCDEFGHIJKLMNOPQRST
UVWXYZ   0123456789   ([{&:;.,!?¿¡*%}]) €$¢£¥ƒ

Futura ND Condensed

Paul Renner
1930
BAUER CLASSICS

Display
abcdefghijklmopqrstuvwxyz ABCDEFGHIJKLMNOPQRST
UVWXYZ   0123456789   ([{&:;.,!?¿¡*%}]) €$¢£¥ fifl

Futura ND Display

Paul Renner
1932
BAUER CLASSICS

Black
abcdefghijklmopqrstuvwxyz ABCDEFGHIJKLMNOPQR
STUVWXYZ   0123456789 ([{&:;.,!?¿¡*%}]) €$¢£¥ƒ fifl

Futura ND Black

Paul Renner
1929
BAUER CLASSICS

Paris ND

Enric Crous Vidal
1953

GRAFÍA LATINA

Light

ABCDEFGHIJKLMNOPQRSTUVWXYZ
1234567890 .,:;-?!¿¡

Medium

ABCDEFGHIJKLMNOPQRSTUVWXYZ
1234567890 .,:;-?!¿¡

Bold

ABCDEFGHIJKLMNOOPQRSTUV
WXYZ 1234567890 .,:;-?!¿¡

VALENCIA

BOLOGNA

PARIS

Flash ND

Enric Crous Vidal
1953

GRAFÍA LATINA

ABCDEFGHIJKLMNOOPQRSTUV
WXYZ 1234567890 .,:;-?!¿¡

Arabescos ND

Enric Crous Vidal
1954

GRAFÍA LATINA

sales@neufville.com

Stage

ABCDEFGHIJKLMNOPQRSTUVW XYZ abcdefghijklmnopqrstu vwxyz 1234567890 -.,:;?!¿¡

Ilerda

Enric Crous Vidal
1945

GRAFÍA LATINA

W841

youth

ABCDEFGHIJKLMNOPQ RSTUVWXYZ abcdefghij klmnopqrstuvwxyz 1234 567890 €$¥ -.,:;?!¿¡

Gaudí ND

Ricard Girald Miracle
1962

GRAFÍA LATINA

MIDKAP

ABCDEFGHIJKLMNOPQRSTUV WXYZ 1234567890 &$ -.,:;?!¿¡

Diagonal ND

Antoni Morillas
1970

GRAFÍA LATINA

NOVICE
NOVICE

abcdefghijklmnopqrst uvwxyz 1234567890 €$£ ~?!

Uncial Romana ND

Ricardo Rousselot
1996

GRAFÍA LATINA

def

abcdefghijklmnopqr stuvwxyz abcdefghijklm nopqrstuvwxyz 1234567890 & €$£ (~.,:;?!¿¡)

CarloMagno ND

Ricardo Rousselot
1997

GRAFÍA LATINA

Rubén Fontana
2001

MODERN COLLECTION
Sistema Fontana: Body Text fonts
·Aa

Character sets supported:
·Windows Latin 1 · MacRoman

Features:
·Old style figures
·Genuine small caps
·Expert set containing special charac-
ters and ligatures

Unicode v3.0 compliant

Aa OsF Light
abcdefghijklmopqrstuvwxyz ABCDEFGHIJKLMNOPQRST
UVWXYZ 0123456789 ([{&:;,.!?¿¡*%}]) €$¢£¥ƒ CHChch fifl

Aa OsF Light Italic
abcdefghijklmopqrstuvwxyz ABCDEFGHIJKLMNOPQRST
UVWXYZ 0123456789 ([{&:;,.!?¿¡%}]) €$¢£¥ƒ CHChchfifl*

Aa SC Light
ABCDEFGHIJKLMOPQRSTUVWXYZ ABCDEFGHIJKLMNOPQRST
UVWXYZ 0123456789 ([{&:;,.!?¿¡*%}]) €$¢£¥ƒ CHChch fifl

Aa OsF Regular
abcdefghijklmopqrstuvwxyz ABCDEFGHIJKLMNOPQRST
UVWXYZ 0123456789 ([{&:;,.!?¿¡*%}]) €$¢£¥ƒ CHChch fifl

Aa OsF Regular Italic
abcdefghijklmopqrstuvwxyz ABCDEFGHIJKLMNOPQRST
UVWXYZ 0123456789 ([{&:;,.!?¿¡%}]) €$¢£¥ƒ CHChchfifl*

Aa SC Regular
ABCDEFGHIJKLMOPQRSTUVWXYZ ABCDEFGHIJKLMNOPQRST
UVWXYZ 0123456789 ([{&:;,.!?¿¡*%}]) €$¢£¥ƒ CHChch fifl

Rubén Fontana
2001

MODERN COLLECTION
Sistema Fontana: Body Text fonts
·Aa
·Cc
·Ee

Aa OsF Regular. 8 pnt
El sosiego, el lugar apacible, la amenidad de los campos, la serenidad de los
cielos, el murmurar de las fuentes, la
quietud del espíritu son grande parte
para que las musas más estériles se
muestren fecundas y ofrezcan partos al
mundo que le colmen de maravilla y de
contento. Acontece tener un padre un
hijo feo y sin gracia alguna, y el amor
que le tiene le pone una venda en los
ojos para que no vea sus faltas, antes

Cc OsF Regular. 8 pnt
El sosiego, el lugar apacible, la amenidad de los
campos, la serenidad de los cielos, el murmurar
de las fuentes, la quietud del espíritu son grande
parte para que las musas más estériles se muestren fecundas y ofrezcan partos al mundo que le
colmen de maravilla y de contento. Acontece
tener un padre un hijo feo y sin gracia alguna, y
el amor que le tiene le pone una venda en los
ojos para que no vea sus faltas, antes las juzga
por discreciones y lindezas y las cuenta a sus
amigos por agudezas y donaires. Pero yo, que,

Ee OsF Regular. 8 pnt
El sosiego, el lugar apacible, la amenidad de los campos,
la serenidad de los cielos, el murmurar de las fuentes, la
quietud del espíritu son grande parte para que las musas
más estériles se muestren fecundas y ofrezcan partos al
mundo que le colmen de maravilla y de contento.
Acontece tener un padre un hijo feo y sin gracia alguna, y
el amor que le tiene le pone una venda en los ojos para
que no vea sus faltas, antes las juzga por discreciones y
lindezas y las cuenta a sus amigos por agudezas y donaires. Pero yo, que, aunque parezco padre, soy padrastro de
Don Quijote, no quiero irme con la corriente del uso, ni

sales@neufville.com

Cc OsF Light

abcdefghijklmopqrstuvwxyz ABCDEFGHIJKLMNOPQRST
UVWXYZ 0123456789 ([{&:;,.!?¿¡*%}]) €$¢£¥ƒ CHChch fifl

Cc SC Light

ABCDEFGHIJKLMOPQRSTUVWXYZ ABCDEFGHIJKLMNOPQRST
UVWXYZ 0123456789 ([{&:;,.!?¿¡*%}]) €$¢£¥ƒ CHCHCH

Cc OsF Regular

abcdefghijklmopqrstuvwxyz ABCDEFGHIJKLMNOPQRST
UVWXYZ 0123456789 ([{&:;,.!?¿¡*%}]) €$¢£¥ƒ CHChch fifl

Cc SC Regular

ABCDEFGHIJKLMOPQRSTUVWXYZ ABCDEFGHIJKLMNOPQRST
UVWXYZ 0123456789 ([{&:;,.!?¿¡*%}]) €$¢£¥ƒ CHCHCH

Cc OsF Semibold

abcdefghijklmopqrstuvwxyz ABCDEFGHIJKLMNOPQRST
UVWXYZ 0123456789 ([{&:;,.!?¿¡*%}]) €$¢£¥ƒ CHChch fifl

Cc OsF Semibold Italic

abcdefghijklmopqrstuvwxyz ABCDEFGHIJKLMNOPQRST
UVWXYZ 0123456789 ([{&:;,.!?¿¡*%}]) €$¢£¥ƒ CHChchfifl

Cc SC Semibold

ABCDEFGHIJKLMOPQRSTUVWXYZ ABCDEFGHIJKLMNOPQRST
UVWXYZ 0123456789 ([{&:;,.!?¿¡*%}]) €$¢£¥ƒ CHChch fifl

Ee SC Light

ABCDEFGHIJKLMOPQRSTUVWXYZ ABCDEFGHIJKLMNOPQRST
UVWXYZ 0123456789 ([{&:;,.!?¿¡*%}]) €$¢£¥ƒ CHCHCH

Fontana ND

Rubén Fontana
2001

MODERN COLLECTION
Sistema Fontana: Body Text fonts
·Aa

Character sets supported:
·Windows Latin 1 · MacRoman

Features:
·Old style figures
·Genuine small caps
·Expert set containing special characters and ligatures

Unicode v3.0 compliant

Neufville Digital

Fontana ND

Rubén Fontana
2001

MODERN COLLECTION
Sistema Fontana: Body Text fonts
·Ee

Fontana ND

Rubén Fontana
2001

MODERN COLLECTION
Sistema Fontana: Body Text fonts
·Ee

Character sets supported:
·Windows Latin 1 · MacRoman

Features:
·Old style figures
·Genuine small caps
·Expert set containing special charac-
ters and ligatures

Unicode v3.0 compliant

Ee OsF Light

abcdefghijklmopqrstuvwxyz ABCDEFGHIJKLMNOPQRST
UVWXYZ 0123456789 ([{&:;.,!?¿¡*%}]) €$¢£¥f CHChch fifl

Ee OsF Regular

abcdefghijklmopqrstuvwxyz ABCDEFGHIJKLMNOPQRST
UVWXYZ 0123456789 ([{&:;.,!?¿¡*%}]) €$¢£¥f CHChch fifl

Ee SC Regular

ABCDEFGHIJKLMOPQRSTUVWXYZ ABCDEFGHIJKLMNOPQRST
UVWXYZ 0123456789 ([{&:;.,!?¿¡*%}]) €$¢£¥f CHChch

Ee OsF Semibold

abcdefghijklmopqrstuvwxyz ABCDEFGHIJKLMNOPQRST
UVWXYZ 0123456789 ([{&:;.,!?¿¡*%}]) €$¢£¥f CHChch fifl

Ee SC Semibold

ABCDEFGHIJKLMOPQRSTUVWXYZ ABCDEFGHIJKLMNOPQRST
UVWXYZ 0123456789 ([{&:;.,!?¿¡*%}]) €$¢£¥f CHChch

Ee OsF Bold

abcdefghijklmopqrstuvwxyz ABCDEFGHIJKLMNOPQRST
UVWXYZ 0123456789 ([{&:;.,!?¿¡*%}]) €$¢£¥f CHChch fifl

Ee OsF Bold Italic

abcdefghijklmopqrstuvwxyz ABCDEFGHIJKLMNOPQRST
UVWXYZ 0123456789 ([{&:;.,!?¿¡*%}]) €$¢£¥f CHChchfifl

Ee SC Bold

ABCDEFGHIJKLMOPQRSTUVWXYZ ABCDEFGHIJKLMNOPQRST
UVWXYZ 0123456789 ([{&:;.,!?¿¡*%}]) €$¢£¥f CHChch

sales@neufville.com

Gg Regular

abcdefghijklmopqrstuvwxyz ABCDEFGHIJKLMNOPQRST
UVWXYZ 0123456789 ([{&:;.,!?¿¡*%}]) €$¢£¥f CHChch fifl

Gg Semibold

abcdefghijklmopqrstuvwxyz ABCDEFGHIJKLMNOPQRST
UVWXYZ 0123456789 ([{&:;.,!?¿¡*%}]) €$¢£¥f CHChch fifl

Gg Bold

abcdefghijklmopqrstuvwxyz ABCDEFGHIJKLMNOPQRST
UVWXYZ 0123456789 ([{&:;.,!?¿¡*%}]) €$¢£¥f CHChch fifl

Gg Black

abcdefghijklmopqrstuvwxyz ABCDEFGHIJKLMNOPQRST
UVWXYZ 0123456789 ([{&:;.,!?¿¡*%}]) €$¢£¥f CHChch fifl

Gg Black Italic

abcdefghijklmopqrstuvwxyz ABCDEFGHIJKLMNOPQRST
UVWXYZ 0123456789 ([{&:;.,!?¿¡*%}]) €$¢£¥f CHChchfifl

Fontana ND

Rubén Fontana
2001

MODERN COLLECTION
·Sistema Fontana: Body Text fonts
·Gg

Character sets supported:
·Windows Latin 1 · MacRoman

Features:
Expert set containing special
characters and ligatures

Unicode v3.0 compliant

Ll Semibold

abcdefghijklmopqrstuvwxyz ABCDEFGHIJKLMNOPQRST
UVWXYZ 0123456789 ([{&:;.,!?¿¡*%}]) €$¢£¥f CHChch fifl

Ll Bold

abcdefghijklmopqrstuvwxyz ABCDEFGHIJKLMNOPQRST
UVWXYZ 0123456789 ([{&:;.,!?¿¡*%}]) €$¢£¥f CHChch fifl

Ll Black

abcdefghijklmopqrstuvwxyz ABCDEFGHIJKLMNOPQRST
UVWXYZ 0123456789 ([{&:;.,!?¿¡*%}]) €$¢£¥f CHChch fifl

Fontana ND

Rubén Fontana
2001

MODERN COLLECTION
Sistema Fontana: Tilting fonts
·Ll

Character sets supported:
·Windows Latin 1 · MacRoman

Features:
·Expert set containing special
characters and ligatures

Unicode v3.0 compliant

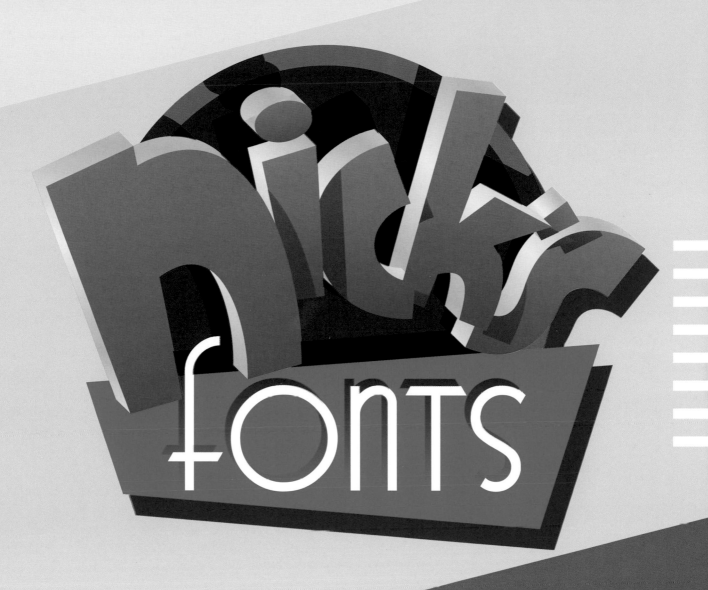

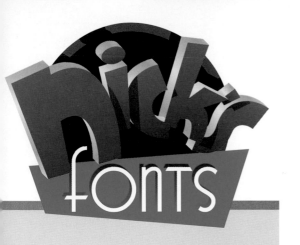

"I would attribute my love of the letterforms of yesteryear to a youth misspent hanging around in too many libraries," says award-winning type designer Nick Curtis. "As a kid, I would spend hours wandering through the stacks, devouring volumes on Currier and Ives prints, silent movies, and other visual expressions of earlier popular culture."

Nick's interest in typography began around age 13 with his discovery of a type specimen book a neighbor had discarded — a big, fat green binder filled with hundreds of fonts. Thereafter, his personal art projects were adorned with handlettering patterned after several of those fonts. Later, his influences expanded to include, among others, Push Pin Studio and the San Francisco rock poster movement.

Professionally, Nick has worked as an art director in advertising agencies, an a/v production company, and broadcast television. "In the early 80s, TV was on the leading edge of what passed for computer graphics at the time. I was fortunate enough to be at the right place at the right time to develop the technical skills that I still use to create electronic type."

Nick began creating freeware fonts in 1997, and expanded into producing commercial fonts in 2001. Two of his commercial releases that year, Jeepers ITC and Woodley Park, were recognized by the Type Directors Club as among the best new type designs of 2001. He adds to his collection of freeware fonts (now over 150) on a regular basis—available at www.nicksfonts.com—as well as his commercial endeavors (currently over 100).

Nick currently resides in the Washington, DC area, where he still hangs around in libraries. He is a registered researcher at the Library of Congress, and also regularly explores the vast virtual library that is the Internet, searching for more historical letterforms to revive and reintroduce to the world.

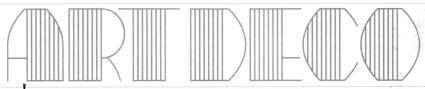

ABCDEFGHIJKLMNOPQRSTUVWXYZabcde
fghijklmnopqrstuvwxyz0123456789!?&$¢£¥ ÆŒØÐ æßðøþ

Astoria Titling NF

Nick Curtis
2001

Influenced by Joan Trochut Blanchard, Gus Oring, and Paul Carlyle.

ABCDEFGHIJKLMNOPQRSTUVWXYZABCDEFGH
IJKLMNOPQRSTUVWXYZ0123456789!?&$¢£€

Big Tent Players NF

Nick Curtis
2002

ABCDEFGHIJKLMNOPQRST
UVWXYZ0123456789!?&$¢

Boogaloo Boulevard NF

Nick Curtis
2002

Based on Harold Holland Day's version of Broadway.

ABCDEFGHIJKLMNOPQRSTUVW
XYZabcdefghijklmnopqrstuvwxyz0123

Day Tripper NF

Nick Curtis
2002

Based on Dignity Roman by Alphonso E. Tripp.

ABCDEFGHIJKLMNOPQRSTUVWXYZabcdefg
hijklmnopqrstuvwxyz0123456789!?&$¢£

Fifth Avenue Salon NF

Nick Curtis
2002

FIVE AND DIME

ABCDEFGHIJKLMNOPQRSTUVWXYZ01234567

Five and Dime NF

Nick Curtis
2002

An architectural font, great for simulating old signs.

Gotham Rail Company NF

Nick Curtis
2002

ABCDEFGHIJKLMNOPQRSTUVWXYZA
BCDEFGHIJKLMNOPQRSTUVWXYZ012

Joost a Gigolo NF

Nick Curtis
2002

Based on the work of Dutch comic
book artist Joost Swarte.

ABCDEFGHIJKLMNOPQR
STUVWXYZ0123456789!

La Moda NF

Nick Curtis
2002

ABCDEFGHIJKLMNOPQRSTUV
WXYZ*abcdefghijklmnopqrst*

Lance Corporal NF

Nick Curtis
2002

ABCDEFGHIJKLMNOPQRSTUV
WXYZABCDEFGHIJKLMNOPQR

Mesa Verde NF

Nick Curtis
2002

ABCDEFGHIJKLMNOPQRST
UVWXYZABCDEFGHIJKLMNO

Modern Art NF

Nick Curtis
2002

Based on the work of Dutch comic
book artist Joost Swarte.

MODERNART
ABCDEFGHIJKLMNOPQRSTU
VWXYZ0123456789!?&$¢£¥¢

Monte Casino NF

Nick Curtis
2002

ABCDEFGHIJKLMNOPQRSTUVW
XYZ0123456789!?&$¢£¥Æ

ABCDEFGHIJKLMNOPQRSTUVWXYZ01
23456789!?&$¢£¥ÆÇÐØÞÆSSÐØÞ

Normal

ABCDEFGHIJKLMNOPQRSTUVWXYZ
0123456789!?&$¢£¥ÆÇÐØÞÆSSÐØ

Bold

ABCDEFGHIJKLMNOPQRSTUVWXYZabcdefghijklmnopq
rstuvwxyz0123456789!?&$¢£¥ÆÇÐØÞæßðøþ

Round Bold

ABCDEFGHIJKLMNOPQRSTUVWXYZabcdefghijklmnopqrstuvw

Square Extralight

ABCDEFGHIJKLMNOPQRSTUVW

Square Light

ABCDEFGHIJKLMNOPQRSTUVW

Square Normal

ABCDEFGHIJKLMNOPQRSTUVW

Square Bold

ABCDEFGHIJKLMNOPQRSTUVWXYZabcdef
ghijklmnopqrstuvwxyz0123456789!?&$

Oldstyle

New Deal Deco NF

Nick Curtis
2002

Risky Business NF

Nick Curtis
2001

Nick's Fonts

Rocketman XV-7 NF

Nick Curtis
2001

ABCDEFGHIJKLMNOPQRSTU
VWXYZabcdefghijklmnopqr

Sabrina Zaftig NF

Nick Curtis
2002

ABCDEFGHIJKLMNO
PQRSTUVWXYZ01234567

Wagner Silhouette NF

Nick Curtis
2002

ABCDEFGHIJKLMNOPQRS
TUVWXYZabcdefghijklmnopqr

Washington Square NF

Nick Curtis
2002

ABCDEFGHIJKLMNO
PQRSTUVWXYZabcdefghijkl
mnopqrstuvwxyz0123456789!?&$¢£¥

White Tie Affair NF

Nick Curtis
2002

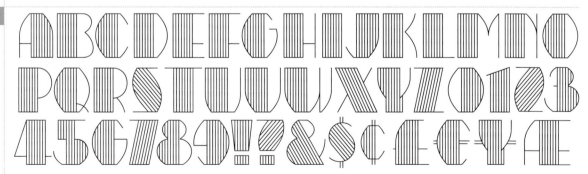

ABCDEFGHIJKLMNO
PQRSTUVWXYZ0123
456789!?&$¢£¥Æ

CLASSIC

ABCDEFGHIJKLMNOP
QRSTUVWXYZabcdefghijklmnopqrstu
vwxyz0123456789!?& $¢£¥ÆĐØÞœß

Classic Typefaces

Londonderry Air NF

Nick Curtis

2002

Based on the old ATF font Canterbury.

ABCDEFGHIJKLMNOPQRSTUVW
XYZ0123456789!?&$¢£¥ÆĐØÞÆ

Persephone NF

Nick Curtis

2002

Based on the old ATF font Pericles.

ABCDEFGHIJKLMNOPQRSTUVWXYZ
AEG0123456789!?&$¢£¥ÆĐØÞÆS

Quadrivium NF

Nick Curtis

2002

Based on Weiss Initial II by Rudolph Weiss.

ABCDEFGHIJKLMNOPQRSTUVWX
YZabcdefghijklmnopqrstuvwxyz0123
456789!?@$¢£¥§†‡ÇÆĐØÞæßðøþ

Saturday Morning Toast NF

Nick Curtis

2001

Based on the old logotype font for *The Saturday Evening Post*.

Slam Bang Theater NF

Nick Curtis

2002

Based on ATF Nubian, designed by Williard T. Sniffin.

DECORATIVE

Annabelle Matinee NF

Nick Curtis
2002

ABCDEFGHIJKLMNO
PQRSTUVWXYZabcdefgh
ijklmnopqrstuvwxyz012345
6789!?&$¢£€¥ ÆŒØÞ æß

Bessie Mae Moocho NF

Nick Curtis
2002

ABCDEFGHIJKLMNOPQRST
UVWXYZ0123456789!?&$¢

Bo Diddlioni Stencil NF

Nick Curtis
2001

ABCDEFGHIJKLMNOPQRSTUVWXY
Zabcdefghijklmnopqrstuvwxyz0123456

Cambridge Pinstripe NF

Nick Curtis
2002

abcdefghijklmnopqrstuvwxyz
0123456789!?&$¢£€¥ ÆŒØÞ æß

Foo Bar Inline NF

Nick Curtis
2002

Based on the Supertipo Veloz series
by Joan Trochut Blanchard.

ABCDEFGHIJKLMNOPQRSTUVWXYZ
0012345678 91!&$£€¥ ÆŒØÞ ß

Marrakesh Express NF

Nick Curtis
2002

ABCDEFGHIJKLMNOPQRS
TUVWXYZ0123456789!?&$¢

ABCDEFGHIJKLMNOPQRSTUVWX
YZabcdefghijklmnopqrstuvwxyz&

Metro Retro Redux NF

Nick Curtis
2001

Based on the typeface Modernistic,
designed by Wadsworth A. Parker.

ABCDEFGHIJKLMNOPQRS.T.UVW.X.YZ
01.23456 7 8.9!?&$¢£¥ ÆÐØÞ ÆSÐØÞ

Olbrich Display NF

Nick Curtis
2002

Based on poster lettering by Joseph
Maria Olbrich.

ABCDEFGHIJKLMNOP
QRSTUVWXYZ!?&01

Partager Caps NF

Nick Curtis
2002

ABCDEFGHIJKLMNOPQR
STUVWXYZ0123456789!

Robot Monster NF

Nick Curtis
2001

ABCDEFGHIJKLMNOPQRSTUVWXYZZ0123
456789!!?&§†‡‡¢£¥¶ÆÐØ ÆSÐØÞ

Super Bob Triline NF

Nick Curtis
2001

Based on the Supertipo Veloz series by
Joan Trochut Blanchard.

ABCDEFGHIJKLMNOPQRSTUVWXYZ
ABCDEFGHIJKLMNOPQRSTUVWXYZ012
3456789!?&$¢£¥ ÆÐØÞ ÆSÐØÞ

Toonerville NF

Nick Curtis
2002

ABCDEFGHIJKLMNOPQRSTUV
WXYZSO0123456789!?&$¢£€

Ziggy Stardust NF

Nick Curtis
2002

Handlettering

Bergling Fantasia NF

Nick Curtis
2002

Based on handlettering by J. M. Bergling.

ABCDEFGHIJKLMNOPQRSTUVWXYZab
cdefghijklmnopqrstuvwxyz0123456789!?

Bergling Fantasia Bold NF

Nick Curtis
2002

Based on handlettering by J. M. Bergling.

ABCDEFGHIJKLMNOPQRSTUVWXYZa
bcdefghijklmnopqrstuvwxyz0123456789

Bundle of Joy NF

Nick Curtis
2002

Based on handlettering by Australian lettering artist C. Milne.

ABCDEFGHIJKLMNOPQRSTUVWX
YZabcdefghijklmnopqrstuvwxyz

Duffy's Tavern NF

Nick Curtis
2002

Based on handlettering by E. C. Matthews.

ABCDEFGHIJKLMNOPQRSTUVWX
YZabcdefghijklmnopqrstuvwxyz012345

East Coast Frolics NF

Nick Curtis
2002

ABCDEFGHIJKLM NOPQRSTUVWX
YZabcdefghijklmnopqrstuvwxyz01

Erehwon Roman NF

Nick Curtis
2002

Based on handlettering by J. M. Bergling.

ABCDEFGHIJKLMNOPQRST
UVWXYZabcdefghijklmnopqrstuvwx

Gasoline Alley NF

Nick Curtis
2002

Based on handlettering by Albanis Ashmun Kelly, 1911.

ABCDEFGHIJKLMNOPQRSTU
VWXYZabcdefghijklmnopqrstuvwxy

ABCDEFGHIJKLMNOPQRSTUVWXYZabc
defghijklmnopqrstuvwxyz&012345678

Heberling Casual NF

Nick Curtis
2002

Based on handlettering by Walter A. Heberling, 1922.

ABCDEFGHIJKLMNOPQRSTUVWXYZab
cdefghijklmnopqrstuvwxyz&0123456

Heberling Casual Bold NF

Nick Curtis
2002

ABCDEFGHIJKLMNOPQRSTUVWX
YZABCDEFGHIJKLMNOPQRSTUVWXYZ

Magic Lantern SW

Nick Curtis
2001

Based on handlettering by Samuel Welo.

ABCDEFGHIJKLMNOPQRSTUVWX
YZabcdefghijklmnopqrstuvwxyz&0123

Mrs. Bathhurst FGC

Nick Curtis
2001

Based on handlettering by Fred G. Cooper.

ABCDEFGHIJKLMNOPQRSTUV
XYZabcdefghijklmnopqrstuvwxy

Roman Holiday Xbold NF

Nick Curtis
2001

ABCDEFGHIJKLMNOPQRSTUVWXYZ
abcdefghijklmnopqrstuvwxyz&01234

Speedball No. 1 NF

Nick Curtis
2002

Based on handlettering by Samuel Welo.

ABCDEFGHIJKLMNOPQRS
TUVWXYZabcdefghijklmnopqrst
uvwxyz&0123456789!?$¢£€

Strongs Draughtsman NF

Nick Curtis
2001

Based on handlettering by Lawrence Strong, ca. 1910.

Thimble Theatre NF

Nick Curtis
2001

Based on handlettering by J. M. Bergling.

ABCDEFGHIJKLMNOPQRSTUV
WXYZabcdefghijklmnopqrstuv

WHG Simpatico NF

Nick Curtis
2002

Based on handlettering by William Hugh Gordon.

ABCDEFGHIJKLMNOPQRSTUVWXY
Zabcdefghijklmnopqrstuvwxyz012345678

Whoopee Cushion SW

Nick Curtis
2002

Based on handlettering by Samuel Welo.

ABCDEFGHIJKLMNOPQRS
TUVWXYZabcdefghijklmnop

Wigwam HB

Nick Curtis
2001

Based on handlettering by Ed and Ben Hunt.

ABCDEFGHIJKLMNOPQRSTUVWX
YZABCDEFGHIJKLMNOPQRSTUVWXYZ0I

All Nick's Fonts have extensive kerning, carefully and thoughtfully applied by hand.

ABCDEFGHIJKLMNOPQRST
UVWXYZabcdefghijklmn
opqrstuvwxyz&012345678

Artemisia NF

Nick Curtis
2002

B. Based on Adonis by ATF.

ABCDEFGHIJKLMNOPQR
STUVWXYZabcdefghijklmn
opqrstuvwxyz&0123456789$

MargaritaVille NF

Nick Curtis
2001

ABCDEFGHIJKLMN
OPQRSTUVWXYZabcdefghi
jklmnopqrstuvwxyz&0123456789$¢

Monte Carlo Script NF

Nick Curtis
2002

B. Based on Médicis Script by Deberny
D. & Peignot.

ABCDEFGHIJKLMNOPQRSTUVW
XYZabcdefghijklmnopqrstuvwxyz&0123

Thai Foon HB NF

Nick Curtis
2001

B. Based on handlettering by Ed and
E. Ben Hunt.

Character Sets

All Nick's Fonts have complete Adobe
character sets, plus the Euro symbol.

!."#$%&'()*+,-./0123456789:

;<=>?@ABCDEFGHIJKLM

NOPQ RSTUVWXYZ[\]^

_`abcdefghijklmnopq rstuv

wxyz{|}~‚ƒ„…†‡^‰Š‹Œ''""•—

—~™š›œŸ¡¢£€¥¦§¨©ª«¬—®¯°

±²³´µ¶·¸¹º»¼½¾¿ÀÁÂÃÄÅ

ÆÇÈÉÊËÌÍÎÏÐÑÒÓÔÕÖ×Ø

ÙÚÛÜÝÞßàáâãäåæçèéêëìíî

ïðñòóôõö÷øùúûü ýþ ÿı˘˙˚˝¸˛ˇ

Additional Macintosh characters

ŁłŽž≠∞≤≥µ∂∑∏π∫Ω

√≅∆◊/⬤ﬁﬂ

Text

ABCDEFGHIJKLMNOPQRSTUVWX
YZabcdefghijklmnopqrstuvwxyz&01234567
89$f†‡¢£€¥!?ÆÐÞßæðøþ™§©®µ¶

Normal

ABCDEFGHIJKLMNOPQRSTUVWXYZ
abcdefghijklmnopqrstuvwxyz&0123456789$f
†‡¢£€¥!?ÆÐÞßæðøþ™§©®µ¶

Normal Italic

ABCDEFGHIJKLMNOPQRSTUVWX
YZabcdefghijklmnopqrstuvwxyz&0123456
789$f†‡¢£€¥!?ÆÐÞßæðøþ™§©®µ¶

Bold

ABCDEFGHIJKLMNOPQRSTUVWXY
Zabcdefghijklmnopqrstuvwxyz&0123456789$
f†‡¢£€¥!?ÆÐÞßæðøþ™§©®µ¶

Bold Italic

Text

McKenna Handletter NF

Nick Curtis
2002

Based on the eponymous text face
designed by Elizabeth Colwell.

Nick's Fonts

WOODTYPE

Brazos WBW Extrabold

Nick Curtis
2001

ABCDEFGHIJKLMNOPQRST
UVWXYZABCDEFGHIJKLMNOP
QRSTUVWXYZ0123456789!?

Dime Box WBW

Nick Curtis
2001

ABCDEFGHIJKLMNOPQRS
TUVWXYZ0123456789!?

Gullywasher WBW

Nick Curtis
2001

ABCDEFGHIJKLMNOPQRSTUV
WXYZ0123456789!?&$¢£€ Æ

Jefferson Pilot WBW

Nick Curtis
2001

ABCDEFGHIJKLMNOPQ
RSTUVWXYZ01234567

Laguna Madre WBW

Nick Curtis
2001

ABCDEFGHIJKLMNOPQRSTUVWXYZabc
defghijklmnopqrstuvwxyz0123456789!?&

himself@nicksfonts.com

ABCDEFGHIJ LI IO Q
RSTUVWXYZ0123456789

ABCDEFGHIJKLMNOPQRST
UVWXYZABCDEFGHIJKLMNOP

ABCDEFGHIJKLMNOPQRS
TUVWXYZ0123456789!?

ABCDEFGHIJKLMNOPQRSTUVWX
YZ0123456789!?&$¢£¥ÆÐØÞÆẞ

ABCDEFGHIJKLMNOPQRSTUV
WXYZabcdefghijklmnopqrstuvw

ABCDEFGHIJKLMNOPQ
RSTUVWXYZabcdefghijkl

ABCDEFGHIJKLMNOPQRSTUVWXYZ012
3456789!?&$f†‡$¢¢¥©®Æ♭♭S

I felt bad because I had no shoes until I met a man who had no Bodoni

No Bodoni Typography
http://www.nobodoni.com
support@nobodoni.com

No Bodoni is a small, independent type design company, inspired by Giambattista Bodoni's dedication and drive to create unique types for his time. No Bodoni believes that a typeface is a functional aesthetic object, designed to signify—rather than represent—meaning, emotion and belief. Typefaces are transcendent as well as historical and cultural. They not only carry information about the text they represent, but about the designer who uses them, the culture they come from, and commentary about the medium of typography itself.

No Bodoni's types are not the tired revivals of standard classics, nor smudged, degraded letterforms missing half the character set. They are not mere fonts, but unique, usable types that are personal responses to putting information on a page.

No Bodoni Typography is a project of
George Everet(t) Thompson.

No Bodoni typefaces are available from Myfonts.com

ITC Oldrichium is available from the
International Typeface Corp.

www.itcfonts.com

AåBbÇçDdÈéFfGgHhIiJjKkLlMmÑñÖôP
pQqRrSsTtÛüVvWwXxYyZz&{}()[]«€1
23456789»$¢£¥%‰o?!¿¡.,:;*"'"'¶‹Œœøø
Æœfiflß›°·@©®™ ſ∫≠≤–›÷=±‹+≥≂ºª·§‡†

ÅBÇDÈFGHÍJKMÑÖPQRSTÛVWXYZã
bçdêfghijklmnòpqrstúvwxyz&{}()[]
«€123456789»$¢£¥%‰o?!¿¡.,:;*"'"'¶
‹ŒœØøÆœfiflß›°·@©®™

ÅBÇDÈFGHIJKLMÑÔPQRSTÜVWXYZ
åbçdèfghíjklmñöpqrstûvwxyz&{}()
[]«€123456789»$¢£¥%‰o?!¿¡.,:;*"'"'¶
‹ŒœØøÆœfiflß›°·@©®™

Claudium

George Everet(t) Thompson
2002

Claudium started as an attempt to create a sans serif version of Garamond, but as time went on, it became a meditation on the nature of French typography from Garamond to Excoffon. A cursive italic was designed, based on Garamond's Greek forms. The original drawings were done in marker on tracing paper with about a 9-inch body height. This was done to make them as gestural and flowing as possible. Only the lowercase italic letters were designed and then mated to the Regular caps like Griffo's original italic.

No Bodoni

Claudium 11/12

In 1833, John Calhoun came from Buffalo, New York, to become the first printer in Chicago. Calhoun had heard about the boom in Chicago from a friend, and so he shipped printing equipment from Buffalo, then followed by boat. His boat was run

Claudium Bold 11/12

In 1833, John Calhoun came from Buffalo, New York, to become the first printer in Chicago. Calhoun had heard about the boom in Chicago from a friend, and so he shipped printing equipment from Buffalo, then followed by boat.

Claudium Italic 11/12

In 1833, John Calhoun came from Buffalo, New York, to become the first printer in Chicago. Calhoun had heard about the boom in Chicago from a friend, and so he shipped his printing equipment from Buffalo,

George Everet(t) Thompson
2001

ITC Oldrichium is based on the calligraphy and typefaces of Czech designer Oldrich Menhart. I'm very enamored of his work, especially his calligraphy, which is much looser and rougher than his type designs. I wanted to design a face with the spirit of both his type and his lettering. I lettered forms in Menhart's style, using his Manuscript face as a beginning guide. The resulting type was too calligraphic, so I redrew it and made the forms more styled. The incised version was based on his Parliament type, which is more elegant and less calligraphic than Oldrichium.

ITC Oldrichium Regular

åbçdèfghijklmñôpqrstüvwxyz1234567890.,:;?!¿¡[]{}()
ÅBÇÉDFGHÌJKLMÑÖPQRSTÛVWXYZæÆœŒfiflß

Pick-Up on Noon Street

A Carrot is as Close as a Rabbit Gets to a Diamond

ITC Oldrichium Demi Italic

åbçdèfghijklmñôpqrstüvwxyz1234567890.,:;?!¿¡[]{}()
ÅBÇÉDFGHÌJKLMÑÖPQRSTÛVWXYZœŒæÆfifl

ITC Oldrichium Light

åbçdèfghijklmñôpqrstüvwxyz1234567890.,:;?!¿¡[]{}()
ÅBÇÉDFGHÌJKLMÑÖPQRSTÛVWXYZœŒæÆfiflß

The Mothers of Invention

If on a winter's night a traveler

ITC Oldrichium Bold

åbçdèfghijklmñôpqrstüvwxyz1234567890.,:;?!¿¡[]
ÅBÇÉDFGHÌJKLMÑÖPQRSTÛVWXYZæÆœŒfifl

Regular 11/12

In 1833, John Calhoun came from Buffalo, New York, to become the first printer in Chicago. Calhoun had heard about the boom in Chicago from a friend, and so he shipped his printing equipment from Buffalo, then followed by boat. His

Italic 11/12

In 1833, John Calhoun came from Buffalo, New York, to become the first printer in Chicago. Calhoun had heard about the boom in Chicago from a friend, and so he shipped printing equipment from New York, then followed by boat. His boat

Demi 11/12

In 1833, John Calhoun came from Buffalo, New York, to become the first printer in Chicago. Calhoun had heard about the boom in Chicago from a friend, and so he shipped his printing equipment from Buffalo, then followed by boat. His

support@nobodoni.com

George Everet(t) Thompson

ITC Oldrichium Italic

abçdèfghijklmñôpqrstüvwxyz1234567890.,:;?!¿¡()[]{}0
ÅBÇÉDFGHÌJKLMÑÖPQRSTÛVWXYZŒœÆæßflfi

ITC Oldrichium Demi

abçdèfghijklmñôpqrstüvwxyz1234567890.,:;?!¿¡()[]{}0
ÅBÇÉDFGHÌJKLMÑÖPQRSTÛVWXYZŒœÆæßfl

Captain Beefheart & His Magic Band
Trouble is My Business

ITC Oldrichium Light Italic

abçdèfghijklmñôpqrstüvwxyz1234567890.,:;?!¿¡()[]{}0
ÅBÇÉDFGHÌJKLMÑÖPQRSTÛVWXYZŒœÆæßflfi

ITC Oldrichium Engraved

abçdèfghijklmñôpqrstüvwxyz1234567890.,:;?!¿¡()[]
ÅBÇÉDFGHÌJKLMÑÖPQRSTÛVWXYZŒœÆæßfl

DM Bob & the Deficits
The Castle of Crossed Destinies

Demi Italic 11/12

In 1833, John Calhoun came from Buffalo, New York, to become the first printer in Chicago. Calhoun had heard about the boom in Chicago from a friend, and so he shipped printing equipment from Buffalo, then followed by boat. His boat was run

Light 11/12

In 1833, John Calhoun came from Buffalo, New York, to become the first printer in Chicago. Calhoun had heard about the boom in Chicago from a friend, and so he shipped printing equipment from Buffalo, then followed by boat. His boat was run

Light Italic 11/12

In 1833, John Calhoun came from Buffalo, New York, to become the first printer in Chicago. Calhoun had heard about the boom in Chicago from a friend, and so he shipped printing equipment from Buffalo, then followed by boat. His boat was run

No Bodoni

George Everet(t) Thompson
2002-2003

Tinman is a humanist sans based on
Goudy's University of California
Oldstyle.

Tinman

ABCDEFGHIJKLMNOPQRSTUVWXYZ?!&@
abcdefghijklmnopqrstuvwxyz1234567890()

Tinman Demibold

ABCDEFGHIJKLMNOPQRSTUVWXYZ?!&
abcdefghijklmnopqrstuvwxyz123456789

Tinman Bold

ABCDEFGHIJKLMNOPQRSTUVWXYZ&
abcdefghijklmnopqrstuvwxyz123456789

Tinman, DemiBold, Bold

Largo Desolato

Largo Desolato

Largo Desolato

Eyes of a Blue Dog

Eyes of a Blue Dog

Eyes of a Blue Dog

support@nobodoni.com

Tinman Italic

ABCDEFGHIJKLMNOPQRSTUVWXYZ&()@
abcdefghijklmnopqrstuvwxyz1234567890?!

Tinman DemiBold Italic

ABCDEFGHIJKLMNOPQRSTUVWXYZ@
abcdefghijklmnopqrstuvwxyz01234567890

Tinman Bold Italic

ABCDEFGHIJKLMNOPQRSTUVWXYZ&@
abcdefghijklmnopqrstuvwxyz123456789?!

Tinman Italic, DemiBold Italic, Bold Italic

Largo Desolato

Largo Desolato

Largo Desolato

Eyes of a Blue Dog

Eyes of a Blue Dog

Eyes of a Blue Dog

No Bodoni

Sleep Tickets

George Everet(t) Thompson
2002-2003

Sleep Tickets is a sans serif based on Georg Trump's Delphin, which was based on Francesco Griffo's original italic. Griffo designed the italic only as a lowercase with no capitals, and used the Bembo capitals with it.

Sleep Tickets

ABCDEFGHIJKLMNOPQRSTUVWXYZ
abcdefghijklmnopqrstuvwxyz
1234567890

Sleep Tickets Bold

ABCDEFGHIJKLMNOPQRSTUVWX
YZabcdefghijklmnopqrstuvwxyz
1234567890

Sleep Tickets

Life During Wartime
Yellow Back Radio Broke Down

Sleep Tickets Bold

Pattern Recognition
Tours of the Black Clock

support@nobodoni.com

DAVIES BROTHERS,
COAL AND WOOD,
162 East 23d Street,
And at the offices of the Mutual District Messenger Co.

COAL and WOOD put in your CELLAR at ONE HOUR'S NOTICE.

PRESENT PRICES, DECEMBER 1st, 1891
Lehigh Coal

Stove or Range,	-	-	-	$5.25
Nut,	-	5.25	Egg, -	5.25
Furnace,	-	-	-	5.25
American Cannel	-	-	-	12.00
INCE HALL English Cannel,			-	16.00

Per ton of 2000 lbs., delivered on the Sidewalk

Floridium

ABCDEFGHIJKLMNOPQRSTUVWXYZ,.;:&@
abcdefghijklmnopqrstuvwxyz123456789

Floridium

ABCDEFGHIJKLMNOPQRSTUVWXYZ,.;:&@
abcdefghijklmnopqrstuvwxyz1234567890

Floridium

ABCDEFGHIJKLMNOPQRSTUVWXYZ,.;:
abcdefghijklmnopqrstuvwxyz123456

Floridium

George Everet(t) Thompson
1999-2002

Floridium grew out of an affection for the old wood types of the 1800s. Painters Roman (issued by both Page and Wells wood type companies–see *American Wood Type: 1828-1900* by Rob Roy Kelly for more information) was the initial inspiration. It was the source for the "banana" and "snake head" serifs. But the design, released by Adobe as Juniper, was too quirky to be very useful. I tried to create a type that was more sophisticated and modern, while keeping the original personality of the nineteenth-century type. A bold weight and an italic, which weren't part of the original wood type, were designed as well.

No Bodoni

George Everet(t) Thompson
2002-2003

Dog Butter is based on an old Barnhart Brothers & Spindler script type variously called Oliphant or Advertisers Upright Script. The original BB&S design was clearly based on some hard lettering that was very inconsistent. Some characters were very nice, but others were dull as dirt. I wanted to make all the characters equally interesting and light-hearted, while making it a monotone script so there could be a wide variety of weights.

Of Grammatology
A Sign is Just a Sign
Travels in Hyper Reality
Semiotics and Structuralism
Course in General Linguisites
Perscpectives in Zoosemiotics
The Raw & the Cooked
The Name of the Rose
The Jealous Potter
Mythologies

Dog Butter ExtraLight

abcdefghijklmnopqrstuvwxyzABCDEFGHIJKLMN
OPQRSTUVWXYZ1234567890?$&

Dog Butter

abcdefghijklmnopqrstuvwxyzABCDEFGHIJK
LMNOPQRSTUVWXYZ123456789?

support@nobodoni.com

George Everet(t) Thompson
2002-2003

Dog Butter Medium

abcdefghijkl mnopqrstuvwxyz ABCDEFGHIJK
LMNOPQRST UVWXYZ123456789?

Dog Butter DemiBold

abcdefghijkl mnopqrstuvwxyz ABCDEFGHIJK
LMNOPQRST UVWXYZ123456789?

Dog Butter Bold

abcdefghijkl mnopqrstuvwxyz ABCDEFGHI
JKLMNOPQRST UVWXYZ123456

Charles Peirce

Jacques Derrida

Roman Jakobson

Claude Levi Strauss

Ferdinand de Sassure

George Everet(t) Thompson
1994-2000

Isbellium is a sans serif version of Dick Isbell's Americana type, the last type cut in metal by the American Type Founders Co. (ATF). Isbell's Americana is an elegant face with a wide stance, and Isbellium tries to maintain that elegance. This is more difficult to achieve in a sans serif than a serif type. It has some of the flair of the serif, but with a quieter voice and a polite authority.

Isbellium is a display face with a Roman and Italique in five weights: Regular, Medium, DemiBold, Bold, and ExtraBold. Small caps versions for each weight are also in progress.

Endless, Nameless
Heart–Shaped Box
Verse Chorus Verse
Smells Like Teen Spirit
Radio Friendly Unit Shifter

Isbellium Italique

åbçdèfghijklmñôpqrstüvuwxyz1234567890.,:;?![]{}()
ÅBÇÉDFGHÌJKLMÑÖPQRSTÛVWXYZœŒæÆfifiß

Isbellium Medium

åbçdèfghijklmñôpqrstüvuwxyz1234567890.,:;?![]{}()
ÅBÇÉDFGHÌJKLMÑÖPQRSTÛVWXYZœŒæÆfifiß

Isbellium DemiBold Italique

åbçdèfghijklmñôpqrstüvuwxyz1234567890.,:;?!()[]
ÅBÇÉDFGHÌJKLMÑÖPQRSTÛVWXYZœŒæÆ

Isbellium Bold

åbçdèfghijklmñôpqrstüvuwxyz1234567890.,?!()
ÅBÇÉDFGHÌJKLMÑÖPQRSTÛVWXYZæÆœŒ

Isbellium ExtraBold Italique

åbçdèfghijklmñôpqrstüvuwxyz1234567890?![]
ÅBÇÉDFGHÌJKLMÑÖPQRSTÛVWXYZœÆŒ

support@nobodoni.com

Swordfishtrombones
Invitation to the Blues
Murder in the Red Barn
Emotional Weather Report
House Where Nobody Lives

Isbellium

åbçdèfghijklmñôpqrstüvwxyz1234567890.,:;?!¿¡()[]{}
ÅBÇÉDFGHÌJKLMÑÖPQRSTÛVWXYZŒœÆæßfifi

Isbellium Medium Italique

åbçdèfghijklmñôpqrstüvwxyz1234567890?![]{}
ÅBÇÉDFGHÌJKLMÑÖPQRSTÛVWXYZŒœÆœßfi

Isbellium DemiBold

åbçdèfghijklmñôpqrstüvwxyz1234567890?!()
ÅBÇDÉDFGHÌJKLMÑÖPQRSTÛVWXYZŒœÆ

Isbellium Bold Italique

åbçdèfghijklmñôpqrstüvwxyz1234567890?!
ÅBÇDÉDFGHÌJKLMÑÖPQRSTÛVWXYZŒœÆ

Isbellium ExtraBold

åbçdèfghijklmñôpqrstüvwxyz1234567890?!
ÅBÇDÉDFGHÌJKLMÑÖPQRSTÛVWXYZŒœÆ

Ms Kitty

George Everet(t) Thompson
2002

Some scribbles on a bar napkin, a note from a cute girl passed in history class—what is there to say but "why not a typeface?" Actually, it's that late-night, "Let's get this typeface done!" madness that causes these flights of fancy. Anything to relieve the boredom of doing all those kerning pairs. Or maybe it's sunspots?

Ms Kitty is all uppercase letterforms with two versions of each letter, one in the cap position, the other in the lowercase position. There are myriad kerning pairs to allow the dots to overlap for better spacing.

Besides the regular and bold weights, there are a bolder and much bolder weight in the works. And perhaps there will be a "too bold to be believed" version. Depends on the sunspots.

Ms Kitty

AABBCCDDEEFFGGHHIIJJKK
LLMMNNOOPPQQRRSSTTUU
VVWWXXYYZZ1234567890?!

Ms Kitty Bold

AABBCCDDEEFFGGHHIIJJK
KLLMMNNOOPPQQRRSSTT
UUVVWWXXYYZZ1234567

Ms Kitty

MARDER & LUSE

Ms Kitty Bold

FREIBERGER, GERING & KRANZ

Ms Kitty

FUST AND SCHÖEFFER

Ms Kitty Bold

SWEYNHEIM & PANNARTZ

support@nobodoni.com

ABCDEFGHIJKLMNOPQRSTUVWXYZa
bcdefghijklmnopqrstuvwxyz1234567890?!

ABCDEFGHIJKLMNOPQRSTUVWXYZ
abcdefghijklmnopqrstuvwxyz123456789

ABCDEFGHIJKLMNOPQRSTUVWXYZ
abcdefghijklmnopqrstuvwxyz1234567

ABCDEFGHIJKLMNOPQRSTUVWXY
Zabcdefghijklmnopqrstuvwxyz12345

Jim Hurtibise **Billy Vukuvich**

Eddie Sachs • ***Roger McCluskey*** • *Gordon Johncock* • Roger Ward

Troy Ruttman *Mario Andretti*

Dick Rathman • **Jim McElreath** • A. J. Foyt • *Tommy Hinnerschitz*

Dick Rathman **Jim McElreath**

Jim Hurtibise • **Billy Vukuvich** • Troy Ruttman • *Mario Andretti*

A. J. Foyt *Tommy Hinnerschitz*

Tommy Hinnerschitz • **Eddie Sachs** • ***Jim Hurtibise*** • Roger Ward

Eddie Sachs ***Roger McCluskey***

Dick Rathman • **Jim McElreath** • A. J. Foyt • *Tommy Hinnerschitz*

Gordon Johncock Roger Ward

Parma Typewriter

George Everet(t) Thompson
1995–2000

Parma is a typewriter-style face with the form and elegance of a Bodoni. Functional beauty was the aim of mating the two ideas in one typeface, creating a utilitarian design with graceful features—unlike most typewriter faces, which have a mechanical feel. This avoids that inelegant, klugey appearance and makes it possible to have an attractive italic version.

I'm converting the keys on my beloved old Olivetti portable to type in Parma. And then I'm going to get a Lambretta scooter to go zipping around in, and maybe one of those front-opening Fiats for drives in the countryside.

No Bodoni

George Everet(t) Thompson
1993-2000

Estiennium is a humanist sans serif with a quirky personality, named for the first family of French printers. The design began with the uppercase O, a modified super-ellipse with its corners clipped off. The bowls of the uppercase and lowercase letters follow the same shape, but stand off from the stems, as if they had been pulled away to show the connective tissue that binds them together.

Estiennium Regular

åbçdèfghijklmñôpqrstüvwxyz1234567890.,:;?!¿¡[]{}()
ÅBÇÉDFGHÌJKLMÑÖPQRSTÛVWXYZœÆœŒfifiß

Estiennium Italique

åbçdèfghijklmñôpqrstüvwxyz1234567890.,:;?!¿¡[]{}()
ÅBÇÉDFGHÌJKLMÑÖPQRSTÛVWXYZœÆœŒfifiß

Estiennium DemiBold

åbçdèfghijklmñôpqrstüvwxyz1234567890.,:;?!¿¡[]{}()
ÅBÇÉDFGHÌJKLMÑÖPQRSTÛVWXYZœŒœÆfifi

Estiennium DemiBold Italique

åbçdèfghijklmñôpqrstüvwxyz1234567890.,:;?!¿¡[]{}()
ÅBÇÉDFGHÌJKLMÑÖPQRSTÛVWXYZœŒœÆfifiß

Estiennium Bold

åbçdèfghijklmñôpqrstüvwxyz1234567890.,:;?!¿¡[]
ÅBÇÉDFGHÌJKLMÑÖPQRSTÛVWXYZœÆœŒfifi

Smokestack Lightnin'
DUST MY BROOM
Standin' at the Crossroads
What's the matter with the mill?

support@nobodoni.com

Estiennium (cont.)

George Everet(t) Thompson
1993-2000

Estiennium ExtraBold

åbçdèfghijklmñôpqrstüvwxyz1234567890,;?!¿¡[]{}()
ÅBÇÉÐFGHÌJKLMÑÖPQRSTÛVWXYZœÆœŒfifiß

Estiennium ExtraBold Italique

åbçdèfghijklmñôpqrstüvwxyz1234567890?![]{}()
ÅBÇÉÐFGHÌJKLMÑÖPQRSTÛVWXYZœÆœŒfifiß

Estiennium Black

åbçdèfghijklmñôpqrstüvwxyz1234567890?![]{}()
ÅBÇÉÐFGHÌJKLMÑÖPQRSTÛVWXYZœŒœÆfifi

Estiennium Black Italique

åbçdèfghijklmñôpqrstüvwxyz1234567890?![]{}()
ÅBÇÉÐFGHÌJKLMÑÖPQRSTÛVWXYZœŒœÆfifiß

Estiennium Bold Italique

åbçdèfghijklmñôpqrstüvwxyz1234567890.,:;?!¿¡[]
ÅBÇÉÐFGHÌJKLMÑÖPQRSTÛVWXYZœÆœŒfifi

Key to the Highway
LEVEE CAMP MOAN
Rollin' and Tumblin'
Keep your hands off her

PAR
KIN
SON

PARKINSON TYPE DESIGN

PARKINSON TYPE DESIGN

Jim Parkinson specializes in the design
of typefaces and typographic logos.
He has designed over 100 typefaces. Half
are exclusives for font companies including
The Font Bureau, Adobe, Agfa/Monotype,
ITC, FontShop and Chank.
The others, shown here, are available from
Parkinson Type Design, Phil's Fonts and MyFonts.

email: parkinson@typedesign.com
visit the website: typedesign.com

PAR
KIN
SON

*People who love ideas must have a love of words,
and that means, given a chance, they will take
a vivid interest in the clothes which words wear.*
– Beatrice Warde

ABCDEFGHIJKLMNOPQRSTUVWXYZ
abcdefghijklmnopqrstuvwxyz &12345

ABCDEFGHIJKLMNOPQRSTUVWXYZ
abcdefghijklmnopqrstuvwxyz &12345

ABCDEFGHIJKLMNOPQRSTUVWXY
abcdefghijklmnopqrstuvwxyz &12345

ABCDEFGHIJKLMNOPQRSTUVWXY
abcdefghijklmnopqrstuvwxyz &12345

We use the letters of our alphabet every day with the utmost ease & unconcern, taking them almost as much for granted as the air we breathe. We do not realize that each of these letters is at our service today only as the result of a long & laboriously slow process of evolution in the age-old art of writing. Douglas C. McMurtrie

Azuza

Jim Parkinson
2001

Medium
Medium Italic
Bold
Bold Italic

Parkinson

Jim Parkinson
2001-2003

Extra Condensed
Condensed
Light
Medium
Bold
Extra Bold
Black
Wide Light
Wide Medium
Wide Bold
Wide Extra Bold
Wide Black

THREE AMBULANCES TAKE BLAST VICTIM TO HOSPITAL

Cops Halt Doughnut Shop Robbery

Missouri Woman Big Winner at Hog Show

Stolen Painting Found by Tree

DEAD MAN GETS JOB BACK

Something Went Wrong in Jet Crash, Expert Says

STEALS CLOCK, FACES TIME

Man Disputes Government Claim He's Dead

PANTS MAN TO EXPAND AT THE REAR

Unwanted Workers Get Shot at Jobs

TWO SOVIET SHIPS COLLIDE, ONE DIES

TREES CAN BREAK WIND

parkinson@typedesign.com

ABCDEFGHIJKLMNOPQRSTUVWXYZ
abcdefghijklmnopqrstuvwxyz & 12345

Wisconsin Bill Would Permit Blind to Hunt Deer

ABCDEFGHIJKLMNOPQRSTUVWXYZ
abcdefghijklmnopqrstuvwxyz & 12345

HOSPITAL SUED BY 7 FOOT DOCTORS

ABCDEFGHIJKLMNOPQRSTUVWXYZ
abcdefghijklmnopqrstuvwxyz & 12345

Iowa Cemeteries Are Death Traps

ABCDEFGHIJKLMNOPQRSTUVWXYZ
abcdefghijklmnopqrstuvwxyz & 12345

RAINS DELAY UMBRELLA SHOW

Parkinson

ABCDEFGHIJKLMNOPQRSTUVWXYZ
abcdefghijklmnopqrstuvwxyz & 12345

Art Causes School Evacuation

ABCDEFGHIJKLMNOPQRSTUVWXYZ
abcdefghijklmnopqrstuvwxyz & 1234

Dead Man Found in Cemetery

ABCDEFGHIJKLMNOPQRSTUVWX
abcdefghijklmnopqrstu & 1234

Apart from the cutters of

GRAVESTONES

the most conservative people in

TYPOGRAPHY

are newspaper people.   W.A. Dwiggins

ABCDEFGHIJKLMNOPQRSTUVWXYZ
abcdefghijklmnopqrstuvwxyz & 12345
Dinosaur Faces Grand Jury Probe

Balboa Wide

Jim Parkinson
2003

Light
Medium
Bold
Extra Bold
Black

ABCDEFGHIJKLMNOPQRSTUVWXYZ
abcdefghijklmnopqrstuvwxyz & 12345

ABCDEFGHIJKLMNOPQRSTUVWXYZ
abcdefghijklmnopqrstuvwxy & 12345
London Man Slain With Turnip

ABCDEFGHIJKLMNOPQRSTUVWXYZ
abcdefghijklmnopqrstuvw & 12345

ABCDEFGHIJKLMNOPQRSTUV
abcdefghijklmnopqrs & 12345
HIGH-SPEED TRAIN
Could Reach Valley in Five Years

Parkinson

Jim Parkinson
2003

Light
Medium
Bold
Extra Bold

ABCDEFGHIJKLMNOPQRSTUVW
abcdefghijklmnopqrstuvwxy &12345

ABCDEFGHIJKLMNOPQRSTUV
abcdefghijklmnopqrstuvw &12345

ABCDEFGHIJKLMNOPQRSTU
abcdefghijklmnopqrstuv &12345

ABCDEFGHIJKLMNOPQRSTU
abcdefghijklmnopqrstuv &12345

The graphic signs called letters are so completely
blended with the stream of written thought that
their presence therein is as unperceived as the
ticking of a clock in the measurement of time.
Only by an effort of attention does the layman
discover that they exist at all. It comes to him as
a surprise that these signs should be a matter
of concern to any one of the crafts of men.
But to be concerned with the shapes of letters is
to work in an ancient and fundamental material.
The qualities of letter forms at their best are the
qualities of a classic time: order, simpicity, grace.
W.A.Dwiggins

parkinson@typedesign.com

ABCDEFGHIJ KLMNOPQRST UVWXYZ & 123

SATURDAY & SUNDAY
MAY 2 & 3

Sutro Black Initials

Jim Parkinson
2003

Caps, figures, accents, and punctuation

ABCDEFGHIJK LMNOPQRSTU VWXYZ & 12345 HOT MINERAL SPRINGS

Sutro Shaded Initials

Jim Parkinson
2003

Caps, figures, accents, and punctuation

Parkinson

ABCDEFGHIJKLMNOPQRSTUVWXYZ
ABCDEFGHIJKLMNOPQRSTUVWXYZ &12345

THE HUMAN PROJECTILE

ABCDEFGHIJKLMNOPQRSTUVWXYZ
ABCDEFGHIJKLMNOPQRSTUVWX & 12345

SHOT THROUGH SPACE

ABCDEFGHIJKLMNOPQRS
ABCDEFGHIJKLMNOP & 12345

AT HIGH VELOCITY

ABCDEFGHIJKLMNOPQRSTUVWXYZ
ABCDEFGHIJKLMNOPQRSTUVWXYZ & 12345

FROM A MONSTER CANNON

parkinson@typedesign.com

ABCDEFGHIJKLMNOPQRSTUVW
ABCDEFGHIJKLMNOPQRSTU & 12345
You Will Be Amazed

Modesto Regular

Jim Parkinson
2001

ABCDEFGHIJKLMNOPQRS
ABCDEFGHIJKLMNOPQ & 12345
Bring the Family

Modesto Expanded

Jim Parkinson
2001

ABCDEFGHIJK
LMNOPQRSTU
VWXYZ & 1234
PICNIC

Modesto Inline

Jim Parkinson
2003

Caps, figures, accents,
and punctuation

Parkinson

Jim Parkinson
2003

ABCDEFGHIJKLMNOPQRSTUVWXYZ
abcdefghijklmnopqrstuvwxyz & 12345

Harmonious Typeface Designs

Jim Parkinson
2003

ABCDEFGHIJKLMNOPQRSTUVWXYZ
abcdefghijklmnopqrstuvwxyz & 12345

For Advertising & Publications

Jim Parkinson
2003

ABCDEFGHIJKLMNOPQRSTUVWXY
abcdefghijklmnopqrstuvwxyz & 12345

Harmonious Typeface Designs

Jim Parkinson
2003

ABCDEFGHIJKLMNOPQRSTUVWXYZ
abcdefghijklmnopqrstuvwxyz & 12345

For Advertising & Publications

parkinson@typedesign.com

We are type designers, punch cutters, wood cutters, type founders, compositors, printers, and book-binders from conviction and with passion, not because we *are insufficiently talented* for other higher things, but *because to us the highest* things stand in closest *kinship to our own crafts.* RUDOLF KOCH

Richmond Family

Jim Parkinson
2003

Condensed Light
Condensed Medium
Condensed Bold
Condensed Extra Bold
Light
Light Italic
Medium
Medium Italic
Bold
Bold Italic
Inlined Initials

Parkinson

Richmond Condensed

Jim Parkinson
2003

Light
Medium
Bold
Extra Bold

ABCDEFGHIJKLMNOPQRSTUVWXYZ
abcdefghijklmnopqrstuvwxyz &12345

ABCDEFGHIJKLMNOPQRSTUVWXYZ
abcdefghijklmnopqrstuvwxyz &12345

ABCDEFGHIJKLMNOPQRSTUVWXYZ
abcdefghijklmnopqrstuvwxyz &12345

ABCDEFGHIJKLMNOPQRSTUVWXYZ
abcdefghijklmnopqrstuvwxyz &12345

Geometry can produce legible letters, but art alone makes them beautiful. Art begins where geometry ends, and imparts to letters a character transcending mere measurement.

Paul Standard

ABCDEFGHIJKLMNOPQRSTUVWXYZ
abcdefghijklmnopqrstuvwxyz &12345

Typography is a servant –

Richmond Light

Jim Parkinson
2003

ABCDEFGHIJKLMNOPQRSTUVWXYZ
abcdefghijklmnopqrstuvwxyz &12345

the servant of thought and

Richmond Light Italic

Jim Parkinson
2003

ABCDEFGHIJKLMNOPQRSTUVWXYZ
abcdefghijklmnopqrstuvwxyz &12345

language to which it gives

Richmond Medium

Jim Parkinson
2003

ABCDEFGHIJKLMNOPQRSTUVWXYZ
abcdefghijklmnopqrstuvwxyz &12345

visible existence. *T.M. Cleland*

Richmond Medium Italic

Jim Parkinson
2003

Parkinson

The "blobby" look is the result of varying pressure on a sharply pointed crow-quill pen nib.

Tears fall at the death of a pet sparrow

(Written by John Skelton, tutor to Henry VIII)

Pla ce bo,
Who is there, who?
Di le xi,
Dame Margery;
Fa, re, my, my,
Wherefore and why, why?
For the sowle of Phyllyp
   Sparowe,

That was late slayn at Carowe,
Among the nones blake,
For that sweet soules sake,
And for all sparowes soules,
Set in our bederolls,
Pater noster qui,
With an Ave Mari,
And with the corner of a Crede
The more shalbe your mede.
I wept and I wayled,
The tearys downe hayled;

But nothing it auayled
To call Phylyp agayne,
Whom Gyb our cat
   hath slayne.
Kyrie, eleison
Christe, eleison
Kyrie, eleison!
For Phylyp Sparowes soule
Set in our bederoll
Let vs now whysper
A Pater noster . . .

ABCDEFGHIJKLMNOPQRSTUVWXYZ
abcdefghijklmnopqrstuvwxyz1234567890
&?!@#$%*()[]{};:.,/""''

Father mourns the death of a promising son

Successive generations of the Oglander family lived at Nunwell on the Isle of Wight for over 800 years. Following is an extract from the diary of Sir John Oglander (1585 - 1655), concerning the loss of his eldest son, who died from smallpox in France in 1632.

On the 21st July, being at Newport, and there busy in many things concerning the good of our Island, I heard a murmuring and sadness amongst the gentlemen and clergy and the rest. Mr. Price of Calbourne told me he hoped the ill news that was come to town was not true. Then I, becoming suspicious, demanded whether he had heard any ill news of any of my family. And he, finding my ignorance, converted it to a loss of the King of Sweden's army. Many more overtures I had, but knew nothing until I was putting my foot in the stirrup. Then Sir Robert Dillington and Sir Edward Dennys came unto me and told me of a flying report, brought by a bark off Weymouth, lately come from France, that my eldest son George was very sick – if not dead. With my tears instead of ink I write these last lines. O George, my beloved George, is dead, and with him most of my terrestrial comforts, although I acknowledge I have good and dutiful sons left. Only with my tears and a foul pen was this written.

ABCDEFGHIJKLMNOPQRSTUVWXYZ
abcdefghijklmnopqrstuvwxyz123456789&0

Indians Sold into Slavery

As Indian captives – men, women, and children – continued to pour into Plymouth, all were sold into slavery, some to local planters, the majority in the West Indies. All the Wampanoag lands were seized and sold "so as to settle plantations thereon in an orderly way to promote the publick worship of God, and our owne publicke good."

"The design of Christ in these last days is not to extirpate nations but to gospelize them," exclaimed John Eliot in bitter protest against these and similar acts throughout the United Colonies. "To sell souls for money seemeth to me a dangerous merchandise."

– George F. Willison: Saints and Strangers

ABCDEFGHIJKLMNOP
QRSTUVWXYZabcdefghijklmnopqrstu
vwxyz1234567890&.,()!?/·@ÿ

Shakespeare, Austen popularize romantic love

Let me not to the marriage of true minds
Admit impediments.
Love is not love which alters when it alteration finds,
Or bends with the remover to remove: -
O no! it is an ever-fixed mark
That looks on tempests, and is never shaken;
It is the star to every wandering bark,
Whose worth's unknown, although his height be taken.

— *William Shakespeare*

"Engagement!" cried Marianne, "there has been no engagement."
"No engagement?"
"No, he is not so unworthy as you believe him. He has broken no faith with me."
"But he told you that he loved you?"
"Yes – no – never absolutely. It was every day implied, but never professedly declared. Sometimes I thought it had been – but it never was."

— *Jane Austen*

ABCDEFGHIJKLMNOPQRST
UVWXYZabcdefghijklmnopqrstuvwxyz
1234567890?!@#$%&*()/;:""

Burns eulogizes love beside a Scottish stream

Flow gently, sweet Afton, among thy green bræs,
Flow gently, I'll sing thee a song in thy praise.
My Mary's asleep by thy murmuring stream,
Flow gently, sweet Afton, disturb not her dream.

Thou stock-dove whose echo resounds thro' the glen
Ye wild whistling blackbirds, in yon thorny den
Thou green-crested lapwing thy screaming forbear
I charge you, disturb not my slumbering Fair.

How lofty, sweet Afton, thy neighbouring hills
Far mark'd with the course of clear, winding rills
There daily I wander as noon rises high,
My flocks and my Mary's sweet cot in my eye.

How pleasant thy banks and green valleys below,
Where, wild in the woodlands, the primroses blow;
There oft, as mild Evning weeps over the lea
The sweet-scented birk shades my Mary and me.

The Afton rises near Cumnock in south-western Scotland and travels only eight miles before emptying into the River Nith. The poem was written by Robert Burns in 1789.

ABCDEFGHIJKLMNOPQRSTU
VWXYZabcdefghijklmnopqrstuvwxyz
&st?!$&1234567890fiflffffifflе_h_m_n

Wordsworth had lovely vision in Lake District

Avocet Light

Ted Staunton
2000

Effective for certificates, menus, invitations, etc.

I wandered lonely as a cloud
That floats on high o'er vales and hills,
When all at once I saw a crowd,
A host of golden daffodils,
Beside the lake, beneath the trees,
Fluttering and dancing in the breeze.

Continuous as the stars that shine
And twinkle on the Milky Way,
They stretched in never-ending line
Along the margin of the bay;
Ten thousand saw I at a glance,
Tossing their heads in sprightly dance.

The waves beside them danced, but they
Outdid the sparkling waves in glee;
A poet could not but be gay,
In such a jocund company;
I gazed - and gazed - but little thought
What wealth to me the show had brought.

For oft, when on my couch I lie,
In vacant or in pensive mood,
They flash upon that inward eye
Which is the bliss of solitude,
And then my heart with pleasure fills,
And dances with the daffodils.

ABCDEFGHIJKL
MNOPQRSTUVWXYZ
abcdefghijklmnopqrstuvwxyz
1234567890

a b b b d d d d e e g g ff fi fl ffi ffl gh k k k l ll l m n
r r s t tt v w w y ct st œ B D L P R S T Th W
& & ⚜ ∝ ae ¶ ⚘ ⚘ ⚘ ⚘

Tyndale

Ted Staunton
2000

One of a series exploring the conver-
gence of Gothic and Roman influences.

They bought his books - only to burn them

WILLIAM TYNDALE was born in Gloucestershire, England between 1490 and 1495. As a young man he attended both Oxford and Cambridge universities. A follower of the 'new learning' being propagated by such scholars as Colet and Erasmus, he wished to translate the Bible into English, but was forced to leave England to do so. Large numbers of his New Testament, printed in Holland, were bought up in England by the Bishop of London - not for distribution, but that they might be burned! The income provided Tyndale with enough capital to begin working on a new translation of the Old Testament, but he was betrayed from his hiding place among the merchants of Antwerp and strangled at the stake October 6, 1536.

It is estimated that about 90 per cent of the King James Authorized Version of 1611 is Tyndale's work.

ABCDEFGHIJK
LMNOPQRSTU
VWXYZ
abcdefghijklmno
pqrstuvwxyz
1234567890
&.,;:'"[]{}()!@#$%^*fifl‡ÆÆæŒœ

Tyndale Xtras

Ted Staunton / Other sources
2002

Arabesque and other ornaments from printed books of the seventeenth and eighteenth centuries, plus extra ligatures for the Tyndale font.

Amelia

Ted Staunton / Other source
2003

Initials in the Victorian style, plus a
selection of wood-engraved blanks
from the eighteenth century, artist
unknown.

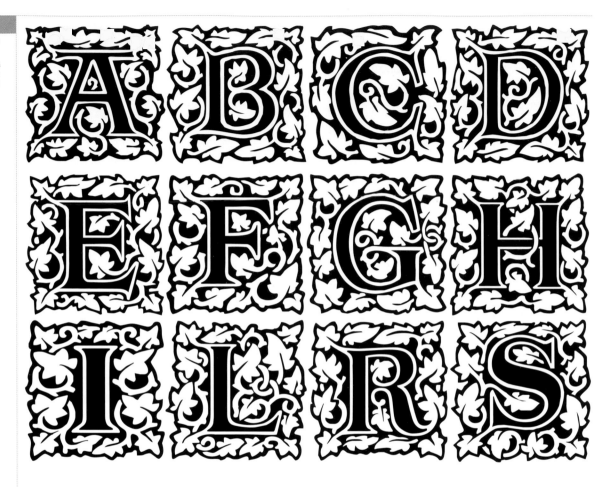

Floriat

Ted Staunton
2003

Sherwood

Mark Simonson

STUDIO

Mark Simonson Studio is a one-person operation offering, among other things, lettering and type design services. Several of Mark's fonts were licensed by FontHaus beginning in 1992, the most popular thus far being Felt Tip Roman,™ based on his own messy handwriting. In 2000, after a several-year break, he resumed typeface design and production in earnest. Many of the typefaces shown here are recent releases.

The M.S.S. collection is eclectic, offering original vintage and contemporary styles for both display and text. All fonts are of high quality with complete character sets (including European accents), careful spacing and extensive kerning tables for care-free setting. Every font is available for both Macintosh or Windows in PostScript™ Type 1 and TrueType formats.

M.S.S. typefaces are available from several different vendors, online and off, or direct from the source. See www.ms-studio.com for details.

In addition to the retail fonts shown here, M.S.S. offers custom font design and development services. Custom lettering for any purpose is also available. Scripts are Mark's specialty. Call or write for details.

Mark Simonson Studio

www.ms-studio.com
mark@ms-studio.com

1496 Raymond Avenue
Saint Paul, Minnesota 55108 USA

651-649-0553

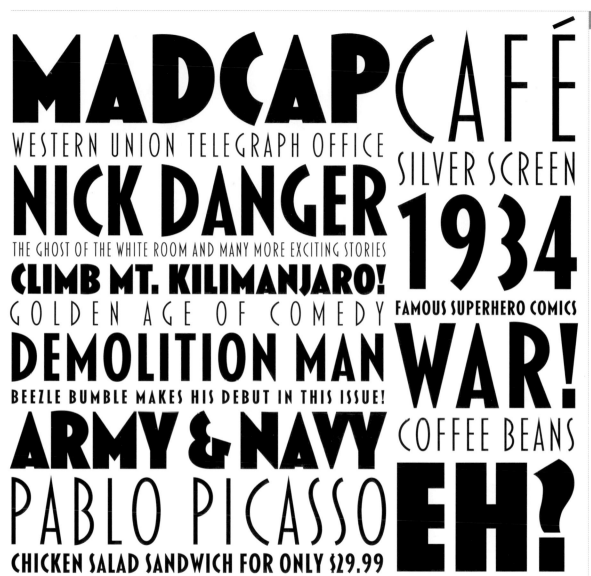

MADCAP CAFÉ

WESTERN UNION TELEGRAPH OFFICE

SILVER SCREEN

NICK DANGER

1934

THE GHOST OF THE WHITE ROOM AND MANY MORE EXCITING STORIES

CLIMB MT. KILIMANJARO!

GOLDEN AGE OF COMEDY

FAMOUS SUPERHERO COMICS

DEMOLITION MAN

WAR!

BEEZLE BUMBLE MAKES HIS DEBUT IN THIS ISSUE!

ARMY & NAVY

COFFEE BEANS

PABLO PICASSO

EH?

CHICKEN SALAD SANDWICH FOR ONLY $29.99

Blakely Light

ABCDEFGHIJKLMNOP
QRSTUVWXYZ 12345678
90 &*$¢£.,:;!?'''""«»()

Blakely Bold

ABCDEFGHIJKLMN
OPQRSTUVWXYZ 12
34567890 &*$.,:;!?(

Blakely Black

ABCDEFGHIJKLM
NOPQRSTUVWX
YZ 1234567890&

Blakely

Mark Simonson
2000–2003

Blakely Light is based on a custom font created in 1994 for the Signals mail order catalog. It is more restrained than other similar Art Deco typefaces, avoiding the typical high- or low-waisted crossbars. The Bold and Black weights are recent additions.

Mark Simonson Studio

Coquette is a hybrid of 1920s-era sans serif faces (Erbar, Kabel, Futura) and traditional French Civilité-inspired scripts (Typo Upright Script, Gando). The result is a face that is original yet familiar. It retains many script-like details and flows like a script, but remains disconnected.

Botticelli
2004
Florida Everglades
Eh?
Holiday Packages
Carriage
Guys
Transportation
Parade

Radio
Arts Décoratifs & Industriels Modernes
World Movie Premiere
·
Lumiere
Le Più Belle Confezioni Per La Donna
Ziegfield Follies of 1933
Azure Sky
Beans Roasted Fresh Daily

Coquette Light

ABCDEFGHIJK
LMNOPQRSTU
VWXYZ abcdefg
hijklmnopqrstuvwxyz
1234567890 &*$¢£.,:;
!?'"" «»( )[ ]{ }@©®/%

Coquette Regular

ABCDEFGHIJK
LMNOPQRSTU
VWXYZ abcdefg
hijklmnopqrstuvwxyz
1234567890 &*$¢£.,:;
!?'"" «»( )[ ]{ }@©®/%

Coquette Bold

ABCDEFGHIJK
LMNOPQRSTU
VWXYZ abcdefgh
ijklmnopqrstuvwxyz
1234567890 &*$¢£.,:;
!?'"" «»( )[ ]{ }@©®/%

mark@ms-studio.com

FITZGERALD

EL PUEBLO DE NUESTRA SENORA LA REINA DE LOS ANGELES DE PORCIUNCULA

Admiral

NEW YORK SUBWAY

VIDEO MELIORA PROBOQVE DETERIORA SEQVOR

WORLD

LITERARY GUILD

Fortune

AN ALTERNATIVE TO THE USUAL MOVIE TITLE

VIRTUE

San Francisco

CHICAGO

City

WINE &

DINE QUARTERLY / SEPTEMBER 2003

Mr.

BRIDGE

Rig

Goldenbook

Mark Simonson
2003

Goldenbook is based on the logotype of a literary magazine from the late 1920s called *The Golden Book Magazine*. It is meant to be used large, and includes both ranging and lining numerals.

Mark Simonson Studio

Goldenbook Light

ABCDEFGHIJKLM
NOPQRSTUVWXY
Z 1234567890 abcdef
ghijklmnopqrstuvwxyz
1234567890(&*$.,:;!?")

Goldenbook Regular

ABCDEFGHIJKLM
NOPQRSTUVWXY
Z 1234567890abcdef
ghijklmnopqrstuvwxyz
1234567890(&*$.,:;!?)

Goldenbook Bold

ABCDEFGHIJKLM
NOPQRSTUVWXY
Z 1234567890abcdef
ghijklmnopqrstuvwxyz
1234567890(&*$.,:;!?)

Mark Simonson
2001

Mostra was inspired by Italian Art Deco posters from the 1920s and '30s. It is a caps-only design, but has up to three alternate forms for many characters, providing a range of looks from the conventional to the more stylized.

RISTORANTE
WIZARD
RISK
SIGARETTE
HA!
GRAN PARADISO
A&E
CAPPUCCINO & ESPRESSO
ROMA

MOSTRA DELLA LUCE
COFFEE
FLORAL ARRANGEMENTS
PRELUDE ON THE AFTERNOON OF A FAUN
SIMPLICITY
BETWEEN THE WARS
MAGAZINE
CIOCCOLATO CARAMELLE & CONFETTVRE
WHAT?

Mostra Light

AAABCCDEEFFGGG
HIJKKLMNOPQQRR
SSSTUVWXYYZ 1234
567890 &*$¢£.,;!?
'""'«»()/%@©®ªº†‡

Mostra Regular

AAABCCDEEFFGGG
HIJKKLMNOPQQRR
SSSTUVWXYYZ 1234
567890 &*$¢£.,;!?
'""'«»()/%@©®ªº†

Mostra Bold

AAABCCDEEFFGG
GHIJKKLMNOPQ
QRRSSTUVWXYYZ
1234567890 &*$¢£
.,;!?'""'«»()/%@©

mark@ms-studio.com

ACCIDENTAL

APPLICAZIONI ELETTRICHE MODERNE

SOAP

LA CAMICIA CHE PORTA QUESTI MARCHI

WAR & PEACE

POUR AVOIR DES CHEVEUX MAGNIFIQUES

SARSAPARILLA

2001

1928

37

396

$4,568.99

Mustra Heavy

AAABCCDEEFFGG
GHIJKLMNOPQQ
RRSSSTUVWXYYZ
1234567890 &*$C£
.,:!?"''""«»()/%@

Mostra Black

AAABCCDEEFFG
GGHIJKLMNOPQ
QRRSSSTUVWXY
YZ1234567890 &
*$C£.,:!?"''""()/%

Mostra

Mark Simonson
2001

Mark Simonson Studio

Metallophile Sp 8

ABCDEFGHIJKLMNOPQRSTUVWXYZ
abcdefghijklmnopqrstuvwxyz 1234567890
&.,:;!?<>''""«»———=+(){}%*#@ $¢£¥©®
åœÆøœéîüñ™fifl¶ºª/

Metallophile Sp 8 Italic

ABCDEFGHIJKLMNOPQRSTUVWXYZ
abcdefghijklmnopqrstuvwxyz 1234567890
&.,:;!?<>''""«»———=+(){}%*#@ $¢£¥©®
åéüœÆøœéîüñ™fifl¶ºª/

HOW IS ONE TO ASSESS AND EVALUATE a type face in terms of its esthetic design? Why do the pace-makers in the art of printing rave over a specific face of type? What do they see in it? Why is it so superlatively pleasant to their eyes? Good design is always practical design. And what they see in a good type design is, partly, its excellent practical fitness to perform its work. It has a "heft" and balance in all of its parts just right for its size, as any good tool has. Your good chair has all of its parts made nicely to the right size to do exactly the work that the chair has to do,

HOW IS ONE TO ASSESS AND EVALUATE a type face in terms of its esthetic design? Why do the pace-makers in the art of printing rave over a specific face of type? What do they see in it? Why is it so superlatively pleasant to their eyes? Good design is always practical design. And what they see in a good type design is, partly, its excellent practical fitness to perform its work. It has a "heft" and balance in all of its parts just right for its size, as any good tool has. Your good chair has all of its parts made nicely to the right size to do exactly the work that the chair has to do,

Metallophile Sp 8

Mark Simonson
2002

Metallophile Sp 8 is a faithful facsimile of an 8-point sans serif typeface as set on a 1940s vintage hot metal typesetting machine. The effect is very different from its modern cousins, which are drawn more rigidly and use one design for all sizes. Metallophile Sp 8 is best if used at or near 8 points. This is the first font in a series.

Sharktooth

Mark Simonson
2000, 2003

Sharktooth began as an attempt to create a sans serif typeface based on the general structure of Felt Tip Roman (facing page). It turned out quite different in the end, though you can still see similarities. It has an unusual structure for a sans serif, with the diagonal stress of the round elements in tension with the perpendicularity of the linear elements. This seeming contradiction gives Sharktooth a lively, unconventional texture. The Bold and Heavy weights are recent additions.

anagram
Go!
SQUARE
2,634
Eccentricity
WASHINGTON
Monster Truck Show

MYSTERIOUS
65TH ST.
Natural Dentistry
TRIG
Mondays
Oh?
Wet & Wild

Woofers & Tweeters
swatches
Fix
PRESENT
$895
Quagmire
SPEED FREAK

GIVE ME the attention of your eyes, and through this one of your senses **I will lead your thinking** into those contemplations and associations that will make the product advertised appear as a thing greatly to be desired, says the modern selling scientist, who has mastered the meaning of Psychology and knows how to apply its force in the business of causing favorable mental impressions for any article of merchandise. The writer of the successful message and the designer work together to develop an effect. They comprehend

GIVE ME the attention of your eyes, and through this one of your senses **I will lead your thinking** into those contemplations and associations that will make the product advertised appear as a thing greatly to be desired, says the modern selling scientist, who has mastered the meaning of Psychology and knows how to apply its force in the business of causing favorable mental impressions for any article of merchandise. The writer of the successful message and the designer work together to develop an

GIVE ME the attention of your eyes, and through this one of your senses I will lead your thinking into those contemplations and associations that will make the product advertised appear as a thing greatly to be desired, says the modern selling scientist, who has mastered the meaning of Psychology and knows how to apply its force in the business of causing favorable mental impressions for any article of merchandise. The writer of the successful message and the designer work to-

Sharktooth Regular

ABCDEFGHIJKLMN
OPQRSTUVWXYZ &
1234567890 abcdefg
hijklmnopqrstuvwxyz
(.,:;!?--—) [/*""] {$@%}

Sharktooth Bold

ABCDEFGHIJKLMN
OPQRSTUVWXYZ &
1234567890 abcdefg
hijklmnopqrstuvwx
yz (.,:;!?-) [/*""] {$@%}

Sharktooth Heavy

ABCDEFGHIJKLMN
OPQRSTUVWXYZ &
1234567890abcdefg
hijklmnopqrstuvwx
yz(.,:;!?-) [/*""] {$@%}

COGITO ERGO SUM

QUOUSQUE TANDEM ABUTERE, CATALINA, patientia nostra? quamdiu nos etiam furor iste tuus eludet? quem ad fin em sese effrenata jactabit audacia? nihilne te nocturnum praesidium pa latii, nihil urbis vigiliae, nihil timor populi, nihil consensus bonorum omnium, nihil hic munitissimus habendi senatus locos, nihil horum ora vultusque moverunt? patere tua consilia non sentis? constrictam jam omnium horum conscientia

Ipso Facto
PLAUDITE CIVES!
gloria

Felt Tip Roman

ABCDEFGHIJKLMNOPQ RSTUVWXYZ abcdef ghijklmnoprstuvwxyz 1234567890 &*$.,:;!?ᵁ⁽‘” @#%( )<>=+-—éàÆ¶

Felt Tip Roman Bold

ABCDEFGHIJKLMNOPQ RSTUVWXYZ abcdef ghijklmnoprstuvwxyz 1234567890 &*$.,:;!?ᵁ⁽‘” @#%( )<>=+-—éàÆ¶

Felt Tip Roman Heavy

ABCDEFGHIJKLMNOP QRSTUVWXYZ abc defghijklmnoprstuv wxyz 1234567890 & *$.,:;!?ᵁ⁽‘”@#%( )<>=+

Mark Simonson
1992, 2003

Felt Tip Roman began as an experiment in 1989–a straight adaptation of the designer's handwriting. The Bold and Heavy weights were added recently to broaden its usefulness.

Felt Tip Woman

ABCDEFGHIJKLMNOPQRS TUVWXYZ abcdefghijklmno prstuvwxyz 1234567890 & *$.,:;!?⁰⁽‘”@#%( )<>=+-

Felt Tip Woman Bold

ABCDEFGHIJKLMNOPQRS TUVWXYZ abcdefghijklmno prstuvwxyz 1234567890 &

ERRARE HUMANUM EST

QUOUSQUE TANDEM ABUTERE, CATALINA, patientia nostra? quamdiu nos etiam furor iste tuus eludet? quem ad fin em sese effrenata jactabit audacia? nihilne te nocturnum praesidium pa latii, nihil urbis vigiliae, nihil timor populi, nihil consensus bonorum omnium, nihil hic munitissimus habendi senatus locos, nihil horum ora vultusque moverunt? patere tua consilia non sentis?

Mark Simonson
2003

Felt Tip Woman is based on the handwriting of designer Patricia Thompson. The name was inspired by a mis-hearing of the name "Felt Tip Roman" by a colleague.

Felt Tip Senior

ABCDEFGHIJKLMN OPQRSTUVWXYZ abcdefghijklmno prstuvwxyz 1234 567890 $*.,:;!?⁶⁾‘‘ @#%()<>=+-[]

DIEM PERDIDI

QUOUSQUE TANDEM ABUTERE, CATALINA, patientia nostra? quamdiu nos etiam furor iste tuus eludet? quem ad fin em sese effrenata jactabit audacia? nihilne te nocturnum praesidium pa latii, nihil urbis vigiliae, nihil timor populi, nihil consensus bonorum omnium, nihil hic munitissimus habendi senatus locos, nihil horum ora vultusque moverunt? patere tua consilia non sentis? constrictam jam

Mark Simonson
2000

Felt Tip Senior is based on the handwriting of Leroy Simonson, father of the designer. It was originally licensed exclusively to Mr. Simonson in 1994, but was made available to the general public in 2000.

Mark Simonson Studio

Mark Simonson
1994

Proxima Sans is a melding of elements found in other sans serif typefaces. It combines the stylistic details of geometric faces such as Futura, Kabel, and Erbar with the proportions of grotesques such as Franklin Gothic, Akzidenz Grotesk, and Helvetica. The oblique members of the family are optically balanced, not simply slanted geometrically.

AMONG THOSE WHO HAVE SERIOUSLY CONSIDERED the *flying saucer* as a mode of flight are aerodynamists who are, unsurprisingly, reluctant to accept my own interplantary explanation. **Nevertheless,** they have not ignored the aerodynamic qualities of disc-shaped aircraft. **It is said** that such aircraft have been built and flown years ago—*it would seem not without some success.* More recently, the press has released information about a saucer-type aircraft being developed in Canada. (*Plate 1.*) The craft is still in the mock-up stage and is said to be nearly forty feet in diameter. **The revolutionary feature** about the plane is not so much the shape of the wing itself, but in *the turbine power plant* which it is claimed rotates within the stationary wing and about the pilot's central capsule thereby giving

AMONG THOSE WHO HAVE SERIOUSLY CONSID-ERED the *flying saucer* as a mode of flight are aerodyna-mists who are, unsurprisingly, reluctant to accept my own interplantary explanation. **Nevertheless,** they have not ignored the aerodynamic quali-ties of disc-shaped aircraft. **Such aircraft** have been built and flown years ago—*it would seem not without some success.* More recently, the press has released information about a saucer-type aircraft being developed in Canada. (*Plate 1.*) The craft is still in the mock-up stage and is said to be nearly 40 feet in diameter. **The revolutionary feature** about the plane is not so much the shape of the wing itself, but in *the turbine power plant* which it is claimed rotates within the stationary wing and about the pilot's central

QUESTION?

STANDARD PROCEDURE

Men's

EDUCATIONAL WORD & LETTER GAMES

Rare Earth

Corporal Punishment

ROCK & ROLL

Proxima Sans

ABCDEFGHIJKLM
NOPQRSTUVWXY
Z 1234567890 abc
defghijklmnopqrst
uvwxyz &*$.,:;!?"“”

Proxima Sans Oblique

*ABCDEFGHIJKLM
NOPQRSTUVWX
YZ 1234567890 a
bcdefghijklmnop
qrstuvwxyz &*$.,:*

Proxima Sans Medium

**ABCDEFGHIJKLM
NOPQRSTUVWXY
Z 1234567890 abc
defghijklmnopqrst
uvwxyz &*$.,:;!?"“”**

Proxima Sans Medium Oblique

***ABCDEFGHIJKLM
NOPQRSTUVWX
YZ 1234567890 a
bcdefghijklmnop
qrstuvwxyz &*$.,:***

mark@ms-studio.com

SPARKLE
CONFIDENTIALITY
Cardinal

Proxima Sans Black

ABCDEFGHIJKLM
NOPQRSTUVWX
YZ 1234567890 a
bcdefghijklmnopq
rstuvwxyz &$.,:;!?

Proxima Sans Black Oblique

ABCDEFGHIJKLM
NOPQRSTUVWX
YZ 1234567890 a
bcdefghijklmnopq
rstuvwxyz &$.,:;!?

AMONG THOSE WHO HAVE SERIOUSLY CON-SIDERED the *flying saucer* as a mode of flight are aerodynamists who are oddly reluctant to accept my own interplantary explanation. Nevertheless, they have not ignored the aerodynamic qualities of a *disc-shaped aircraft.* It is said that such aircraft have been built and flown years ago—it would seem not without some success. Recently, the press has released information about a saucer-type aircraft being developed in Canada. (Plate 1.) The craft is still in the mock-up stage and is said to be *nearly forty feet in diameter.* The revolutionary feature about the plane is not so much the shape of the wing itself, but in the turbine power plant

Proxima Sans

Mark Simonson
1994

Mark Simonson Studio

MONOSPACED

`clipA.loadMovie("section1.swf"); // Load a document into clipA`

`>>> T = [(1,2),(3,4)]`

Code Head

OBJECT-ORIENTED PROGRAMMING
"Typewriter Quotes"

Anonymous™

ABCDEFGHIJKLMNOPQRSTUVWXYZ 1234567890 %°$¢£€ƒ¥
abcdefghijklmnopqrstuvwxyz (&$.,:;!?¿¡---*«»/)
[' " ‚ ‶‷† ‡] {@©®™•º₀+−=≠÷±<>≤≥¬|\^#∫√≈ΩΔ∂Σπ∏}
(áàâäãåæçéèêëíìîïñóòôöõøœúùûüÿﬁﬂÁÀÂÄÃÅÆÇÉÈÊËÍ)

MOTION PICTURES AND PERSISTENCE OF VISION.--The motion picture projector is simply a projection lantern that casts a series of pictures on a screen in rapid succession. To the eye, the pictures seem to blend into one another, thus producing the illusion of continuous motion. The reason for this blending is that the impression made upon the retina of the eye by a given picture persists for about one-sixteenth of a second after the picture has been removed. Hence, when pictures are shown one after another at the rate of sixteen or more per second, the image of any one picture will not have time to fade from the retina before the next one appears. The motion projector is simply a projection lantern that casts a series of pictures on a

Anonymous™

Mark Simonson
2001

Anonymous started as a 9-point Macintosh bitmap font designed by Susan Lesch and David B. Lamkins. It was intended as a more legible alternative to the Monaco system font. Mark Simonson developed the outline version shown here. The goal was to interpret the simple bit patterns of the originally typographically.

ANONYMOUS
Original bitmap font
ANONYMOUS
Typographic interpretation

Storm Type Foundry was founded in Prague in 1993 with the aim to restore the values of classical typography for the benefit of digital technologies. *"Back to the roots" is a tendency which characterizes a large part of our production, inspired by the Renaissance, Baroque, and Neo-classical periods. Our catalogue includes a group of Baroque type families which have been digitized for the first time in the world, and whose shape is almost intact.* We started by drawing alphabets which could be used in book printing, then we proceeded to alphabets for film- and photosetting, and, nowadays, in the era of computers, we use the experience we have gained to make digital typefaces more human.
Our current TypoKatalog5 contains over 490 original fonts.

visit us on **www.stormtype.com**
*buy online on **www.myfonts.com***

ABCDEFGHJKLMNOPabcdefghjklmnop
qrstuvwxyzQRSTUVWXYZ&0123456789
AaBbCcDdEeFfGgHhJjKkLlMmNn
PpQqRTwYyffſtſtctſſfitt)0123456789

Antique Ancienne

František Štorm
1998

Inspired by eighteenth-century type
specimens.

Baroque typography deserves anything else but the attribute "transitional". In the first half of the 18th-century, besides persons whose names are prominent and well-known up to the present, as was Baskerville or Caslon, there were many type founders who did not manage to publish their manuals or forgot to become famous in some *other way. They often imitated the typefaces of their more experienced contemporaries, but many of them arrived at a quite strange, even weird originality, which ran completely outside the mainstream of typographical art. The prints from which we have drawn inspiration for these six digital designs come from Paris, Vienna and Prague, from the period*

Antique Ancienne 11 pt.

František Štorm
1998

Inspired by eighteenth-century type
specimens.

Gloria patri & *filii* & *spiritui* Sancto.

Antique Moderne

František Štorm
1998

Inspired by eighteenth-century type
specimens.

Antique Regent: ABCDEFG HJKLMNOPabcdefghjklmno pqrstuvwxyzQRSTUVWXYZ &0123456789*AaBbCcDdEeFfG gHhJjKkLlMmNnPpQqRTw YyffvfiꝐ0123456789*

Antique Moderne: ABCDEF GHJKLMNOPabcdefghjklm nopqrstuvwxyzQRSTUVW XYZ&0123456789*AaBbCcD dEeFfGgHhJjKkLlMmNnPp QqRTwffſtfiꝐ0123456789*

Ant. Regent & Moderne

František Štorm
1998

Inspired by eighteenth-century type
specimens.

Storm Type Foundry

František Štorm
2002

Regular

OpenType font with full range
of features.

ABCDEFGHIJKLMNOPQRSTUVWXYZ
abcdefghijklmnopqrsßtuvwxyzfiflfkstctsfttfüfjsp
ABCDEFGHIJKLMNOPQRSTUVWXYZ0123456789
+@!?€£&,0123456789→0123456789

František Štorm
2002

Italic

ABCDEFGHIJKL MNPQR STUVWXYZ
abcdefghijklmnopqrsßtuvwxyz & Swash & Endings
ABCDEFGHIJKLMNQRSTUVWX bdfghjklpqrsßstuvwx yz
+@!?€£&,0123456789→0123456789 rsßtu vz

František Štorm
2002

Bold

ABCDEFGHIJKLMNOPQRSTUVWXYZ
abcdefghijklmnopqrsßtuvwxyzfiflfkstctsfttfüfjsp
ABCDEFGHIJKLMNOPQRSTUVWXYZ0123456789
+@!?€£&,0123456789→0123456789

František Štorm
2002

Bold Italic

ABCDEFGHIJKLMNOPQRSTUVWXYZ
abcdefghijklmnopqrsßtuvwxyzfiflfkstctsfttfüfjsp
ABCDEFGHIJKLMNOPQRSTUVWXYZ0123456789
+@!?€£&,0123456789→0123456789

mail@stormtype.com

c'est *une*

Jannon Text 137 pt.

occafion faite

Jannon Text 68 pt.

pour l'amplification d'idée progreſsiſte

Jannon Antiqua 32 pt.

de **Jannon.** *Jannon* redresse l'axe des hachures, supprime les

Jannon Antiqua 19 pt.

courbes et les subſtitue par les lignes droites. Il n'a pas peur d'incorporer les éléments tout à fait ſtatiques dans l'ensemble parfaitement dynamique d'antique, ce qu'eſt le cas de la plupart des majuscules. Il dessine hardiement l'italique d'une façon nouvelle avec l'angle d'inclinaison irregulier. Notre transcription digitale précédente contenait également tels annomalies, comme la minuscule „z" en italique, posée trop haut (ce qu'eſt peut-être une pittoresque faute de compositeur), élargissement léger de la partie moyenne des tiges verticales et quelques autres défauts. En somme: c'est une fonte trop beau et trop orientée vers ses origines, qui ne corresponde pas tout à fait au exigeances contemporai-

nes. JANNON TEXT MODERNE SOLUTIONNE LES POINTS FAIBLES DES VERSIONS DIGITALES PRÉCÉDENTES. *Tous les traits fins sont accentués et la hauteur medium des minuscules eſt légerement plus petite en comparaison avec Jannon Text. En suivant l'eſprit cristallin et presque froid de Jannon, nous avons approché notre alphabet de baroque, mais aussi des exigeances des leċteurs contemporains. Jannon Text Moderne compte naturellement huit styles de base avec petite capitales, & en plus les chiffres non-tabulés, italiques décoratives, ligatures et vignettes d'époque. Nous éditons cette fonte comme l'alternative entre les autres répliques postgaramondiennes, convenable à toutes les genres de la littérature, qui fera digestibles même les romans gigantesques.* Jannon T Moderne OT 9 pt.

Jannon T Moderne OT 42 pt.

Jannon Antiqua

Elqa&

Jannon Text

Elqa&

Jannon T Moderne

Elqa&

Jannon

František Štorm
1995-2002

The engraver Jean Jannon ranks among the significant representatives of French typography of the first half of the seventeenth century. He was born in 1580, apparently in Switzerland. He trained as punchcutter in Paris. From 1610, he worked in the printing office of the Calvinist Academy in Sedan, where he was awarded the title "Imprimeur de son Excellence et de l'Academie Sédanoise." He began working on his own alphabet in 1615, so that he would not have to order type for his printing office from Paris, Holland, and Germany, which at that time was rather difficult. The other reason was that not only the existing typefaces but also the respective punchers were rapidly wearing out.

Their restoration was extremely painstaking, not to mention the fact that the result would have been just a poor shadow of the original elegance. Thus, a new typeface came into existence, standing on a traditional basis, but with a life-giving sparkle from its creator. In 1621, Jannon published a Roman typeface and italics, derived from the shapes of Garmond's typefaces. As late as the start of the twentieth century, Jannon's typeface was mistakenly called Garamond, because it looked like that typeface at first sight. Jannon's Early Baroque Roman typeface, however, differs from Garamond in contrast and in having grander forms. Jannon's italics rank among the most successful italics of all time—they are brilliantly cut and elegant.

Storm Type Foundry

Baskerville Ten OT

František Štorm
2002

Regular

OpenType face with full range
of features.

ABCDEFGHIJKLMNOPQRSTUVWXYZ
abcdefghijklmnopqrsßtuvwxyzfiflfkstctfstfüisp
ABCDEFGHIJKLMNOPQRSTUVWXYZ0123456789
+@!?€£&,0123456789→0123456789

ABCDEFGHIJKLMNOPQRSTUVWXYZ
abcdefghijklmnopqrsßtuvwxyzfiflfkstctfstfüisp
ABCDEFGHIJKLMNOPQRSTUVWXYZ0123456789
+@!?€£&,0123456789→0123456789

ABCDEFGHIJKLMNOPQRSTUVWXYZ
abcdefghijklmnopqrsßtuvwxyzfiflfkstctfstfüisp
ABCDEFGHIJKLMNOPQRSTUVWXYZ0123456789
+@!?€£&,0123456789→0123456789

ABCDEFGHIJKLMNOPQRSTUVWXYZ
abcdefghijklmnopqrsßtuvwxyzfiflfkstctfstfüisp
ABCDEFGHIJKLMNOPQRSTUVWXYZ0123456789
+@!?€£&,0123456789→0123456789

Bask | Bask

J Baskerville Original

Baskerville Ten OT

An analytical
transcription is also
to remove any potential
shortcomings of the source of inspiration
and must not take over mechanically all details of the design.

An analytical
transcription is also
to remove any potential
shortcomings of the source of inspiration
and must not take over mechanically all details of the design.

John Baskerville Original

ABCDEFGJKLMNPQR
STUVWXYZabcdefghjk
mnopqrstuwxyzABCDEFGJK
LMNOPQRSTUVWXYZ+@!?
0123456790I3456789
ßffiſtſtætæœ&

John Baskerville

František Štorm
2000-2002

Until recently, the story of this typeface ended with mediocre digital versions that did not get at the root of its inspiration. We selected as the most successful models of the digitalization of this typeface its roman and italics in the size of about today's 14 points, which Baskerville used for the printing, among other things, of his folio Bible in 1763, and Vergil's works in Latin in 1757. These were large-size, stately prints on paper smoothed out by hot copper calendar rollers. His engraver, John Handy, was given the task to make the typeface different from the then-fashionable Caslon, which was a surprise for a certain part of typophiles of the period. Baskerville's production in this way perhaps prepared the public also for some ideas of Bodoni and Didot, which is why nowadays everybody calls it a "transitory" phenomenon. A detailed examination of Baskerville's heritage, however, remains a task for historians. An analytical transcription is also needed to remove any potential shortcomings of the source of inspiration, and must not take over mechanically all details of the design. Even creators of genius, however, make mistakes sometimes, and therefore, in spite of the fact that we officially speak about "a transcription," what was involved in the case of all complementary designs was fairly fundamental reworking. Our aim was not so much to be reverently faithful to the original, as to preserve the spirit of the typeface and to breathe new life into it. Baskerville is a typeface with the character of a gentleman, a typeface of sober elegance and clear design. Its nature is remote from drastic contrasts, as we know them from the Continental typography of the Late Baroque period. A project of a typeface family that includes twenty designs cannot rely on a single pair of tired eyes; that is why we are again grateful to Otakar Karlas for his valuable advice, especially when putting the finishing touches to the typeface.

Storm Type Foundry

285

Walbaum Text OT

František Štorm
2002

Regular

OpenType font with full range
of features.

ABCDEFGHIJKLMNOPQRSTUVWXYZ
abcdefghijklmnopqrsßtuvwxyzfiflfkstctſſtfüfjsp
ABCDEFGHIJKLMNOPQRSTUVWXYZ0123456789
+@!?€£&,0123456789→0123456789

ABCDEFGHIJKLMNOPQRSTUVWXYZ
abcdefghijklmnopqrsßtuvwxyzfiflfkstctſſtfüfjsp
ABCDEFGHIJKLMNOPQRSTUVWXYZ0123456789
+@!?€£&,0123456789→0123456789

ABCDEFGHIJKLMNOPQRSTUVWXYZ
abcdefghijklmnopqrsßtuvwxyzfiflfkstctſtfüsp
ABCDEFGHIJKLMNOPQRSTUVWXYZ0123456789
+@!?€£&,0123456789→0123456789

ABCDEFGHIJKLMNOPQRSTUVWXYZ
abcdefghijklmnopqrsßtuvwxyzfiflfkstctſtfüsp
ABCDEFGHIJKLMNOPQRSTUVWXYZ0123456789
+@!?€£&,0123456789→0123456789

J.E.W. MINOR
irregularities
& the soft
details

Walbaum Text OT

František Štorm
2002

Just like the teacher of calligraphy, designer of gravestones, and painter-craftsman of Baskerville, Justus Erich Walbaum also came to typography from another—this time much more distant—profession. He was born in 1768 as a parson's son, and was apprenticed to a confectioner in his young days. From engraving confectioner's molds, it was only a short step to cutting type punches and typefounder's tools. Renaissance graphic artists, to be sure, were fellows of a different caliber—they started their careers by engraving weapons! Walbaum's name, however, does not appear in any imprint lines, because he probably never printed books himself. The same typefaces were used by other printers of that period, for example, Unger or Prillwitz. Maybe the last fine Walbaum typeface was used to print Berthold's Specimen Book of 1923, which also includes a specimen text in the size of 12 points, on which our transcription draws.

In contradistinction to the strictly rational Didot or the elegant Bodoni, Walbaum, at first sight, does not possess any features that might lead to a brief attribute. In any case, however, it is an outstanding work, a far cry from chocolate wafer cakes or cream horns. The expression of the typeface is robust, as if it had been seasoned with the spicy smell of the dung of Saxon cows somewhere near Weimar, where the author had his type foundry in the years 1803-39. Its typical features are: a firm skeleton of the design of the individual letters, in some cases supported by a square scheme; daring triangular serifs on S, s, C, and G; K, and R standing, like grumblers, with one foot placed forward; and rather conservative italics. An especially unsuccessful solution for its time was the design of the italic figures. Nevertheless, they were blindly taken over by the Berthold Company in 1919, together with the other shortcomings.

Storm Type Foundry

Walbaum Text OT 36 pt. (above) and 10pt. (bottom)

UNSERE TEXT-WALBAUM HAT EINE KLASSIZISTISCH ANGEMESSENE MINUSKELMITTELHÖHE, IN Bezug auf die Barockexperimente mit Proportionen. Die untere Schriftlinie ist relativ lang, die obere korrespondiert mit den Versalien. *Bei den Kursiven sind die Minuskeltypen um einen geringen Grad mehr als die Versalien geneigt: dies ist eine typische Erscheinung der meisten historischen Schriften, und wir haben uns daran im Laufe der Hunderte von Jahren bereits gewöhnt.* **Feine Unregelmäßigkeiten und weiche Details** sind für angenehmes Lesen behalten. Die schon erwähnten *Kursivenziffern* sind zur Erhaltung des zeitgemäßen Charakters der Schriftfamilie völlig neu bearbeitet. Alle Schriftbilder sind für kleine Schriftkegel unter 12 Punkte ausbalanciert. Diese wuchtige leibartige Schrift kann für alle Arten der schöngeistigen Literatur angewendet werden, insbesondere für deutsche Novellen der Romantik aus dem ländlichen Milieu.

Underneath

THE CONTEMPORARY-LO.OKING DESIGN OF BIBLON,

one can conjecture

a Baroque play,

with the shifting of shadows,

intentional overstatement,

or absolute simplification of forms.

Regular	ABDEGJKLMQRSTUWXYZabcdefghjklnopqrstuwxyz&1234567890
Italic	*ABDEGJKLMQRSTUWXYZabcdefghjklnopqrstuwxyz&1234567890*
Bold	**ABDEGJKLMQRSTUWXYZabcdefghjklnopqrstuwxyz&1234567890**
Bold Italic	***ABDEGJKLMQRSTUWXYZabcdefghjklnopqrstuwxyz&1234567890***
Small Caps	ABDEGJKLMQRSTUWXYZABCDEFGHJKLNOPQRSTUWXYZ&1234567890
Small Caps Bold	**ABDEGJKLMQRSTUWXABCDEFGHJKLNOPQRSTUWXYZ&1234567890**
Swash Italic	*ABDEGJKLMQRSTUWXYZabcdefghjklnopqrstuwxyz&1234567890*
Swash Italic Bold	***ABDEGJKLMQRSTUWXYZabcdefghjklnopqrstuwxyz&1234567890***

mail@stormtype.com

another *variation*

on the RENAISSANCE-BAROQUE ROMAN FACE,
it extends the seleċtion
of text typefaces.

Serapion **Italics** *are inspired
partly by the Renaissance
Cancelleresca.*

ABDEGJKLMQRSTUWYabcdefghjklnopqrstuwxyz&1234567890	Regular
ABDEGJKLMQRSTUWXYZabcdefghijklmnopqrstuwxyz&1234567890	Italic
ABDEGJKLMQRSTUabcdefghjklnopqrstuwxyz&1234567890	Bold
ABDEGKLMQRSTUWXYabcdefghjklmnopqrstuwxyz&1234567890	Bold Italic
ABDEGKLMQRSTUABCDEFGHJKLNOPQRSTUWXYZ&1234567890	Small Caps
ABDEGKLMQRSTUWABCDEFGHJKLNOPQRSTUWXYZ&1234567890	Small Caps Bold
ABDEGJKLMQRABCDEFGHJKLNOPQRSTUWXYZ&1234567890	Swash Italic
ABDEGJKLMQRTABCDEFGHJKLNOPQRSTUWXYZ&1234567890	Swash Italic Bold

František Štorm
2001

The idea of a brand-new grotesk is certainly rather foolish–there are already lots of these typefaces in the world, and, quite simply, nothing is more beautiful than the original Gill. The sans serif chapter of typography is now closed by hundreds of technically perfect imitations of Syntax and Frutiger, which are, however, for the most part based on the cool DIN aesthetics. The only change, when looking for inspiration, is to go very far...

A grotesk does not afford such a variety as a serif typeface; it is dull and can soon tire the eye. This is why books are not set in sans serif faces. A grotesk, however, is always welcome for expressing different degrees of emphasis, for headings, marginal notes, captions, registers, and so on; in short, for any service accompaniment of a book, including its titlings. We also often come across a text in which we want to distinguish the individual speakers or writing persons by the use of different typefaces. The condition is that such grotesk should blend in perfectly with the proportions, color, and above all, with the expression of the basic serif typeface. In the area of nonfiction typography, what we appreciate in sans serif typefaces is that they are clamorous in inscriptions and economic in the setting. John Sans is to be a modest servant and at the same time an original loudspeaker; it wishes to inhabit libraries of educated persons and to shout from billboards.

A year ago, we completed the transcription of the typefaces of John Baskerville, whose heritage still stands out vividly in our memory. Baskerville cleverly incorporated certain constructional elements in the design of the individual letters of his typeface. These elements include, above all, the alternation of soft and sharp stroke endings. The frequency of these endings in the text and their rhythm produce a balanced impression. The anchoring of the letters on the surface varies, and they do not look monotonous when they are read. We attempted

ABDEGJKMQRSTUWXYZabcdefghjknoprstuwxyz&123567890
ABDEGJKMQRSTUWXYZabcdefghjknoprstuwxyz&123567890
ABDEGJKMQRSTabcdefghijklmnopqrstuvwxyz&1234567890
ABDEGJKMQRSTabcdefghijklmnopqrstuvwxyz&1234567890

ABDEGJKMQRSTUWXYZabcdefghjknoprstuwxyz&123567890
ABDEGJKMQRSTUWXYZabcdefghjknoprstuwxyz&123567890
ABDEGJKMQRSTabcdefghijklmnopqrstuvwxyz&1234567890
ABDEGJKMQRSTabcdefghijklmnopqrstuvwxyz&1234567890

ABDEGJKMQRSTUWXYZabcdefghjknoprstuwxyz&123567890
ABDEGJKMQRSTUWXYZabcdefghjknoprstuwxyz&123567890
ABDEGJKMQRSTabcdefghijklmnopqrstuvwxyz&1234567890
ABDEGJKMQRSTabcdefghijklmnopqrstuvwxyz&1234567890

ABDEGJKMQRSTUWXYZabcdefghjknoprstuwxyz&123567890
ABDEGJKMQRSTUWXYZabcdefghjknoprstuwxyz&123567890
ABDEGJKMQRSTabcdefghijklmnopqrstuvwxyz&1234567890
ABDEGJKMQRSTabcdefghijklmnopqrstuvwxyz&1234567890

Can John survive without SERIFS?

mail@stormtype.com

ABDEGJKMQRSTUWXYZabcdefghjknoprstuwxyz&123567890
ABDEGJKMQRSTUWXYZabcdefghjknoprstuwxyz&123567890
ABDEGJKMQRSTUWXYZabcdefghjknoprstuwxyz&123567890
ABDEGJKMQRSTUWXYZabcdefghjknoprstuwxyz&123567890

ABDEGJKMQRSTUWXYZabcdefghjknoprstuwxyz&123567890
ABDEGJKMQRSTUWXYZabcdefghjknoprstuwxyz&123567890
ABDEGJKMQRSTUWXYZabcdefghjknoprstuwxyz&123567890
ABDEGJKMQRSTUWXYZabcdefghjknoprstuwxyz&123567890

ABDEGJKMQRSTUWXYZabcdefghjknoprstuwxyz&123567890
ABDEGJKMQRSTUWXYZabcdefghjknoprstuwxyz&123567890
ABDEGJKMQRSTABCDEFGHIJKLMNOPQRSTUVWXYZ&1234567890
ABDEGJKMQRSTABCDEFGHIJKLMNOPQRSTUVWXYZ&1234567890

ABDEGJKMQRSTUWXYZabcdefghjknoprstuwxyz&123567890
ABDEGJKMQRSTUWXYZabcdefghjknoprstuwxyz&123567890
ABDEGJKMQRSTABCDEFGHIJKLMNOPQRSTUVWXYZ&1234567890
ABDEGJKMQRSTABCDEFGHIJKLMNOPQRSTUVWXYZ&1234567890

John Sans

František Štorm
2003

to use these tricks also in the creation a sans serif typeface. Except that, if we wished to create a genuine "Baroque grotesk," all the decorativeness of the original would have to be repeated, which would result in a parody. On the contrary, to achieve a mere contrast with the soft Baskerville, it is sufficient to choose any other hard grotesk and not take a great deal of time designing a new one. Between these two extremes, we chose a path starting with the construction of an almost monolinear skeleton, to which the elements of Baskerville were carefully attached. After many tests of the text, however, some of the flourishes had to be removed again. Anything that is superfluous or ornamental is against the substance of a grotesk typeface. The monolinear character can be impinged upon in those places where any consistency would become a burden. The fine shading and softening is for the benefit of both legibility and aesthetics. The more marked incisions of all crotches are a characteristic feature of this type, especially in the bold design. The color of the Text, Medium, and Bold designs is commensurate with their serif counterparts. The White and X-Black designs already exceed the framework of book graphics, and are suitable for use in advertisements and magazines.

Also, the inclusion of nonaligning figures in the basic designs and aligning figures in the small caps serves the purpose of harmonization of the sans serif families with the serif types. nonaligning figures link up better with lowercase letters in the text.

If John Sans looks like many other modern typefaces, it is just as well. It certainly is not to the detriment of a Latin typeface as a means of communication, if different typographers in different places of the world arrive in different ways at a similar result.

Storm Type Foundry

Baskerville Ten OT

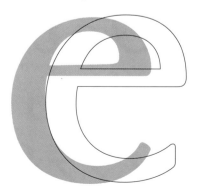

John Sans

Teuton

František Štorm
2002

Inspired by a gravestone lettering, suitable for communication systems, posters, and technical literature.

Kaufmann *nicht* *unter* 25 Jahre alt, mit Kenntnissen der *doppelten* *Buchführung* und Korrespondenz, für Metallwarenfabrik zum *Eintritt per 15.* *Januar 1906 gesucht.* Bewerbungen mit Gehaltsforderungen unter K 25 an die Expedition. Teuton hat 14 Schriftschnitte.

Plagwitz

František Štorm
2000

Plagwitz is a part of Leipzig, where the ATypI Congress in 2000 was held.

Zwei Herzen in Dreivierteltakt aus Plagwitz zusammen gebracht ABCFGRST@☞✠&0123456789ßfff

Monarchia

František Štorm
1996

Modeled freely after Rudolf Koch's Frühling.

Eine Schwalbe macht kein Sommer (oder Frühling). ABCDabcd@&123456789ffi

mail@stormtype.com

Juvenis

Josef Týfa and František Štorm
2002

Under the name Juvenis, Josef Tyfa
published an original concept of a
sans serif typeface in the past half-
century. It had a large x-height,
space-saving proportions, and daring
semi-serifs. Later, in 2001, Tyfa came
with numerous new sketches and
refreshing variations. In summer
2002, we made extra bold versions,
interpolated weights, and new italics.
The result is a contemporary typeface with good legibility. Juvenis def-
initely exceeds its original intention
as type for children's literature, and
it can be used for longer texts and
periodicals.

AaBbCcDdEeFfGgHhIiJ
jKkLlMmNnOoPpQqRr
SsTtUuVvWwXxYyZzf
iflfk!?€£&0123456789

Light EFGHIJKLMPQRSTUabcdefghjklnopqrstuwxyz&1234567890
ABCDEFGHIJKLMPQRSTUabcdefghjklnopqrstuwxyz&1234567890
ABCDEFGJKLMPQRSTabcdefghjklnopqrstuwxyz&1234567890
ABCDEFGJKLMPQRSTabcdefghjklnopqrstuwxyz&1234567890
Book EFGHIJKLMPQRSTUabcdefghjklnopqrstuwxyz&1234567890
ABCDEFGHIJKLMPQRSTUabcdefghjklnopqrstuwxyz&1234567890
ABCDEFGJKLMPQRSabcdefghjklnopqrstuwxyz&1234567890
ABCDEFGJKLMPQRSabcdefghjklnopqrstuwxyz&1234567890
Text EFGJKLMPQRSTUabcdefghjklnopqrstuwxyz&1234567890
ABCDEFGJKLMPQRSTabcdefghjklnopqrstuwxyz&1234567890
ABCDEFGJKLMPQabcdefghjklnopqrstuwxyz&1234567890
ABCDEFGJKLMPQabcdefghjklopqrstuwxyz&1234567890
Medium GJKLMPQRSabcdefghjklnopqrstuwxyz&1234567890
ABCDEFGJKLMPQRSabcdefghjklnopqrstuwxyz&1234567890
ABCDEFGJKLMPabcdefghjklopqrstuwxyz&1234567890
ABCDEFGJKLQabcdefghjklnopqrstuwxyz&1234567890

Storm Type Foundry

terminaldesign

Terminal Design, Inc., is an independent type design and lettering studio, creating original and custom work for advertising, editorial, corporate, publishing and government clients. Our work ranges from complex road guide sign type systems and custom font development to magazine logo and book jacket lettering. We are particularly interested in developing large, legible type families that can be applied over a broad range of applications. Our library of retail fonts is growing, and licenses are available for any installation.

Terminal Design, Inc.
125 Congress Street Brooklyn, NY 11201
V: 718-246-7069 • F: 718-246-7085
www.terminaldesign.com • type@terminaldesign.com

Started by James Montalbano in 1990, Terminal Design, Inc., is currently located on the terminal moraine in Brooklyn, NY. Montalbano's professional career began as a public school graphic arts teacher, trying to get his young students interested in letterpress, offset and silk screen printing. When told he would also have to teach wood shop, he went off to graduate school and taught graphic arts to college students along the way. Seeing no real difference between teaching 8th grade or college undergraduates, he returned to NYC and found work in the wild world of type shops and magazine art departments. It was during this time that he took a lettering course with Ed Benguiat, which changed everything. Montalbano's career continued as a magazine art director, then as the design director responsible for 20 trade magazines (whose subject matter no one should be required to remember). He tried his hand at designing pharmaceutical packaging, but that only made him ill. When his nausea subsided, he started Terminal Design, Inc., and hasn't been sick since.

Featured text:
A Descent into the Maelstrom
by Edgar Allan Poe

We had now reached the summit of the loftiest crag. For some minutes the old man seemed too much exhausted to speak. "Not long ago," said he at length, "and I could have guided you on this route as well as the youngest of my sons; but, about three years past,

Giacomo Light

James Montalbano
2002

OpenType: Contains Tabular & Oldstyle Figures, Fractions, Superior & Inferior Figures, and Ligatures.

There happened to me an event such as never happened before to mortal man, or at least such as no man ever survived to tell of, and the six hours of deadly terror which I then endured have broken me up body and soul. You suppose me a very old man,

Giacomo Light Italic

James Montalbano
2002

OpenType: Contains Tabular & Oldstyle Figures, Fractions, Superior & Inferior Figures, and Ligatures.

But I am not. It took less than a single day to change these hairs from a jetty black to white, to weaken my limbs, and to unstring my nerves, so that I tremble at the least exertion, and am frightened at a shadow. Do you know I can scarcely look over this little cliff

Giacomo Regular

James Montalbano
2002

OpenType: Contains Tabular & Oldstyle Figures, Fractions, Superior & Inferior Figures, and Ligatures.

Without getting giddy?" The "little cliff," upon whose edge he had so carelessly thrown himself down to rest that the weightier portion of his body hung over it, while he was only kept from falling by the tenure of his elbow on its extreme and slippery edge, this

Giacomo Regular Italic

James Montalbano
2002

OpenType: Contains Tabular & Oldstyle Figures, Fractions, Superior & Inferior Figures, and Ligatures.

Terminal Design

Giacomo Medium

James Montalbano
2002

OpenType: Contains Tabular &
Oldstyle Figures, Fractions, Superior &
Inferior Figures, and Ligatures.

"Little cliff" arose, a sheer unobstructed precipice of black shining rock, some fifteen or sixteen hundred feet from the world of crags beneath us. Nothing would have tempted me to be within half a dozen yards of its brink. In truth so deeply was I

Giacomo Medium Italic

James Montalbano
2002

OpenType: Contains Tabular &
Oldstyle Figures, Fractions, Superior &
Inferior Figures, and Ligatures.

Excited by the perilous position of my companion, that I fell at full length upon the ground, clung to the shrubs around me, and dared not even glance upward at the sky, while I struggled in vain to divest myself of the idea that the very foundations

GiacomoBold

James Montalbano
2002

OpenType: Contains Tabular &
Oldstyle Figures, Fractions, Superior &
Inferior Figures, and Ligatures.

Of the mountain were in danger from the fury of the winds. It was long before I could reason myself into sufficient courage to sit up and look out into the distance. "You must get over these fancies," said the guide, "for I have brought you

Giacomo Bold Italic

James Montalbano
2002

OpenType: Contains Tabular &
Oldstyle Figures, Fractions, Superior &
Inferior Figures, and Ligatures.

Here that you might have the best possible view of the scene of that event I mentioned, and to tell you the whole story with the spot just under your eye. We are now," he continued, in that particularizing manner which distinguish him,

"We are now close upon the Norwegian coast, in the sixty-eighth degree of latitude, in the great province of Nordland, and in the dreary district of Lofoden. The mountain upon whose top we sit is Helseggen, the Cloudy. Now raise

Giacomo Heavy

James Montalbano
2002

OpenType: Contains Tabular & Oldstyle Figures, Fractions, Superior & Inferior Figures, and Ligatures.

Yourself up a little higher, hold on to the grass if you feel giddy so, and look out, beyond the belt of vapor beneath us, into the sea." I looked dizzily, and beheld a wide expanse of ocean, whose waters wore so inky a hue as to bring at

Giacomo Heavy Italic

James Montalbano
2002

OpenType: Contains Tabular & Oldstyle Figures, Fractions, Superior & Inferior Figures, and Ligatures.

Once to my mind the Nubian Geographer's account of the Mare Tenebrarum. A panorama more deplorably desolate no human imagination can conceive. To the right and left, as far as the eye could reach, there lay

Giacomo Black

James Montalbano
2002

OpenType: Contains Tabular & Oldstyle Figures, Fractions, Superior & Inferior Figures, and Ligatures.

Out stretched, like ramparts of the world, lines horridly black and beetling cliff, whose character of gloom was but the more forcibly illustrated by the surf which reared high up against it, its white and ghastly

Giacomo Black Italic

James Montalbano
2002

OpenType: Contains Tabular & Oldstyle Figures, Fractions, Superior & Inferior Figures, and Ligatures.

Terminal Design

Rawlinson Regular

James Montalbano
2002

OpenType: Contains Tabular,
Proportional & Oldstyle Figures,
Fractions, Superior & Inferior Figures,
and Ligatures.

Crest, howling and shrieking forever. Just opposite the promontory upon whose apex we were placed, and at a distance of some five or six miles out at sea, there was visible a small, bleak-looking island; or, more properly, its position was discernible

Rawlinson Italic

James Montalbano
2002

OpenType: Contains Tabular,
Proportional & Oldstyle Figures,
Fractions, Superior & Inferior Figures,
and Ligatures.

Through the wilderness of surge in which it was enveloped. About two miles nearer the land, arose another of small size, hideously craggy and barren, and encompassed at various intervals by a cluster of dark rocks. The appearance of the ocean, in the space

Rawlinson Medium

James Montalbano
2002

OpenType: Contains Tabular,
Proportional & Oldstyle Figures,
Fractions, Superior & Inferior Figures,
and Ligatures.

Between the more distant island and the shore, had something very unusual about it. Although, at the time, so strong a gale was blowing landward that a brig in the remote offing lay to under a double reefed trysail, and constantly plunged her

Rawlinson Med Italic

James Montalbano
2002

OpenType: Contains Tabular,
Proportional & Oldstyle Figures,
Fractions, Superior & Inferior Figures,
and Ligatures.

Whole hull out of sight, still there was here nothing like a regular swell, but only a short, quick, angry cross dashing of water in every direction, as well in the teeth of the wind as otherwise. Of foam there was little except in the immediate vicinity of the

718-246-7069

Rocks. "The island in the distance," resumed the old man, "is called by the Norwegians Vurrgh. The one midway is Moskoe. That a mile to the northward is Ambaaren. Yonder are Islesen, Hotholm, Keildhelm, Suarven, and Buckholm.

Rawlinson Bold

James Montalbano
2002

OpenType: Contains Tabular, Proportional & Oldstyle Figures, Fractions, Superior & Inferior Figures, and Ligatures.

Further off, between Moskoe and Vurrgh, are Otterholm, Flimen, Sandflesen, and Stockholm. These are the true names of the places, but why it has been thought necessary to name them at all, is more than either you or I can understand.

Rawlinson Bold Italic

James Montalbano
2002

OpenType: Contains Tabular, Proportional & Oldstyle Figures, Fractions, Superior & Inferior Figures, and Ligatures.

Do you hear anything? Do you see any change in the water?" We had now been about ten minutes upon the top of Helseggen, to which we had ascended from the interior of Lofoden, so that we had caught no glimpse of the sea until it had

Rawlinson Heavy

James Montalbano
2002

OpenType: Contains Tabular, Proportional & Oldstyle Figures, Fractions, Superior & Inferior Figures, and Ligatures.

Burst upon us from the summit. As the old man spoke, I became aware of a loud and gradually increasing sound, like the moaning of a vast herd of buffaloes upon an American prairie; and at the same moment I perceived that what

Rawlinson Heavy Italic

James Montalbano
2002

OpenType: Contains Tabular, Proportional & Oldstyle Figures, Fractions, Superior & Inferior Figures, and Ligatures.

Terminal Design

Rawlinson Cn Regular

James Montalbano
2002

OpenType: Contains Tabular,
Proportional & Oldstyle Figures,
Fractions, Superior & Inferior
Figures, and Ligatures.

Seamen termed the chopping character of the ocean beneath us, was rapidly changing into a current which set to the eastward. Even while I gazed, this current acquired a monstrous velocity. Each moment added to its speed, to its head long impetuosity. In five minutes the whole sea, as far

Rawlinson Cn Italic

James Montalbano
2002

OpenType: Contains Tabular,
Proportional & Oldstyle Figures,
Fractions, Superior & Inferior
Figures, and Ligatures.

As Vurrgh, was lashed into ungovernable fury, but it was between Moskoe and the coast that the main uproar held its sway. Here the vast bed of the waters, seamed and scarred into a thousand conflicting channels, burst suddenly into phrensied convulsion, heaving, boiling, hissing, gyrating in gigantic and

Rawlinson Cn Medium

James Montalbano
2002

OpenType: Contains Tabular,
Proportional & Oldstyle Figures,
Fractions, Superior & Inferior Figures,
and Ligatures.

Innumerable vortices, and all whirling and plunging on to the eastward with a rapidity which water never elsewhere assumes, except in precipitous descents. In a few minutes more, there came over the scene another radical alteration. The general surface grew somewhat more smooth,

Rawlinson Cn Med Italic

James Montalbano
2002

OpenType: Contains Tabular,
Proportional & Oldstyle Figures,
Fractions, Superior & Inferior
Figures, and Ligatures.

And the whirlpools, one by one, disappeared, while prodigious streaks of foam became apparent where none had been seen before. These streaks, at length, spread out to a great distance, and entering into combination, took unto themselves the gyratory motion of the subsided vortices,

718-246-7069

And seemed to form the germ of another more vast. Suddenly, very suddenly, this assumed a distinct and definite existence, in a circle of more than a mile in diameter. The edge of the whirl was represented by a broad belt of gleaming spray; but no particle of this slipped into the

Rawlinson Cn Bold

James Montalbano
2002

OpenType: Contains Tabular, Proportional & Oldstyle Figures, Fractions, Superior & Inferior Figures, and Ligatures.

Mouth of the terrific funnel, whose interior, as far as the eye could fathom it, was a smooth, shining, and jet-black wall of water, inclined to the horizon at an angle of some forty-five degrees, speeding dizzily round and round with a swaying and sweltering motion, and sending forth to

Rawlinson Cn Bold Italic

James Montalbano
2002

OpenType: Contains Tabular, Proportional & Oldstyle Figures, Fractions, Superior & Inferior Figures, and Ligatures.

The winds an appalling voice, half shriek, half roar, such as not even the mighty cataract of Niagara ever lifts up in its agony to Heaven. The mountain trembled to its very base, and the rock rocked. I threw myself upon my face, and clung to the scant herbage in

Rawlinson Cn Heavy

James Montalbano
2002

OpenType: Contains Tabular, Proportional & Oldstyle Figures, Fractions, Superior & Inferior Figures, and Ligatures.

An excess of nervous agitation. "This," said I at length, to the old man, "this can be nothing else than the great whirlpool of the Maelstrom. So it is sometimes termed," said he. "We Norwegians call it the Moskoe-strom, from the island of Moskoe in the Midway."

Rawlinson Cn Hvy Italic

James Montalbano
2002

OpenType: Contains Tabular, Proportional & Oldstyle Figures, Fractions, Superior & Inferior Figures, and Ligatures.

Terminal Design

ClearviewOne XThin

*James Montalbano,
Donald Meeker, Chris O'Hara*
1999

Tabular, Proportional
& Oldstyle Figures.

The ordinary account of this vortex had by no means prepared me for what I saw. That of Jonas Ramus, which is perhaps the most circumstantial of any, cannot impart the faintest conception either of the magnificence, or of the

ClearviewOne Thin

*James Montalbano,
Donald Meeker, Chris O'Hara*
1997

Tabular, Proportional
& Oldstyle Figures.

Horror of the scene or of the wild bewildering sense of the novel which confounds the beholder. I am not sure from what point of view the writer in question surveyed it, nor at what time; but it could neither have been

ClearviewOne Light

*James Montalbano,
Donald Meeker, Chris O'Hara*
1997

Tabular, Proportional
& Oldstyle Figures.

From the summit of Helseggen, nor during a storm. There are some passages of his description, nevertheless, which may be quoted for their details, although their effect is exceedingly feeble in conveying

ClearviewOne Book

*James Montalbano,
Donald Meeker, Chris O'Hara*
1997

Tabular, Proportional
& Oldstyle Figures.

An impression of the spectacle. "Between Lofoden and Moskoe," he says, "the depth of the water is between thirty-six and forty fathoms; but on the other side, toward Ver (Vurrgh) this depth

ClearviewOne Medium

*James Montalbano,
Donald Meeker, Chris O'Hara*
1997

Tabular, Proportional
& Oldstyle Figures.

Decreases so as not to afford a convenient passage for a vessel, without the risk of splitting on the rocks, which happens even in the calmest weather. When it is flood, the stream runs up the

ClearviewOne Bold

*James Montalbano,
Donald Meeker, Chris O'Hara*
1997

Tabular, Proportional
& Oldstyle Figures.

Country between Lofoden and Moskoe with boisterous rapidity; but the roar of its impetuous ebb to the sea is scarce equalled by the loudest and most dreadful cataracts; the

ClearviewOne Heavy

*James Montalbano,
Donald Meeker, Chris O'Hara*
1997

Tabular, Proportional
& Oldstyle Figures.

Noise being heard several leagues off, and the vortices or pits are of such an extent and depth, that if a ship comes within its attraction, it is inevitably absorbed and carried

ClearviewOne Black

*James Montalbano,
Donald Meeker, Chris O'Hara*
1999

Tabular, Proportional
& Oldstyle Figures.

Down to the bottom, and there beat to pieces against the rocks; and when the water relaxes, the fragments there of are thrown up again. But these intervals of

Tranquillity are only at the turn of the ebb and flood, and in calm weather, and last but a quarter of an hour, its violence gradually returning. When the stream is most boisterous, and its fury heightened by a storm, it is dangerous

ClearviewOne XThin Ital

James Montalbano, Donald Meeker, Chris O'Hara
1999

Tabular, Proportional & Oldstyle Figures.

To come within a Norway mile of it. Boats, yachts, and ships have been carried away by not guarding against it before they were carried within its reach. It likewise happens frequently, that whales come too near the

ClearviewOne Thin Ital

James Montalbano, Donald Meeker, Chris O'Hara
1997

Tabular, Proportional & Oldstyle Figures.

Stream, and are overpowered by its violence; and then it is impossible to describe their howlings and bellowings in their fruitless struggles to disengage themselves. A bear once, attempting to swim from Lofoden

ClearviewOne Light Ital

James Montalbano, Donald Meeker, Chris O'Hara
1997

Tabular, Proportional & Oldstyle Figures.

To Moskoe, was caught by the stream and borne down, while he roared terribly, so as to be heard on shore. Large stocks of firs and pine trees, after being absorbed by the current, rise again broken

ClearviewOne Book Ital

James Montalbano, Donald Meeker, Chris O'Hara
1997

Tabular, Proportional & Oldstyle Figures.

And torn to such a degree as if bristles grew upon them. This plainly shows the bottom to consist of craggy rocks, among which they are whirled to and fro. This stream is regulated by

ClearviewOne Med Ital

James Montalbano, Donald Meeker, Chris O'Hara
1997

Tabular, Proportional & Oldstyle Figures.

The flux and reflux the sea it being constantly high and low water every six hours. In the year 1645, early in the morning of Sexagesima Sunday, it raged with such noise and impetuosity

ClearviewOne Bold Ital

James Montalbano, Donald Meeker, Chris O'Hara
1997

Tabular, Proportional & Oldstyle Figures.

That the very stones of the houses on the coast fell to the ground." In regard to the depth of the water, I could not see how this could have been ascertained at all in the

ClearviewOne Hvy Ital

James Montalbano, Donald Meeker, Chris O'Hara
1997

Tabular, Proportional & Oldstyle Figures.

Immediate vicinity of the vortex. The "forty fathoms" must have reference only to portions of the channel close upon the shore either of Moskoe or Lofoden. The depth in

ClearviewOne Black Ital

James Montalbano, Donald Meeker, Chris O'Hara
1999

Tabular, Proportional & Oldstyle Figures.

Terminal Design

The centre of the Moskoe-strom must be unmeasurably greater; and no better proof of this fact is necessary than can be obtained from even the sidelong glance into the abyss of the whirl which may be had from the highest crag of Helseggen. Looking

Down from this pinnacle upon the howling Phlegethon below, I could not help smiling at the simplicity with which the honest Jonas Ramus records, as a matter difficult of belief, the anecdotes of the whales and the bears, for it appeared to me,

In fact, a self-evident thing, that the largest ships of the line in existence, coming within the influence of that deadly attraction, could resist it as a feather the hurricane, and must disappear bodily and at once. The attempts to account for

The phenomenon, some of which I remember, seemed to me sufficiently plausible in perusal, now wore a very different and unsatisfactory aspect. The idea generally received is that this, as well as three smaller vortices

Among the Ferroe Islands, "have no other cause than the collision of waves rising and falling, at flux and reflux, against a ridge of rocks and shelves, which confines the water so that it precipitates itself like

A cataract; and thus the higher the flood rises, the deeper must the fall be, and the natural result of all is a whirlpool or vortex, the prodigious suction of which is sufficiently known by lesser

Experiments." These are the words in the Encyclopaedia Britannica. Kircher and others imagine that in the centre of the channel of the maelstrom is an abyss penetrating the globe, and

Issuing in some very remote part the Gulf of Bothnia being somewhat decidedly named in one instance. This opinion, idle in itself, was the one to which, as I gazed, my imagina-

718-246-7069

Most readily assented; and, mentioning it to the guide, I was rather surprised to hear him say that, although it was the view almost universally entertained of the subject by the Norwegians, it nevertheless was not his own. As to the former notion he confessed his

ClearviewOne XThn Cn It

James Montalbano,
Donald Meeker, Chris O'Hara
1999

Tabular & Proportional Figures.

Inability to comprehend it; and here I agreed with him for, however conclusive on paper, it becomes altogether unintelligible, and even absurd, amid the thunder of the abyss. "You have had a good look at the whirl now," said the old man, "and if

ClearviewOne Thin Cn It

James Montalbano,
Donald Meeker, Chris O'Hara
1997

Tabular & Proportional Figures.

You will creep round this crag, so as to get in its lee, and deaden the roar of the water, I will tell you a story that will convince you I ought to know something of the Moskoe-strom." I placed myself as desired, and he proceeded. "Myself and

ClearviewOne Lt Cn It

James Montalbano,
Donald Meeker, Chris O'Hara
1997

Tabular & Proportional Figures.

My two brothers once owned a schooner, rigged smack of about seventy tons burthen, with which we were in the habit of fishing among the islands beyond Moskoe, nearly to Vurrgh. In all violent eddies at sea there is good

ClearviewOne Book Cn It

James Montalbano,
Donald Meeker, Chris O'Hara
1997

Tabular & Proportional Figures.

Fishing, at proper opportunities, if one has only the courage to attempt it; but among the whole of the Lofoden coastmen, we three were the only ones who made a regular business of going out to the

ClearviewOne Med Cn It

James Montalbano,
Donald Meeker, Chris O'Hara
1997

Tabular & Proportional Figures.

Islands, as I tell you. The usual grounds are a great way lower down to the southward. There fish can be got at all hours, without much risk, and therefore these places are preferred. The choice spots

ClearviewOne Bold Cn It

James Montalbano,
Donald Meeker, Chris O'Hara
1997

Tabular & Proportional Figures.

Over here among the rocks, however, not only yield the finest variety, but in far greater abundance; so that we often got in a single day, what the more timid of the craft could not scrape

ClearviewOne Hvy Cn It

James Montalbano,
Donald Meeker, Chris O'Hara
1997

Tabular & Proportional Figures.

Together in a week. In fact, we made it a matter of desperate speculation, the risk of life standing instead of labor, and courage answering for capital. "We kept the smack in a cove

ClearviewOne Blk Cn It

James Montalbano,
Donald Meeker, Chris O'Hara
1999

Tabular & Proportional Figures.

Terminal Design

Underware

is a (typo)graphic designstudio focusing on designing and producing typefaces. These are published for retail sale or are specially tailor-made. The studios are based in Den Haag, Amsterdam and Helsinki.

Dolly™ and Sauna™ are trademarks of Underware.

The stories which are shown here can be more extensively read in the original type specimens. The *Dolly* and *Sauna* fonts are also fully shown in a more extensive way in these two type specimens.

Dolly, a book typeface with flourishes contains many different stories about the dog Dolly, written by many different people like Markus Brilling, Somi Kim, Michael Rock, Ewan Lentjes, Anne Knopf, Guy Tavares, Edwin Smet, Eike Menijn, Wilbert Leering & Lennart Wienecke. The preface is written by Erik Spiekermann. The book is designed by Faydherbe/de Vringer (Wout de Vringer).

Read naked is a sauna proof book which doesn't only contain stories about sauna's, but can also be read inside the sauna. Even better, some stories only become visible inside the sauna at 80 degrees Celsius or higher. The preface is written by Henrik Birkvig. The book is designed by Piet Schreuders in cooperation with Underware.

The book *Dolly, a book typeface with flourishes* (ISBN 90-76984-01-8) and the book *Read naked* (ISBN 90-76984-03-4) are available in specialized bookshops.

Underware
Schouwburgstraat 2
2511 VA Den Haag
the Netherlands

T +31-(0)70 42 78 117
F +31 (0)70 42 78 116
E info@underware.nl
www.underware.nl

Dolly

a book typeface
with flourishes

Underware
2001

Dolly Roman is neutral and useful for long texts. It has old-style figures.

Dolly Italic is narrower and lighter in color than the roman, and so it can be used to emphasize words within roman text.

Dolly Bold is also useful for emphasizing works within roman text. It also works well as a display type.

Dolly Small Caps are intended for setting whole words or strings of characters, whereas roman capitals are used only for the first letter in a word. They match the roman in weight and have figures that align with the x-height.

5.10 If you put on the dog, you behave in an unpleasant, grand way that suggests you think that you are much more important or intelligent than anyone else; used in informal American English. **5.11** If you say that something is going to the dogs (thanks to *The Boys*; if you don't understand this, just put the cd which is included in the Dolly book in your cd-player, pump up the volume and there you go!), you mean that it is losing the good qualities that it had. EG. *This country is going to the dogs!* **5.12** · To fight like cat and dog: see cat. · raining cats and dogs: see rain. **6** See also dogged.

dogcart, dogcarts; often spelled with a hyphen (thanks Robin). A dogcart is a light cart with two wheels pulled by a horse, which people can ride in.

dog-eared. A book or piece of paper that is dog-eared has been used so much that the corners of the pages are turned down or torn.

dogfight, dogfights. A dogfight is **1** A fight between fighter planes, in which they fly close to one another and manoeuvre very fast. **2** A fight between dogs, especially one that has been organized by human beings for entertainment, although in The Hague this is illegal.

dogged means showing determination to continue with something however difficult it is. EG. *...his dogged refusal to admit defeat... ...dogged determination.* · doggedly. EG. They persisted doggedly in their campaign against the law. · doggedness.

doggerel is poetry which is silly or funny, often written quickly and not intended to be serious. EG. *She wrote some doggerel on the subject in 1883.*

doggie paddle; also spelled with a hyphen. The doggie paddle or dog paddle is a swimming stroke in which the arms and legs are moved up and down rapidly, with short strokes under the water; an informal term. The doggie paddle is often used by children who are learning to swim.

doggo. If you lie doggo, you lie still and keep very quiet so that people will not find you; an informal expression. EG. *I lay doggo in my tent in Norway at my own lake (thanks Ietje).*

doggone is an informal American word that's used to emphasize what you are saying. EG. *It's a doggone shame.*

doggy, doggies. See doggie.

dog-house. If you are in the dog-house, you are in disgrace and people are annoyed with you; an informal expression. EG. *Poor Martin Gaus is in the dog-house.*

dogma, dogmas. A dogma is a belief or a system of beliefs which is accepted as true and which people are expected to accept, without questioning it. EG. *He had no time for political or other dogmas... ...Christianity in the early days when there was less dogma.*

dogmatic. Someone who is dogmatic is convinced that they are right and gives their personal opinions without looking at the evidence and without considering that other opinions might be justified. EG. *He was so dogmatic about it that I almost believed what he was saying... His friends were all intensely dogmatic political theoreticians... She was not impressed by his dogmatic assertions.* · dogmatically. EG. *'This stone,' he said dogmetically, 'is far older than the rest.'*

dogmatism is a strong and confident assertion of opinion, which is made without looking at the evidence and without considering that different opinions might be justified. EG. *His education has taught him a distrust of dogmatism.* · Dogmatist. EG. *England inherited the worst dogmas and dogmatists of the women's movement from America.*

do-gooder, do-gooders. A do-gooder is someone who does things which they think will help other people, although others think they are interfering; used showing disapproval.

dog paddle means the same as doggie paddle.

dogsbody, dogsbodies. A dogsbody is a person who had to do all the unpleasant or boring jobs that nobody else wants to do; an informal British word. EG. *He was employed as a general dogsbody on the project.*

dog-tired. If you are dog-tired, you are extremely tired; used in informal English. EG. *Joeri and Ilone were dog-tired that evening.*

doings. Someone's doings are their activities at a particular time. EG. *Bas gave an admiring account of Sami's doings.*

do-it-yourself. See d.i.y. EG. *You can't get this font from good do-it-yourself shops.*

dole, doles, doling, doled. In Britain, the dole is money that is given by the government to people who are unemployed. It is given at regular intervals, for example every two weeks. EG. *How much is the dole now, 20 quid?... There was no dole for farm labourers.* · Someone who is on the dole is registered as unemployed and receives money regularly from the government. EG. *They made him redundant but he wouldn't go on the dole... He's spent the last year on the dole.*

doleful. A doleful expression, manner, voice, etc is depressing and miserable. EG. *'Things are getting desperate,' he said in a doleful monotone.* › used of people. EG. *...his rapid transformation from senator to doleful night-club comic.* · dolefully. EG. *Hogan nodded dolefully.*

doll, dolls, dolling, dolled. A doll is **1** A smart child's toy which looks like a small person or baby. **2** A girl or young woman, especially one who is pretty; used especially in informal American English. EG. *Who's the doll over there?*

doll up. If a woman dolls herself up, she puts on smart or fashionable clothes in order to try and look attractive for a particular occasion; used in informal British English. EG. *She dolled herself up to meet her new boyfriend.* · dolled up. EG. *She was all dolled up in the latest fashion.*

dollar, dollars. A dollar is a unit of money used in the USA, Canada, and other countries, which is divided into one hundred smaller units called cents. EG. *They spent half a million dollars on the font... The pound fell more than 25 percent against the dollar.*

dolly, dollies. **1** Dolly is a child's word for a doll. **2** A dolly or dolly bird is a young woman who is considered to be very pretty but not very intelligent. EG. *He was too busy chasing the teenage dollies of Paris.* **3** A little very ugly french bulldog, always angry, never satisfied, originally from The Hague, loves to play with Martin Gaus (thanks Edgar).

dolphin, dophins. A dolphin is a mammal which lives in the sea and looks like a large fish with a pointed mouth. 7,5/9 pts.

dolt, dolts. A dolt is a stupid person. EG. *You would have to be a*

OVER THE COURSE OF FOUR OR FIVE MONTHS, Dolly started to limp. I couldn't really find any reason for it, no thorn in her paw, for instance, or improperly executed manicure. One day she simply stopped walking on her right hind leg altogether. She would hold it daintily an inch or so off the ground and lope along on three legs.

Dolly tended to be a long-suffering girl, and never would she actively complain about some malady. She would bear her pain in silence, occasionally tossing a watery-eyed glance my way to indicate her general misery. Finally the situation seemed dire enough to warrant a visit to the veterinarian and the ensuing x-ray revealed a *displaced knee-cap* that required surgery to repair it. Her convalescence involved three months in a bright purple cast which held her leg straight out to the side like a chicken wing and out of the end of which her little tuft of a foot stuck like a tribal fetish.

When her cast was finally removed, her little leg was revealed, completely atrophied and as spindly as a toothpick. Dolly tentatively touched her foot 9/10,5 pts.

to the ground, looked up in disgust and went right on limping along on all-threes. Well, this limping went on all Fall, and each day her useless little leg grew increasingly soft and ineffectual. I was growing concerned and every morning I would draw her foot, which was now covered with long fur from lack of friction, to the pavement and rub her uncalloused pad on the ground to remind her of the sensation.

One day on our morning walk, in frustration, I called out in a gruff voice: '*Dolly, would you please walk on that leg!*' 11/13 pts.

Dolly

Underware
2001

All Dolly fonts have Adobe Standard Encoding and a full Western European character set.

Dolly is no ordinary émigré. She is a jindo, the indigenous breed prized as Korea's Natural Treasure No. 53, a symbol of national pride (an abundant Korean resource). When I flew back from Seoul to L.A. with a jindo pup, my husband and I had no idea what lay ahead. To our dismay, Dolly was embraced by the Kim side of the family as a surrogate grandchild and a direct link to a deceased aunt. We attempted to distance ourselves emotionally from our canine ward by giving her a different surname. We chose a flower: *Dolly Dahlia.* No confusing interspecies hyphenation for us. Some have accused us of latent hippiedom, but that is so not true. 12/15 pts.

Dolly

These texts are parts of stories published in the book *Dolly, a book typeface with flourishes.* These stories are written by many different people.

Korean Angelenos like to frequent the hilly trails of Griffith Park. Rarely do we pass them without triggering exclamatory superlatives: "*Oh-hoh! Jindo-gae! Best dog in the world!*" Clearly Koreans esteem the jindo above all other dogs. But one person's esteem is another's tasty treat. An encyclopedic jindo web site states: "*Even though Korea still has a custom of eating dogs, there is a strict distinction of pet dogs and dogs for eating.*" Best... tasting? 15/18 pts.

Dolly

Dolly

Underware
2001

These four fonts provide a good basis for most of the problems of book typography. If you meet a particular problem that could be solved by adding to or adapting these fonts, please contact Underware.

MAYBE WE HAD SAVED **Dolly** from a savory end. Jindos are notable for their loyalty and borderline domestication. The latter alarmed us as novice dog handlers. *Dolly was like a little bucking bronco the first times we tried to leash her.* Sometimes in the early weeks Markus and I would look at each other 36/42 pts.

+31 (0)70 4278117

bored &
lazy dog
& FAT ?
bulldog

Dolly

Underware
2001

Dolly is designed to be set in very small sizes. Because of this purpose, the font has a low contrast. However, the font contains subtle details that are not visible at small sizes. This example is set at 120 points.

» THE CHAPTERS IN THIS SPREAD are from **Marja Jalava's** whole article *'Getting intellectual'* in *Read naked* -book. » More about *Read naked* -book on Underware's website » www.underware.nl

SAUNA HAS BEEN SACRED – restricted and isolated – spatially, temporally and **socially**. This has been evident already in the way the sauna has been built apart from the everyday sphere. Nor has the sauna been entered on a whim, since the heating of traditional stoves has taken hours as well as skill passed from generation to generation. Taking off one's clothes before going into the hot sauna is besides an obvious necessity also a sign of passing into a sacred place. Along with the clothes, the bather symbolically removes his social roles and gets **a temporary relief** from their demands. Furthermore, baring one's body is a display of trust toward the fellow bathers. Even nowadays, bathers often have in common a rare feeling of equality and consensus. In public saunas, this makes possible a spontaneous, at times even very downright personal exchange of thoughts between complete strangers. [...]

+31 (0)70 4278117

Sauna

Underware
2002

Sauna–A typeface for all sizes.

Sauna has a warm and comfortable feeling. The straight lines and sharp corners work as a contrast to round forms; they give a dynamic kick and make the round forms look even rounder.

shown on this page:
Sauna-Dingbats (multicolor)
Sauna-Black
Sauna-BoldItalicSwash
Sauna-Bold
Sauna-SmallCaps
Sauna-Roman
Sauna-Italic

Sauna

A typeface for all sizes.

IN THE OLD AGRICULTURAL SOCIETY sauna has marked out the borders between everyday life and **Sundays**, and the turning points of an individual's life-span and the four seasons. In the sauna, babies were born, brides were bathed, corpses were washed, spells were recited, magic was made and the sick were healed. In these rituals, the sauna represented **the borderline between this life and the hereafter**, the microcosm and the macrocosm. *Löyly*, the steam rising from the hot stove stones, was what especially joined the bathers with the afterlife. In addition to signifying this special type of steam, in many Finno-Ugric languages the word *löyly* has stood for a power of life associated with breathing. Fundamentally, this power has been **ambivalent**, at the same time reforming and destroying human life. It brought relief to the tired and the sick, but it could also cause incurable diseases and ailments. This is referred to by the expression *löylynlyömä* (hit by *löyly*), used in vernacular speech as a synonym for mental illness or retardation. ¶

Sauna

Underware
2002

The Sauna family contains three
weights. Every weight has two italics:
a standard italic and a fancy swash
italic. One this page, the lightest
weight is shown. This weight can be
used for small size and can be combined with the bold weight (previous
spread). The lightest weight contains
small caps.

shown on this page:
Sauna-Roman
Sauna-Italic
Sauna-ItalicSwash
Sauna-SmallCaps

Sauna Dingbats-Solo

My dear grandfather *used to challenge* his fellow saunamen *into a competition.*

IF IT ENDED LIKE IT USUALLY DID, *that he won and was the last man in the sauna,* HE WENT DOWN ON THE FLOOR, *into the cool space under the benches, and threw* ANOTHER PAILFUL OF WATER ON THE STONES, YELLING:

"*Now it's time* to steam up!"

His companions were in an awe,
thinking Grandpa was still sitting on the top bench. *Perkele!*

¶ Jussi Karjalainen (27), a player of cardboard box drum, performs in Helsinki, Finland.

+31 (0)70 4278117

The tolerance varies;

During a sauna session one of our company's foreign workers was asking: 'Is it a part of the experience to black-out?'.

{We carried him outside to recover.}

¶ Ville Repo (31), a construction worker lifting heavy objects at Nastola, Finland.

Sauna

Underware
2002

The bold weight, which is shown on this page, can be combined with the lightest weight (opposite page) in small sizes. Of course, it also works as a display font.

shown on this page:
Sauna-Bold
Sauna-BoldItalic
Sauna-BoldItalicSwash

Underware

Sauna

Underware
2002

The black weight is designed for display use, for big and extremely big sizes. Therefore, it is individual and cannot be combined with regular and bold weights in small sizes.

shown on this page:
Sauna-Black

Always, when I'm visiting my parents, going to sauna is a polite way to escape their over'enthusiasm.

+31 (0)70 4278117

Sauna

Underware
2002

shown on this page:
Sauna-BlackItalic

Underware

I just switch the sauna on, wait for half an hour and I've got a perfect excuse to spend an hour only with my boyfriend.

¶ Agnes Magnusson (24), a student/cheerleader in the University of Uppsala, Sweden.

One time I pee on the rocks and it smelt ten times worse than normal pee smell…

¶ Ashley Ringrose (21), a game programmer in Sydney, Australia.

+31 (0)70 4278117

Don't tell me more, please.

Sauna

Underware
2002

Scale it bigger, and you get even more details!

Each Sauna italic swash font contains a set of twenty-six ligatures, including the double "l" shown on this page. All lightweight ligatures are shown below.

shown on this spread:
Sauna-BlackItalicSwash
Sauna Ligatures-BlackItalicSw

Th Qu Qu
fb ff fh fi fj
fk fl ft ffi ffl
ch ck cl ct
sh sk sl st
kk ll ss tt zz

Sauna Ligatures-ItalicSwash

Underware

Unionfonts.com: Buy and Download 24-7

magma

magma

magma

Magma

Samy Halim
2002

Magma Light

buckets and spoons dug trenches of thought into hard luck stories where cars ignore the laybys and whys because in clanking madness the hissing fury controls no past no future disrupts the present with grinders of steam and rivets of fire and no one around except the sky and the ground bare beauty of thought

Magma Light Condensed

buckets and spoons dug trenches of thought into hard luck stories where cars ignore the laybys and whys because in clanking madness the hissing fury controls no past no future disrupts the present with grinders of steam and rivets of fire and no one around except the sky and the ground bare beauty of thought in fields of yellow.

Magma Regular

buckets and spoons dug trenches of thought into hard luck stories where cars ignore the laybys and whys because in clanking madness the hissing fury controls no past no future disrupts the present with grinders of steam and rivets of fire and no one around except the sky and the ground bare beauty of thought in fields of

Magma Condensed

buckets and spoons dug trenches of thought into hard luck stories where cars ignore the laybys and whys because in clanking madness the hissing fury controls no past no future disrupts the present with grinders of steam and rivets of fire and no one around except the sky and the ground bare beauty of thought in fields of yellow.

Magma Bold

buckets and spoons dug trenches of thought into hard luck stories where cars ignore the laybys and whys because in clanking madness the hissing fury controls no past no future disrupts the present with grinders of steam and rivets of fire and no one around except the sky and the ground bare beauty of thought in fields of yellow.

Magma Bold Condensed

buckets and spoons dug trenches of thought into hard luck stories where cars ignore the laybys and whys because in clanking madness the hissing fury controls no past no future disrupts the present with grinders of steam and rivets of fire and no one around except the sky and the ground bare beauty of thought in fields of yellow.

Lee Fasciani
2003

Headroom Regular

HEADROOM

Headroom Bold

HEADROOM

Headroom Hard Regular

HEADROOM

Headroom Hard Bold

HEADROOM

Headroom Regular 24pt

BUCKETS AND SPOONS DUG TRENCHES
OF THOUGHT INTO HARD LUCK

Headroom Regular 18pt

BUCKETS AND SPOONS DUG TRENCHES OF THOUGHT
INTO HARD LUCK STORIES WHERE CARS IGNORE

Headroom Regular 12pt

BUCKETS AND SPOONS DUG TRENCHES OF THOUGHT INTO HARD LUCK
STORIES WHERE CARS IGNORE THE LAYBYS AND WHYS BECAUSE IN CLANKING

Headroom Regular 12pt

BUCKETS AND SPOONS DUG TRENCHES OF THOUGHT INTO HARD LUCK STORIES WHERE CARS IGNORE
THE LAYBYS AND WHYS BECAUSE IN CLANKING MADNESS THE HISSING FURY CONTROLS NO PAST NO

Chube Thin

chube

buckets and spoons dug trenches of thought into hard luck stories where cars ignore the laybys and whys because in clanking madness the hissing fury controls no past no future disrupts the present with grinders of steam and rivets of fire and no one around except the sky and the ground bare beauty of thought in fields of yellow.

Chube Thin Italic

chube

buckets and spoons dug trenches of thought into hard luck stories where cars ignore the laybys and whys because in clanking madness the hissing fury controls no past no future disrupts the present with grinders of steam and rivets of fire and no one around except the sky and the ground bare beauty of thought in fields of yellow.

Chube Fat

chube

buckets and spoons dug trenches of thought into hard luck stories where cars ignore the laybys and whys because in clanking madness the hissing fury controls no past no future disrupts the present with grinders of steam and rivets of fire and no one around except the sky and the ground bare beauty of thought in fields of yellow.

Chube Fat Italic

chube

buckets and spoons dug trenches of thought into hard luck stories where cars ignore the laybys and whys because in clanking madness the hissing fury controls no past no future disrupts the present with grinders of steam and rivets of fire and no one around except the sky and the ground bare beauty of thought in fields of yellow.

Chube Tubby

chube

buckets and spoons dug trenches of thought into hard luck stories where cars ignore the laybys and whys because in clanking madness the hissing fury controls no past no future disrupts the present with grinders of steam and rivets of fire and no one around except the sky and the ground bare beauty of thought in fields of yellow.

Chube Tubby Italic

chube

buckets and spoons dug trenches of thought into hard luck stories where cars ignore the laybys and whys because in clanking madness the hissing fury controls no past no future disrupts the present with grinders of steam and rivets of fire and no one around except the sky and the ground bare beauty of thought in fields of yellow.

Chube

Lee Fasciani
2003

Lee created Chube by formalizing his handwriting.

Swingo Regular

SWINGO

Swingo Bold

SWINGO

Swingo

Samy Halim
2002

Furby Light

FURBY

buckets and spoons dug trenches of thought into hard luck stories where cars ignore the laybys and whys because in clanking madness the hissing fury controls no past no future disrupts the present with grinders of steam and rivets of fire and no one around except the sky and the ground

Furby Regular

FURBY

buckets and spoons dug trenches of thought into hard luck stories where cars ignore the laybys and whys because in clanking madness the hissing fury controls no past no future disrupts the present with grinders of steam and rivets of fire and no one around except the sky and the ground

Furby Bold

FURBY

buckets and spoons dug trenches of thought into hard luck stories where cars ignore the laybys and whys because in clanking madness the hissing fury controls no past no future disrupts the present with grinders of steam and rivets of fire and no one around except the sky and the ground

Furby

Jonathan Nicol
2003

Jorge Alderete
2003

Prolific Argentinean Jorge Alderete is one of South America's leading illustrators, animators, and comic book artists.

Rubias Morenas Pelirojas is the Spanish expression "Blondes, Brown, and Red hair girls."

AMP Light

abcdeFghijklmnopqrstuvwxyz0123456789
ABCDEFGHIJKLMNOPQRSTUVWXYZ@E$%&

AMP Regular

abcdeFghijklmnopqrstuvwxyz0123456789
ABCDEFGHIJKLMNOPQRSTUVWXYZ@E$%&

AMP Bold

abcdeFghijklmnopqrstuvwxyz0123456789
ABCDEFGHIJKLMNOPQRSTUVWXYZ@E$%&

AMP Outline

abcdeFghijklmnopqrstuvwxyz0123456789
ABCDEFGHIJKLMNOPQRSTUVWXYZ@E$%&

AMP

Neil Summerour
2002

Eva Normal | Eva Normal Italic | Eva Bold | Eva Bold Italic

EVA EVA EVA EVA

EVA

Neil Summerour
2003

Ixtan

Heiko Hoos
2003

IXTAN

Ixtan Light

abcdefghijklmnopqrstuvwxyz
ABCDEFGHIJKLMNOPQRSTUVWXYZ

Ixtan Medium

abcdefghijklmnopqrstuvwxyz
ABCDEFGHIJKLMNOPQRSTUVWXYZ

Ixtan Bold

abcdefghijklmnopqrstuvwxyz
ABCDEFGHIJKLMNOPQRSTUVWXYZ

Ixtan Light Italic

abcdefghijklmnopqrstuvwxyz
ABCDEFGHIJKLMNOPQRSTUVWXYZ

Ixtan Medium Italic

abcdefghijklmnopqrstuvwxyz
ABCDEFGHIJKLMNOPQRSTUVWXYZ

Ixtan Bold Italic

abcdefghijklmnopqrstuvwxyz
ABCDEFGHIJKLMNOPQRSTUVWXYZ

Lee Fasciani
2003

"During recent years I have grown
to recognize and appreciate the
real subtleties in type design and
concentrate on text fonts."
—Lee Fasciani

Dispose

Dispose

Dispose

Dispose Light

buckets and spoons dug trenches of thought
into hard luck stories where cars ignore the
laybys and whys because in clanking
madness the hissing fury controls no past no
future disrupts the present with grinders of
steam and rivets of fire and no one around
except the sky and the ground bare beauty of
thought in fields of yellow.

Dispose Light Oblique

*buckets and spoons dug trenches of thought
into hard luck stories where cars ignore the
laybys and whys because in clanking
madness the hissing fury controls no past no
future disrupts the present with grinders of
steam and rivets of fire and no one around
except the sky and the ground bare beauty of
thought in fields of yellow.*

Dispose Regular

buckets and spoons dug trenches of thought
into hard luck stories where cars ignore the
laybys and whys because in clanking
madness the hissing fury controls no past no
future disrupts the present with grinders of
steam and rivets of fire and no one around
except the sky and the ground bare beauty of
thought in fields of yellow.

Dispose Oblique

*buckets and spoons dug trenches of thought
into hard luck stories where cars ignore the
laybys and whys because in clanking
madness the hissing fury controls no past no
future disrupts the present with grinders of
steam and rivets of fire and no one around
except the sky and the ground bare beauty of
thought in fields of yellow.*

Dispose Heavy

**buckets and spoons dug trenches of thought
into hard luck stories where cars ignore the
laybys and whys because in clanking
madness the hissing fury controls no past no
future disrupts the present with grinders of
steam and rivets of fire and no one around
except the sky and the ground bare beauty of
thought in fields of yellow.**

Dispose Heavy Oblique

*buckets and spoons dug trenches of thought
into hard luck stories where cars ignore the
laybys and whys because in clanking
madness the hissing fury controls no past no
future disrupts the present with grinders of
steam and rivets of fire and no one around
except the sky and the ground bare beauty of
thought in fields of yellow.*

Kanister Kanister

Kanister

Martin Fewell
2003

Kryptk Flash

abcdefghijklmnopqrstuvwxyz0123456789
ABCDEFGHIJKLMNOPQRSTUVWXYZ@€$%&

Kryptk Flash

Neil Summerour
2002

Designed for use in Macromedia Flash MX.

ARE YOU IN

Are You In

Arjen Noordeman
2003

CharifaSans

abcdefghijklmnopqrstuvwxyz0123456789
ABCDEFGHIJKLMNOPQRSTUVWXYZ@£$%&

Charifa Sans

Heiko Hoos
2003

Union Fonts

Paul Davidson
2003

cosmorton

cosmorton

Cosmorton

buckets and spoons dug trenches of thought into hard luck stories where cars ignore the laybys and whys because in clanking madness the hissing fury controls no past no future disrupts the present with grinders of steam and

Cosmorton Bold

buckets and spoons dug trenches of thought into hard luck stories where cars ignore the laybys and whys because in clanking madness the hissing fury controls no past no future disrupts the present with grinders of

Paul Davidson
2003

EPOCH

Von R. Glitschka
2003

www.unionfonts.com

Squirrel *Squirrel* Squirrel *Squirrel*

Squirrel

Maurice van de Stouwe
2003

buckets and spoons dug trenches of thought into hard luck stories where cars ignore the laybys and whys because in clanking madness the hissing fury controls no past no future disrupts the present with grinders of steam and rivets of fire and no one around except the sky and the ground bare beauty of thought in fields of yellow.

EXHAUST LIGHT
EXHAUST REGULAR

Exhaust

Martin Fewell
2003

buckets and spoons dug trenches of thought into hard luck stories where cars ignore the laybys and whys because in clanking madness the hissing fury controls no past no future disrupts the present with grinders of steam and rivets of fire and no one around except the sky and the ground bare beauty of thought in fields of yellow.

EXHAUST BOLD
EXHAUST BLACK

buckets and spoons dug trenches of thought into hard luck stories where cars ignore the laybys and whys because in clanking madness the hissing fury controls no past no future disrupts the present with grinders of steam and rivets of fire and no one around except the sky and the ground bare beauty of thought in fields of yellow.

Datastream

Martin Fewell
2003

'80s revival font.

Datastream Regular

DATASTREAM

Datastream Oblique

DATASTREAM

Airbrake

Martin Fewell
2002

AIRBRAKE REGULAR
AIRBRAKE OBLIQUE

buckets and spoons dug trenches of thought into hard luck stories where cars ignore the laybys and whys because in clanking madness the hissing fury controls no past no future disrupts the present with grinders of steam and rivets of fire and no one around except the sky and the ground bare beauty of thought in fields of yellow.

AIRBRAKE ROUNDED
AIRBRAKE ROUNDED OBLIQUE

buckets and spoons dug trenches of thought into hard luck stories where cars ignore the laybys and whys because in clanking madness the hissing fury controls no past no future disrupts the present with grinders of steam and rivets of fire and no one around except the sky and the ground bare beauty of thought in fields of yellow.

Union Fonts

ThisIsTheTypefaceShowingFromYourFriendsAt:
http://www.youworkforthem.com

All our typefaces are available 24-7 on our website. Once you place an order, they are instantly ready for you to download and use!

ABCDEFGHIJKLMNOPQRSTUVWXYZabcd
efghijklmnopqrstuvwxyz123456789

ABCDEFGHIJKLMNOPQRSTUVWXYZabCd
efghijklmnopqrstuvwxyz123456789

6x7oct-Light

ABCDEFGHIJKLM
NOPQRSTUVWXY
Zabcdefghijklm

6x7oct-LightAlternate

ABCDEFGHIJKLM
NOPQRSTUVWXY
Zabcdefghijklm

6x7oct-Bold

ABCDEFGHIJKLM
NOPQRSTUVWXY
Zabcdefghijklm

6x7oct-Bold Alternate

ABCDEFGHIJKLM
NOPQRSTUVWXY
ZabCdefghijklm

6x7oct-Black

ABCDEFGHIJKLM
NOPQRSTUVWXY
Zabcdefghijklm

6x7oct-BlackAlternate

ABCDEFGHIJKLM
NOPQRSTUVWXY
ZabCdefghijklm

6x7oct

YouWorkForThem
1998

Twelve typestyles in family:
ExtraLight, Light, Regular, Bold,
ExtraBold, Black, ExtraLight Alternate,
Light Alternate, Bold Alternate,
ExtraBold Alternate, Black Alternate

Alloy-Regular

ABCDEFGHIJKLMNOPQRSTUVWXYZabcde
fghijklmnopqrstuvwxyz1234567890!?&

Alloy ExtraLight

ABCDEFGHIJKLMNOPQRSTUVWXYZabcd
efghijklmnopqrstuvwxyz1234567890!?

Alloy-ExtraBold

ABCDEFGHIJKLMNOPQRSTUVWXYZabcdefg
hijklmnopqrstuvwxyz1234567890!?&.,#$((

Alloy Light

ABCDEFGHIJKLMN
OPQRSTUVWXYZa
bcdefghijklmnop

Alloy-SemiBold

ABCDEFGHIJKLMNO
PQRSTUVWXYZabc
defghijklmnopqrst

Alloy-Bold

ABCDEFGHIJKLMNO
PQRSTUVWXYZabc
defghijklmnopqrst

Alloy

YouWorkForThem
1998

Six typestyles in family:
ExtraLight, Light, Regular, SemiBold,
Bold, ExtraBold

YouWorkForThem

YouWorkForThem
2001

Four typestyles in family:
Light, Regular, Bold, ExtraBold

Blackgold-Light

ABCDEFGHIJKLMNOPQRSTUVWXYZ
abcdefghijklmnopqrstuvwxyz1

Blackgold-Regular

ABCDEFGHIJKLMNOPQRSTUVWXYZ
abcdefghijklmnopqrstuvwxyz

Blackgold-Bold

ABCDEFGHIJKLMNOPQRSTUVWXYZ
abcdefghijklmnopqrstuvwxyz

Blackgold-ExtraBold

ABCDEFGHIJKLMNOPQRSTUVWXYZ
abcdefghijklmnopqrstuvwxyz

YouWorkForThem
2001

Six typestyles in family:
ExtraLight, Light, Regular, SemiBold,
Bold, ExtraBold

Blessed-ExtraLight

ABCDEFGHIJKLMNOPQRSTUVWXYZabc
defghijklmnopqrstuvwxyz123456789

Blessed-Regular

ABCDEFGHIJKLMNOPQRSTUVWXYZabc
defghijklmnopqrstuvwxyz123456789

Blessed-ExtraBold

ABCDEFGHIJKLMNOPQRSTUVWXYZabcd
efghijklmnopqrstuvwxyz1234567890

Blessed-Light

ABCDEFGHIJKLMN
OPQRSTUVWXYZa
bcdefghijklmnop

Blessed-SemiBold

ABCDEFGHIJKLMNO
PQRSTUVWXYZab
cdefghijklmnopq

Blessed-Bold

ABCDEFGHIJKLMNO
PQRSTUVWXYZab
cdefghijklmnopq

info@youworkforthem.com

Caliper-Regular
ABCDEFGHIJKLMNOPQRSTUVWXYZabcd
efghijklmnopqrstuvwxyz123456789

Caliper-ExtraWide
ABCDEFGHIJKLMNOPQRSTUVWXY
zabcdefghijklmnopqrstuvwx

Caliper-Stairstep
ABCDEFGHIJKLMNOPQRSTUVWXYZabcdef
ghijklmnopqrstuvwxyz1234567890!?

Caliper-Wide
ABCDEFGHIJKL
MNOPQRSTUVW
XYZabcdefghi

Caliper-LightCubed
ABCDEFGHIJKLMN
OPQRSTUVWXYZa
bcdefghijklm

Caliper-Alternate
ABCDEFGHIJKLMN
OPQRSTUVWXYZa
bcdefghijklm

Caliper

YouWorkForThem
1998

Eight typestyles in family:
Alternate, ExtraWide, Light Cubed,
Regular, Regular Cubed, Stairstep,
Unicase, Wide

Cam-Light
ABCDEFGHIJKLMNOPQRSTUVWXYZABC
DEFGHIJKLMNOPQRSTUVWXYZ1234567

Cam-Regular
ABCDEFGHIJKLMNOPQRSTUVWXYZABC
DEFGHIJKLMNOPQRSTUVWXYZ1234567

Cam-ExtraBold
ABCDEFGHIJKLMNOPQRSTUVWXYZABC
DEFGHIJKLMNOPQRSTUVWXYZ1234567

Cam-Bold
ABCDEFGHIJKL
MNOPQRSTUVWX
YZABCDEFGHIJK

Cam-Oblique
ABCDEFGHIJKL
MNOPQRSTUVWX
YZABCDEFGHIJK

Cam-ExtraBoldOblique
ABCDEFGHIJKLM
NOPQRSTUVWXY
ZABCDEFGHIJKL

Cam

YouWorkForThem
1997

Eight typestyles in family:
Light, Regular, Bold, ExtraBold, Light
Oblique, Oblique, Bold Oblique,
ExtraBold Oblique

YouWorkForThem

Novum-Light

ABCDEFGHIJKLMNOPQRSTUVWX
YZABCDEFGHIJKLMNOPQRSTU

Novum-Regular

ABCDEFGHIJKLMNOPQRSTUVWX
YZABCDEFGHIJKLMNOPQRSTU

Novum-Bold

ABCDEFGHIJKLMNOPQRSTUVWX
YZABCDEFGHIJKLMNOPQRST

Novum-ExtraBold

ABCDEFGHIJKLMNOPQRSTUVWX
YZABCDEFGHIJKLMNOPQRST

OneCross-Light

ABCDEFGHIJKLMNOPQRSTUVWXYZabcdef
ghijklmnopqrstuvwxyz1234567890!?&

OneCross-Bold

ABCDEFGHIJKLMNOPQRSTUVWXYZabcde
fghijklmnopqrstuvwxyz1234567890!?

OneCross-Black

ABCDEFGHIJKLMNOPQRSTUVWXYZabcd
efghijklmnopqrstuvwxyz1234567890

OneCross-Right

ABCDEFGHIJKLMNOP
QRSTUVWXYZabcde
fghijklmnopqrstuv

OneCross-SemiBold

ABCDEFGHIJKLMNOP
QRSTUVWXYZabcde
fghijklmnopqrstuv

OneCross-UltraBold

ABCDEFGHIJKLMNO
PQRSTUVWXYZabcd
efghijklmnopqrst

YouWorkForThem
1999

Twelve typestyles in family:
ExtraLight, Light, Regular, SemiBold,
Bold, ExtraBold, and Oblique versions
of the same weights

Overcross-Extra Light

Overcross-Light

Overcross-Regular

Overcross-Semi-Bold

YouWorkfForThem
2001

Ten typestyles in family:
Regular, SemiBold, Bold, ExtraBold,
Black, and Condensed versions of
the same weights

YouWorkForThem

Pakt-Condensed

ABCDEFGHIJKLMNOPQRSTUVWXYZabcdefghijklmnopqrstuvwxyz1234567890&$.,:!@
#%^*[[{+=\<™©®£fc¥S¶–†‡0ø¿?!iÀÁÄÂÃÉÈËÊÌÍÏÎÒÓÖÔÕÙÚÜÛÑàáäâãèéëêìíïî

Pakt-SemiBoldCondensed

ABCDEFGHIJKLMNOPQRSTUVWXYZabcdefghijklmnopqrstuvwxyz1234567890&$.,:!@#
%^*[[{+=\<™©®£fc¥S¶–†‡0ø¿?!iÀÁÄÂÃÉÈËÊÌÍÏÎÒÓÖÔÕÙÚÜÛÑàáäâãèéëêìíïîó

Pakt-BoldCondensed

ABCDEFGHIJKLMNOPQRSTUVWXYZabcdefghijklmnopqrstuvwxyz1234567890&$.,:!@#
%^*[[{+=\<™©®£fc¥S¶–†‡0ø¿?!iÀÁÄÂÃÉÈËÊÌÍÏÎÒÓÖÔÕÙÚÜÛÑàáäâãèéëêìíïîó

Pakt-BlackCondensed

ABCDEFGHIJKLMNOPQRSTUVWXYZabcdefghijklmnopqrstuvwxyz1234567890&$.,:!@%^
*[[{+=\<™©®£fc¥S¶–†‡0ø¿?!iÀÁÄÂÃÉÈËÊÌÍÏÎÒÓÖÔÕÙÚÜÛÑàáäâãèéëêìíïîó

YouWorkForThem
2001

Ten typestyles in family:
Regular, SemiBold, Bold, ExtraBold,
Black, and Condensed version of the
same weights

Pakt-Regular

ABCDEFGHIJKLMNOPQRSTUVWXYZabcdefghijklmnopqrstuvwxyz1234567890&$.,!@#%^*[[{+=\<™©®€£¢¥§¶–†‡0ø¿?!iÀÁÄÂ

Pakt-SemiBold

ABCDEFGHIJKLMNOPQRSTUVWXYZabcdefghijklmnopqrstuvwxyz1234567890&$.,!@#%^*[[{+=\<™©®€£¢¥§¶–†‡0ø¿?!iÀÁÄ

Pakt-ExtraBold

ABCDEFGHIJKLMNOPQRSTUVWXYZabcdefghijklmnopqrstuvwxyz1234567890&$.,!@#%^*[[{+=\<™©®€£¢¥§¶–†‡0ø¿?!i

Pakt-Black

ABCDEFGHIJKLMNOPQRSTUVWXYZabcdefghijklmnopqrstuvwxyz1234567890&$.,!@#%^*[[{+=\<™©®€£¢¥§¶–†‡0ø¿?!i

YouWorkForThem
1998

Seven typestyles in family:
Thin, ExtraLight, Light, Regular,
SemiBold, Bold, ExtraBold

Praun-Thin

ABCDEFGHIJKLMNOPQRSTUVWXYZabcdefghijklmnopqrstuvwxyz1234567890&$.,!

Praun-Regular

ABCDEFGHIJKLMNOPQRSTUVWXYZabcdefghijklmnopqrstuvwxyz1234567890&$.,!ra#%^+cc

Praun-ExtraBold

ABCDEFGHIJKLMNOPQRSTUVWXYZabcdefghijklmnopqrstuvwxyz1234567890&$.,!ra#%^+ccc+=\<™c

Praun-ExtraLight

ABCDEFGHIJKLMNOPQRSTUVWXYZabcdefghijklmnopqrst

Praun-Light

ABCDEFGHIJKLMNOPQRSTUVWXYZabcdefghijklmnopqrstu

Praun-Bold

ABCDEFGHIJKLMNOPQRSTUVWXYZabcdefghijklmnopqrstuvwx

info@youworkforthem.com

ABCDEFGHIJKLMNOPQRSTUVWXYZabcdefghijkl
mnopqrstuvwxyz1234567890&$.,!@#%^*[[{+=

ABCDEFGHIJKLMNOPQRSTUVWXYZabcdefghijklm
nopqrstuvwxyz1234567890&$.,!@#%^*[[{+=\<™

ABCDEFGHIJKLMNOPQRSTUVWXYZabcdefghijklm
nopqrstuvwxyz1234567890&$.,!@#%^*[[{+=\<™

ABCDEFGHIJKLMNOP
QRSTUVWXYZabcdef
ghijklmnopqrstuvw

ABCDEFGHIJKLMNOPQ
RSTUVWXYZabcdefg
hijklmnopqrstuvwxy

ABCDEFGHIJKLMNOP
QRSTUVWXYZabcdef
ghijklmnopqrstuvw

Proce55ing

YouWorkForThem
1998

Six typestyles in family:
Light, Regular, Bold, Pro55-Light,
Pro55-Regular, Pro55-Bold

Reversion

YouWorkForThem
1997

Twelve typestyles in family:
Thin, ExtraLight, Light, Regular,
SemiBold, Bold, ExtraBold. Includes
a "Broken" Series with Thin,
ExtraLight, Light, Regular, and
SemiBold versions also.

YouWorkForThem

An unexpected tour

There are fine books on the history of typefaces, charting when they were first cut or used, and what we still may not know. But the history and variety of letterforms is far deeper. Artists working with letters have been busy over the past two thousand years. Their efforts, whether cut in stone, worked into metal, woven in fabric, or written on vellum, can be astonishing. This is a tour going around the corners and down the side streets of letterforms, without neglecting familiar landmarks. The notes in these books, whether in the main text or following the pictures, are your expert commentary. Both Nicolete Gray and Jan Tschichold want to make sure that you appreciate the sights.

Nicolete Gray. *A History of Lettering: Creative Experiment and Letter Identity.* Boston: David R. Godine, 1986. London: Phaidon Press, 1986.

Jan Tschichold. *Treasury of Alphabets and Lettering.* New York: Reinhold, 1966; New York: Design Press, McGraw-Hill, 1992; and New York: W. W. Norton, 1995.

Essay questions

What is typography for, really? Why print something? What purposes does that serve? Gutenberg's invention of movable type changed Western society. Elizabeth Eisenstein's readable, scholarly account of the original demand for and effects of print offers a valuable perspective on this true paradigm shift. It will spur your thinking into the roles of electronic writing.

Robin Kinross takes a different tack, examining typography in the context of design and practice, with special attention to the past century. The story of how designers and typographers developed their ideas makes his book compelling. The reproductions are carefully captioned, adding a visual counterpart to the narrative. If you read both books, you're sure to be a hit at cocktail parties near campus.

Elizabeth Eisenstein. *The Printing Press as an Agent of Change.* London and New York: Cambridge University Press, 1979.

Robin Kinross. *Modern Typography: An essay in critical history.* London: Hyphen Press, 1992.

A few closing words

Blah, blah-blah blah, blah blah-ah, blah, bluh. Without words, type wouldn't be any fun; it wouldn't have much meaning, either. Language is the flip side of typography. How the two relate, and exploring the methods used in typography, are the subjects of Cal Swann's deceptively simple book. He covers everything from decision-making charts to linguistic theories of meaning in a clear, unpretentious way.

Cal Swann. *Language and Typography.* New York: Van Nostrand Reinhold, 1991.

Write on, and keep on typographing.

Peter Bain is principal of Incipit (www.incipit.com), a New York design studio whose practice is built upon letters. Projects undertaken for clients include custom typefaces, logotypes, handlettering, and typographic design. Bain has studied, specified, collected, curated, and lectured on typography, and still likes it.

PostScript, TrueType, and/or OpenType formats are included or available for the Mac OS and/or Windows operating systems. Not all foundries provide fonts in all available formats/platforms on this CD-ROM.

P-Type Publications is not responsible for errors, omissions or technical problems inherent in the font software or in its accompanying documentation. Please contact the individual foundries for more information on licensing, upgrades or support.

Font Type Key
Mac PS = Macintosh PostScript
Mac TT = Macintosh TrueType
Win PS = Windows PostScript
Win TT = Windows TrueType
OT = OpenType (cross-platform)

Foundry	Mac Fonts	Win Fonts	Font Name
Atomic Media	Mac PS	Win PS	GENETICA
Atomic Media	Mac PS	Win PS	GENETICA BOLD
Feliciano	Mac PS	Win TT & PS	Galápagos
Galápagos	Mac TT & PS	Win TT & PS	Nikki New Roman GD
Holland Fonts	Mac TT & PS	Win TT & PS	MaxMix
Holland Fonts	Mac TT & PS	Win TT & PS	Chip-1
Identikal	Mac PS	Win PS	ID-01 Left
Identikal	Mac PS	Win PS	ID-01 Right
ingoFonts	Mac TT & PS	Win TT & PS	Charpentier Renaissance
ingoFonts	Mac TT & PS	Win TT & PS	Deutsche Schrift Solling
ingoFonts	Mac TT & PS	Win TT & PS	Fixgum
ingoFonts	Mac TT & PS	Win TT & PS	Josef Normal
ingoFonts	Mac TT & PS	Win TT & PS	KLEX
Jukebox	Mac TT & PS	Win TT & PS	Fairy Tale JF
Jukebox	Mac TT & PS	Win TT & PS	WALCOTT GOTHIC-SUNSET
Mark Simonson	Mac TT	Win TT	Anonymous
Mark Simonson	Mac TT & PS	Win TT & PS	MOSTRA ONE REGULAR
Mark Simonson	Mac TT & PS	Win TT & PS	MOSTRA TWO REGULAR
Mark Simonson	Mac TT & PS	Win TT & PS	MOSTRA THREE REGULAR
Neufville	Mac TT & PS	Win TT & PS	Futura ND Medium
Neufville	Mac TT & PS	Win TT & PS	Futura ND Medium Oblique
Nick's Fonts	Mac TT & PS	Win TT & PS	Annabelle Matinee NF
No Bodoni	Mac PS	Win TT & PS	Claudium
Sherwood	Mac TT	Win TT	Founders

Foundry	Mac Fonts	PC Fonts	Font Name
Storm Type Foundry	Mac TT & PS	Win TT & PS	Lido
Storm Type Foundry	Mac TT & PS	Win TT & PS	*Lido Italic*
Storm Type Foundry	Mac TT & PS	Win TT & PS	**Lido Bold**
Storm Type Foundry	Mac TT & PS	Win TT & PS	***Lido Bold Italic***
Storm Type Foundry	Mac TT & PS	Win TT & PS	Lido Condensed
Storm Type Foundry	Mac TT & PS	Win TT & PS	**Lido Condensed Bold**
Storm Type Foundry	OT	OT	*Walbaum Text Italic OT*
Terminal	OT	OT	Rawlinson OT
Underware	Mac TT		Unibody-8 Roman
Underware	Mac TT		Unibody-8 Italic
Underware	Mac TT		UNIBODY-8 SC
Underware	Mac TT		**Unibody-8 Black**
Union Fonts	Mac TT	Win TT	HOT METAL
YouWorkForThem	Mac PS	Win TT	biblah regular

PostScript Type 1 was developed by Adobe Systems for use with PostScript output devices. In Mac OS, a Type 1 font consists of an outline font (printer font) and a bitmap font (screen font) that also carries the metrics data. In Windows, a Type 1 font also uses two files, one containing the outlines (.PFB), and one containing the printer font metrics (.PFM). Thousands of PostScript fonts have been developed for use with both Mac OS and Windows, although the same font files can not be used interchangeably on both platforms.

TrueType, developed by Apple and intended for use with Mac OS 7, was also adopted by Microsoft for use with Windows (.TTF). TrueType fonts consist of a single file used for both screen display and printing, eliminating the need for separate outline and bitmap fonts. TrueType font files also cannot be used interchangeably on both platforms.

OpenType, developed jointly by Adobe and Microsoft, is a font format designed to combine the best of TrueType and PostScript into a single format for use on both Macintosh and Windows platforms. OpenType allows for up to 65,000 glyphs and conditional letter combinations, with easier access to full expert set characters, facilitating multilingual and advanced typography. An OpenType font consists of one font file that can be installed on either the Mac OS or Windows, eliminating the need for a separate font file for each platform.

Appendix C

Index

The following is a combined index of both volumes of *Indie Fonts*. To differentiate between the two books, page numbers from this volume are listed in bold face.

Legal Information

Acknowledgments

We'd like to express our gratitude to those who assisted in the creation of *Indie Fonts 2*. Their efforts and encouragement were essential to the well-being of the project.

Eternal thanks to our Project Manager, Carima El-Behairy, for keeping everything on track.

Additional thanks to Jared Benson, Jimy Chambers, Stephen Coles, Jon Coltz, Allan Haley, Joe Pemberton, and Claudio Piccinini.

Thanks to the terrific group of type designers we have worked with on the *Indie Fonts* series—it's been a real pleasure.

And to the rest of you out there, making letters and numbers and symbols and more—keep up the good work. The world *does* need more fonts.

The Editors

Colophon

This book was designed by
James Grieshaber.

The text face is *Alisal*,
designed by Matthew Carter
from Carter & Cone.

The headlines and labeling are set
in various weights of *Faceplate*,
designed by Rodrigo Xavier
Cavazos from Psy/Ops.